THE BIBLICAL WORLD VIEW

AN APOLOGETIC

THE BIBLICAL WORLD VIEW

AN APOLOGETIC

DANIEL C. JUSTER

International Scholars Publications
San Francisco - London
1995

Copyright © 1995 by
Daniel C. Juster

International Scholars Publications
4720 Boston Way
Lanham, Maryland 20706

12 Hid's Copse Rd.
Cumnor Hill, Oxford OX2 9JJ

Library of Congress Cataloging-in-Publication Data

Juster, Daniel C.-
The Biblical world view : an apologetic / Daniel C. Juster.
p.   cm.

Includes bibliographical references and index.
1. Apologetics. 2. Bible—Evidences, authority, etc. I. Title.
BT1102.J87   1995   239—dc20   95-9577 CIP

ISBN 1-57309-025-5 (cloth: alk. ppr.)
ISBN 1-57309-024-7 (pbk: alk. ppr.)

⊖™ The paper used in this publication meets the minimum
requirements of American National Standard for Information
Sciences—Permanence of Paper for Printed Library Materials,
ANSI Z39.48—1984

DEDICATION

This book is dedicated to the three professors who most greatly influenced my thinking. Arthur F. Holmes of Wheaton College pressed me to think clearly and to write with persuasion. Stuart C. Hackett, during Wheaton days, opened the world of Eastern and Western religious philosophies with his usual incisive analysis. David L. Wolfe, formerly of the King's College, Wheaton College, and Gordon College, was excellent in integrating the various disciplines of the liberal arts and sciences. He also gave valuable time to me as a young and confused student and provided the tools for sorting out the complex world of human thought.

In addition, I would also like to thank my wife, Patty, for her unfailing support in life as well as in the creation of this study.

Dr. Daniel Juster has taught apologetics since 1971 in various schools, including Trinity College (Deerfield), Messiah Biblical University (Maryland), the Union of Messianic Jewish Congregations Yeshiva and colleges in Korea and Brazil. His academic background is a B.A. in Philosophy, Wheaton; M-Div., McCormick Seminary; Philosophy of Religion Graduate Program, Trinity Evangelical Divinity School, and Th.D., New Covenant International Seminary.

TABLE OF CONTENTS

INTRODUCTION

THE PIVOTAL QUESTIONS OF LIFE ARE RELIGIOUS. Religious-truth questions require disciplined thinking, but such truth-questions are not merely of intellectual import. Rather they impinge upon the whole of life. A person's world view influences the whole of his life. A world view has vast implications for one's understanding of science, anthropology, sociology, psychology, law, politics, literature, and numerous other areas of human understanding. The question "What is man?" *is*, despite those who bury their head in the sand, the all-important question. It is a centrally religious question. Is man a specially created being made in the image of God? Or is man simply an amazing configuration of physical-chemical constituents produced by chance? Is this life the only life we have to live, or is there life after death? Can the Bible or other purported "revelations" commend themselves as giving trustworthy information to answer these questions? Can we answer these questions by reason, without revelation? These are the kinds of questions William James called "forced issues." We have to answer them, since our decision will determine how we live and will significantly alter our lives. To not decide is delusion: for suspending judgment will orient us to unbelief as a way of life.

These questions, and their implications for the arts and sciences, were the central concerns of my life for a ten-year period. The first half of this period was difficult indeed. Doubt and skepticism were devastating. Yet I was determined to find out if these questions could be answered. By God's grace, I was privileged to have access to fine libraries, helpful professors, and the time to pursue the issues. I have come to conclusions which satisfied me. I do believe that I came to grasp the limits and values of reason in settling these issues. I write from the perspective of biblical faith, but I do not assume that the reader is "in the faith." Rather, I write to satisfy those who stand where I once stood. I believe I have an obligation to seek to bolster the maturity and understanding of those within the biblical faith as well.

It has now been many years since the publication of any work on biblical apologetics which has attempted to combine philosophical, cultural, and historical considerations and to form a strong intellectual case for biblical faith. A comprehensive up-to-date survey was greatly desired during my own years of searching. May God grant that this book provide just such a survey. By *comprehensive* we do not mean either exhaustive or lengthy. Rather we seek to summarize many of the key issues which apologetics must face. These include such questions as: What is truth? How does one test religious truth claims? What does modern culture say in regard to religious truth questions? What are the implications of various world views in our societies and in the disciplines of study in the arts and sciences? Can objections to the biblical faith be handled adequately? What is the historical evidence for the biblical faith? What is the present evidence from the lives of the people of faith?

Teaching apologetics has been a great joy. Not only did I gain from reviewing the material, but I have been privileged to see students pass from unbelief to faith and from a weak faith to a strong faith. Although I acknowledge that there is an important intellectual component to faith, I fully recognize that all faith comes only by the Holy Spirit and His work of conviction in the heart that hears the Word of God. Hence, one of the primary questions to be answered concerns the validity of and place of intellectual argument in relation to the work of the Spirit of God. This question will not be avoided.

This is a book for people who want to think. It assumes a reasonably decent education in the arts and sciences, which, despite the decline of educational standards today, should be the possession of most college graduates. The first chapter to follow deals with the issues of those who question the apologetic endeavor. We recommend that those who are either unfamiliar with the issues involved or unschooled in basic philosophical issues skip Chapter One and go directly into Chapter Two. The second chapter begins the presentation of our own apologetic, whereas Chapter One defines and defends the endeavor.

PART ONE

PROLEGOMENA

TO BIBLICAL EVIDENCES

WHAT IS APOLOGETICS?

*A*POLOGETICS IS A TERM DERIVED FROM A GREEK LANGUAGE ROOT MEANING "defense." It does not connote defensiveness or being sorry as in apologizing. *Apologetics is simply a forceful presentation of the biblical world and life view which addresses the question of the validity or truthfulness of that viewpoint.* Apologetics is akin to preaching, yet it is not, strictly speaking, preaching. Apologetics, though containing elements of the proclamation of the Gospel common in preaching, emphasizes the implications of the Gospel in its more fully "world view"–ish dimensions, giving special attention to the issue of the *truth* of the world view. Apologetics and preaching are thus complementary; both require the work of the Spirit of God in the hearts of persons if conviction is to arise in the heart.

There have been great apologetic works in this mode in this past century. A few are James Orr's *A Christian View of God and the World*, William Temple's *Nature, Man, and God*, the amazing tapestry of the writings of C. S. Lewis, and the writings of Edward John Carnell, especially *An Introduction to Christian Apologetics, A Philosophy of The Christian Religion*, and *Christian Commitment*. Many others could be named. However, the last thirty years has seen a dearth of comprehensive works in apologetics from a conservative biblical perspective, although there have been significant writings addressing some of the areas of apologetic concern.

The scope of apologetics is really quite broad. It includes first of all, *cultural apologetics*. Cultural apologetics asks, What do man's art, literature, and music say in regard to beliefs or world views, and what are their implications for human fulfillment and direction? Do art and literature in some way confirm the truth of the biblical world view? Francis Schaeffer, Hans Rookmaaker, and Os Guiness have made this area of apologetics well known. Others, however, have also written on these themes.

There is, secondly, the broad dimension of *philosophical apologetics*. This includes questions of the validity of arguments for the existence of God outside of the evidence stemming from the special revelation of the Bible. Classically, this was the central concern of philosophical apologetics, but it really includes much more. Philosophy is really a comprehensive academic discipline which interprets and ties together all areas of human study in the arts and sciences. Hence, philosophical apologetics evaluates objections to the biblical faith from the natural sciences (biology, geology, astronomy, physics, and chemistry) and from the social sciences (psychology, sociology, and anthropology). It is not the job of apologetics to provide a full integration of these sciences with the biblical world view. This is the job of astute believers who are experts in their fields and are philosophically and theologically sophisticated. Yet, apologetics must deal with the issues and objections to our faith raised by these disciplines, since these most basic objections are relevant to the question of the truth-value of our world view. We shall ask, Does our world view provide a coherent philosophical integration of the various sciences? Philosophical apologetics thus needs to touch on: questions arising from the creation-evolution debate; the vastness of the universe discovered in astronomy; mechanist explanations of man in the natural and social sciences; and psychological and sociological explanations of the content and origin of all world views.

Philosophical apologetics also deals with the issue of the comparative validity of various world views. Recently, Stuart Hackett provided an excellent exposition and evaluation of Eastern religions from a biblical point of view. James Sire has provided a fine summary and evaluation of the basic prominent world views in the late twentieth century. His book, *The Universe Next Door*, merits attention.

Thirdly, the area of *historical apologetics* includes issues such as the archaeological and historical accuracy of the Bible; arguments from fulfilled prophecy (ancient and recent), and the historical evidences for the life, death, and resurrection of Yeshua (Jesus).

Last is the evidence from the testimonies of all believers from the earliest days of Church history, up to and including our own day.

As can be seen from our outline, an apologist should have a basic understanding of many disciplines. Beyond this, as Francis Schaeffer well pointed out, the apologist needs to be well aware of the communications barriers which make it difficult to speak into the contemporary culture. Some words have lost currency, and others have changed in meaning for many people. Many have little comprehension of concepts such as sin and redemption. Others have reinterpreted basic biblical concepts. "Christ" has become an experience of the authentic self divorced from the historical Jesus. Resurrection has been reinterpreted as a renewal in our subjective lives rather than the historic act of God in raising Jesus from the dead. To speak adequately, we must be careful to define our terms.

APPROACHES TO APOLOGETICS

THE PRESUPPOSITIONAL APPROACH

There are great differences of approach to the issues of apologetics among various schools of thought. Some approaches even call the classical endeavor of apologetics itself into question. Such approaches to apologetics we call subjectivist views or at least views which are subjectivist in tendency. It is argued by some that unbelievers exist in a totally different perspective than believers. Furthermore, it is argued that all viewpoints are to be judged from the perspective of the biblical faith. Therefore, to assume that one can judge between world views including the biblical faith is to assume that there is a criterion of judgment superior to the Bible itself by which all world views can be judged. Yet nothing stands above the Bible to judge it. Therefore, the task of apologetics is simply to expose the inadequacies of non-biblical viewpoints from a biblical perspective. However, there is no common ground with unbelievers which can be used to convince them of the truth of our faith. Only the work of the Holy Spirit convincing the heart causes a change of perspective. Indeed, it is even argued that the unbeliever and believer live in two different worlds of interpretation so that no "fact" leads to a change of interpretation. All is perceived in a grid of interpretation. Apologetics must therefore start on the basis of biblical presuppositions. It must simply exhibit the biblical world view and its critique of other perspectives from a biblical base if perchance the Holy Spirit might convince the heart of the hearer. Yet this convincing is wholly apart from anything previously believed by the unbeliever.

The greatest proponent of this view in America has been Cornelius Van Til, who, through several powerful books, has argued for this perspective (see *The Defense of the Faith* and *A Christian Theory of Knowledge*). Van Til argues that all criteria (testing measures) for weighing anything are already part of the world view adopted, so that one can not argue for the truth of the biblical faith with an unbeliever as if there are independent criteria or measures for testing. Gordon Clark has argued in a similar vein in *Religion, Reason, and Revelation*.

However, by far the most powerful presentation of this view has been from Herman Dooyweerd in his monumental *A New Critique of Theoretical Thought*. Dooyweerd was for many years a professor at the Free University of Amsterdam. In my estimation, Dooyweerd was, if not *the* greatest, certainly one of the greatest Christian philosophers of the twentieth century. His writings brilliantly present a biblical interpretation of the nature of existence with reference to most areas of human study. The natural and social sciences are deftly dealt with in his schema. In addition, Dooyweerd provides a devastating critique of all un-biblical viewpoints in philosophy and science. He reveals the arbitrariness of their starting from un-biblical and anti-biblical presuppositions. He also shows the many puzzles, contradictions (antinomies), and points of incoherence to be found in these viewpoints. Yet, despite all this, Dooyweerd echoes as well the impossibility of finding common ground with the unbeliever. Reason must be seen as limited; faith decisions at the heart of our interpretative framework are not the product of the operation of independent reason.

A RESPONSE TO PRESUPPOSITIONALISM

How shall we respond to these arguments? First of all it needs to be pointed out that these men, especially Dooyweerd, have challenged the myth of objectivity in the social sciences and philosophy. They have shown, as will be reflected in this work, how many of the perspectives in these fields arise from anti-biblical biases. The very so-called facts themselves are seen through our world-view values structure. It is impossible to separate the areas of factuality and valuation. Dooyweerd also shows the immense and superior interpretive power of the biblical presuppositions and perspective over all other perspectives.

All of this, however, raises a crucial issue. That is, does the work of Dooyweerd commend itself in any way to the unbeliever? By the gift of God's common grace, is man in his thinking ability able to perceive the superior coherence and freedom from antinomy in the biblical schema of interpretation? Granted, man is dependent upon God's revelation in the Bible. He would never discover the basic biblical ground concepts by his own *unaided* reason. Reason only works with what is revealed to our perception; it does not discover the content of meaning within itself. Yet once man thinks his way through the various world views, as Dooyweerd does, and critically compares them, showing un-biblical views to be full of problems while the biblical view has far fewer inconsistencies, has he not given evidence for the biblical view? Indeed, might we not say of Dooyweerd's great work that it is a case for biblical Christianity and that it commends itself to believers and unbelievers? Is there an element in it which we might call objective? Either this is so, or we have no reason to judge Dooyweerd's philosophy superior to past Christian and non-Christian elaborations. If it is not so, then Dooyweerd is asking us simply to accept his philosophy if we are irrationally moved to do so. Otherwise, Dooyweerd's philosophy commends itself on some more universal rational ground.

We should also note the influence of Sören Kierkegaard, the nineteenth-century Danish Christian philosopher, and Karl Barth, the great German theologian.[1] Both emphasize the centrality of subjective decision and passionately reject the concept of reasons for faith to commend the faith to the unbeliever.[2] Kierkegaard was the great influence on all modern varieties of existential philosophy.

THE OBJECTIVIST (EVIDENTIALIST) APPROACH

Opposed to subjectivist viewpoints are what we might call objectivist perspectives. Objectivists believe that there are universal criteria of evidence and logic by which one can argue for truth in science and religion. These criteria are independent of any viewpoint and are used to test all viewpoints in any field. The great medieval theologian Thomas Aquinas is the classical example of this view. In the twelfth century, he set forth his "objective" arguments. They included arguments for a first cause of creation, from design, and from the moral nature of man to prove the existence of God. His arguments claimed to be based upon observation and logic. Others sought to prove God's existence as necessarily deduced from the idea of God in the mind. These included Anselm (who gave this argument its classical form), Descartes, Leibnitz, and, in our own period, Charles Hartshorn of the University of Texas and Norman Malcolm of Cornell University.

However, most of today's objectivists have been greatly influenced by the empirical method of science. They have sought to base the case for biblical faith upon the ground of historical evidence. This historical evidence is discovered through an empirical approach to the biblical documents and parallel documents of history and archaeology. Such arguments center on the evidences for the resurrection of Jesus (Yeshua) and upon arguments from fulfilled prophecy both in biblical times and in our own day. The accuracy of Scripture, where it can be checked with archaeological evidence, is also used to bolster confidence in the trustworthy nature of the Scriptures. Arguments from prophecy and the resurrection are found in the biblical texts as well as in the writings of the church fathers. Today's historical objectivists include John W. Montgomery, the late Wilbur Smith, Bernard Ramm (in his *Protestant Christian Evidences*), Josh McDowell, and J. N. D. Anderson. A combination of philosophical and historical evidences is found in the classical systematic theology works of the nineteenth century (Shedd, Hodge, and Strong). In Edward John Carnell we find a mixture of objective and subjective apologetic viewpoints that never are quite reconciled. His early writings especially reflect the influence of his two professors, subjectivist Cornelius Van Til and objectivist E. S. Brightman.

The objectivist believes that he can push the unbeliever to the wall by the powerful nature of the objective evidence. The evidence is such that if it is logically presented, the conclusions are inescapable. John Montgomery, who is an excellent debater, once said to me that he could so push the unbeliever with such evidence that all would see that the conclusions were valid. Would this be the case, however, if he were debating someone whose quick-witted mind matched his own?

A RESPONSE TO THE OBJECTIVIST

C. S. Lewis in our own day has provided a tremendously powerful objectivist apologetic both from philosophical and historical arguments. His writings are important for any student of apologetics.

How shall we respond to the objectivist? It should first of all be noted that the objectivist puts too much stock in the universal nature of empirical evidence, logic, and the conclusions that can be derived from these criteria. The concept of the universality of the evidence requires pre-theoretical commitments concerning the value of the empirical world, the nature and importance of logic, and the ability of a scientific approach to reality in discovering truth. Yet all of this would seem strangely unimportant to the Eastern mind, which has decided that real contradiction is part of existence, that logic must be transcended if one is to experience religious truth, and that empirical events are all part of the illusion of experience which can have no value in proving anything religious. What if it is denied that our minds discover anything about the real world other than what we read into this world from our subjective stance? Some argue that we create the world (Aldous Huxley and Timothy Leary, the sixties drug guru, etc.).

Secondly, as George Mavrodes has shown in *Belief in God*, there is no conclusion which cannot be avoided simply by denying the premises of the argument involved. For example, take the argument for the resurrection of Jesus. It is argued that it is highly improbable that the disciples would die for their testimony for the resurrection if they were not convinced that He really arose. Hence, on the basis of probability, it should be concluded that Jesus rose from the dead. This can be placed in syllogistic form.

> Premise #1: Men do not die for a testimony that is false.
> Premise #2: The disciples died for their testimony of the resur
> rection.
> Conclusion: Therefore the disciples' testimony is true, and Jesus
> rose from the dead.

However, a hardened naturalist can simply say that improbable things happen all the time. In this case, he believes that the disciples died for a testimony that was false. Either they were deceived or they had reasons to lie that we may not know or be able to figure out. He simply denies the universal truth value of the first premise and is not forced to the conclusion. Certainly, his own world-view bias leads the naturalist to this denial. However, one can not get at the bias without examining his whole perspective. Indeed, because of his perspective, all the evidence adduced for the resurrection *seems to him* to be highly unconvincing. This leads to an important point. Evidence only *discloses* itself to a person whose stance allows an empathetic appreciation of its significance. This is true in any philosophical or scientific field. The weighing of evidence is the function of a whole person, including all of his biases; it is not the function of a mind understood as an objective computer independent of the whole person.

Thirdly, from a biblical perspective, we need to deal seriously with the effect of sin on man's ability to weigh evidence and to come to conclusions on the basis of evidence. This effect is more manifest as we progress from mathematics to the natural sciences and the social sciences and finally to questions of world-view perspectives. Bias is manifest at every level, but more especially in disciplines that have significant implications for world views. Sin affects the emotions, will, and *the mind*.

Fourthly, Scripture makes it clear that without the work of the Holy Spirit, real faith in God and biblical truth are not possible. Although a few might come to a mere intellectual ascent to biblical propositions, most will not intellectually draw conclusions that go against the tenor of their pre-theoretical commitments. Hence, apologetics needs to give more careful attention to the limits of these four factors. It is my conviction that light is shed on this subject from an examination of scriptural passages that bear on the issue of truth and evidence.

SCRIPTURE AND APOLOGETICS

In Scripture we find two sets of passages; one set which seems negative to the desire for empirical evidence and the other which seems positive. In Matthew 12:38,39 Jesus says that "a sinful and adulterous generation seeks after a sign." This rebuke was given shortly after Jesus' great miracle of multiplying bread and fish in the feeding of the five thousand during Passover season. In John 20:29 Jesus says, "Blessed are those who believe but have not seen." In other words, blessed are those who believe without the empirical evidence Thomas, the disciple of Jesus, required. These verses, and others of this type, are often quoted by the subjective-minded apologists.

Yet there are other passages as well which seem to appeal to an empirical kind of evidence. Jesus says that the people are to believe Him "for the very works' sake" or on the basis of the evidences of his miraculous works. Of course, Jesus presents Himself to his disciples after the resurrection, and this convinces those who doubted the testimonies of the women who were first at the empty tomb. That the resurrection convinced the disciples is reflected in all four gospel accounts. John believes before seeing the risen Messiah on the basis of the evidence of the grave clothes (John 20:6–10).

The same duality is found in the New Testament epistles. Paul, in I Corinthians 2:14, says, "The unspiritual (natural) man does not receive the gifts of the Spirit of God, for they are folly to him and he is unable to understand them because they are spiritually discerned."

I Corinthians 1:18–25 is also well worth quoting:

> For the word of the cross is folly to those who are perishing, but to us who are being saved it is the power of God.
> For it is written, "I will destroy the wisdom of the wise and the cleverness of the clever I will thwart." Where is the wise man? Where is the scribe? Where is the debater of this age? Has God not made foolish the wisdom of the world? For since in the wisdom of God, the world did not know God through wisdom, it pleased God through the folly of what we preach to save those who believe.

On the surface, many take these passages to be calling into question the whole apologetic endeavor which uses reason and evidence to convince people of the truth. Yet, just the same, there are amazingly forceful passages which seem to appeal to empirical evidence to at least convince doubters or those turning to false perspectives. In I Corinthians 15, Paul wrote to those who were denying the real resurrection from the dead. He states,

> For I delivered to you as of first importance what I also received, that Messiah died for our sins in accordance with the Scriptures, that He was buried, that He was raised on the third day in accordance with the Scriptures, and that He appeared to Cephas, then to the twelve. Then He appeared to more than five hundred brethren at one time, most of whom are still alive, though some have fallen asleep.

In the light of the evidence of this testimony Paul asks, "How can you say that there is no resurrection of the dead." Paul evidently is appealing to the evidence of this testimony to convince his opponents. Peter as well reflects a similar point of view when he says,

> For we did not follow cleverly devised myths when we made known to you the power and coming of our Lord Jesus the Messiah, but we were eyewitnesses of his majesty . . . we heard this voice borne from heaven, for we were with Him on the holy mountain. (II Peter 1:16–18)

Are these biblical passages compatible with those which seem to disparage the value of the evidence? We believe they are and that the issue is resolved through the teaching of Jesus in John, Chapter 7. In this passage Jesus makes a startling claim concerning religious truth. He says, "If any man's will is *to do His will*, he shall know whether the teaching is from God or whether I am speaking on my own authority."

The context of this passage is the disagreement among his people occasioned by Jesus' teaching and miracles. Jesus states that our problem is not the adequacy of the evidence. Rather, our moral stance determines our ability to weigh evidence. If a person does not want to do the will of God, he will not be able to perceive the weightiness of apologetic evidence. As Dooyweerd rightly discerned, our heart response to the religious core of existence determines everything. How well I remember first noting how many rejected the biblical faith and found anti-biblical arguments convincing *after* they had rationalized sin in their lives, whether bitterness, adultery, or greed. Hence, Yeshua uses both

logic and evidence as part of his Holy-Spirit–empowered ministry. He appeals
to His works to encourage faith. Miracles are evidential disclosures that en-
gender faith in the heart opened by and to the Spirit. Yet He is adamant against
the "show me" attitude that arises from pride, unbelief, and sin. For such a person, even one rising from the dead will be inadequate evidence (Luke 16:31). A
sinful generation says "give me a sign" but remains unconvinced after it is given.

JESUS USES LOGIC

We also see that Jesus uses the laws of logic in his discussion with opponents.
He seeks to awaken them to see their own sin by appealing to the *contradictory*
nature of their behavior. They rage against Him for breaking the Law when He
did not while they plot to commit murder (John 7:19–24). These discussions
would be foolish if the subjectivist perspective was totally correct.

PAUL EXPLAINS WHY EVIDENCE IS NOT PERCEIVED

Paul understood the moral dimension that pervades knowing. In his profound
description in Romans 1 and 2, we read that God has adequately revealed Himself to all men. However, men have suppressed the truth due to their moral corruption. In one sense they know the truth, yet in their conscious state they
seem to not know it. Men do not desire to repent and come to know the truth.
Rather, they flee the knowledge of God to make an immoral life easier to maintain and so that they can live for self without feeling guilty. They create a religion in which they can manipulate the gods rather than to bow before their infinite Creator-Lawgiver. Unbiblical philosophies help us to live unbiblical lives.
Yet, if we would repent, we would find the truth to be clear. Paul's own words
are worth quoting, but the student should read the whole of Romans 1 and 2.

> For what can be known about God is plain to them, be-
> cause God has shown it to them. Ever since the creation of
> the world, his invisible nature, namely his eternal power and
> deity, has been clearly perceived in the things that have been
> made. So they are without excuse, for although they knew
> God, they did not honor Him as God or give thanks to Him ...
> They exchanged the truth about God for a lie and worshipped
> and served the creature rather than the Creator who is blessed
> forever. . . . And since they did not see fit to acknowledge God,
> God gave them up to a base mind, and to improper conduct.
> They were filled with all manner of wickedness, evil, covetous-
> ness, and malice. . . .

Men in such a state claim to be wise, but are fools. They are natural, unspiritual men for whom the very wisdom of God revealed in the cross and resurrection seem foolish. There is *nothing really foolish* about the Gospel, but to foolish people it seems so. Yet for the lover of God, the Gospel reveals itself in its power, wisdom, and coherence. For an individual to see the evidence requires a beginning of moral repentance. He must entertain the notion that his stance has been wrong, that he might have to change his life and to seek after the truth with a willingness *to do the truth* when it is discovered. Of course, for a person to come to such a stance proves that the Spirit of God is at work in the heart. Perhaps the love and testimony of believers has awakened this incipient heart repentance through the work of the Spirit. Truly, to such a person the evidence will be found adequate, and God's promise applies that if we seek Him with our hearts we shall find Him.

Therefore there is common ground to the extent that a person is open to the Spirit of God. This is not always externally apparent to the apologist. Yet, God uses evidence as part of His revelatory work in revealing Himself to the one who is turning toward Him. This explains why the evidence convinces some, but why we get nowhere with the person who wishes to fight belief in the Gospel. Faith is the work of God's Spirit.

PETER AND PAUL APPEAL TO EVIDENCE

Peter, in his preaching, appeals to the evidence of fulfilled prophecy and the resurrection (Acts 2). Paul connects the unknown god of the stoics of Areopagus to the God who revealed Himself powerfully in the life, death, and resurrection of Yeshua, Jesus the Messiah. Yet these evidences are not calculated to independently convince the adamant unbeliever, but are parts of the message of Jesus through which the Spirit of God will convict the heart of the willing. Paul knew as well that, despite the fall, man *qua* man still maintained dimensions of knowledge which partially reflected truth. He would therefore emphasize his understanding of the listeners by appealing to such content that was held to be true by them as a motivation for them to listen to new evidence for God's revelation. The *common grace* of God enables partial truth to be discovered even by the unregenerate mind. Hence, points of mutual understanding can be found, but only the willing will be led on to further truth.

CONCLUSION

The apologetic task is valid as a tool of the Holy Spirit in bringing the unregenerate to a knowledge of the truth. However, it is also valuable in demonstrating the wisdom and exhibiting the truth value of our faith to the believer. It is a raw kind of prejudice that causes the unbelief of those fools who think they are wise in calling the Gospel foolish. Our task is now to exhibit the nature of evidence and the limits of argument, and to lay out a carefully constructed case for biblical belief. This will show that both objectivists and subjectivists perceive something significant, but their perspectives alone are inadequate.

CHAPTER ONE: STUDY QUESTIONS

1. Put in your own words your understanding of what you think a subjectivist believes about the apologetic endeavor.

2. Describe in your own words your understanding of what an objectivist believes about the apologetic endeavor.

3. At times the teaching of Jesus seems positive toward the presentation of evidence for faith. At other times, He seems negative. Explain why this might be so.

4. Summarize the nature of Paul's use of argument and evidence for the truth of the Gospel.

TRUTH AND THE

NATURE OF VERIFICATION

HISTORICISM AND RELATIVISM

PILATE SKEPTICALLY ASKED, "What is truth?" This question, raised at the trial of Jesus, has been the subject of philosophical debate for millennia. The question "What is truth?" has often been confused with the question "How shall we determine what is true?" Today there is a relativistic spirit concerning truth in religious and philosophical matters. This spirit argues that nothing is really true or false—that something may be true for me but false for you, and vice versa. If it is useful to you, call it truth. This is similar to a belief concerning morals: "Nothing is either right or wrong, but thinking makes it so."

In just such a way, some would repeat this saying and substitute the words "either true or false." In the philosophy of history, this relativism is reflected in a movement known as "historicism," a movement defended by William Dilthey. The historicist never seems to tire of showing us how our belief systems are products of various historical cultures. In the historicist view, there is no way to determine which cultural belief system is more reflective of "the truth." Truth is thus relative to the particular culture of which we belong. It varies from culture to culture.

This spirit of relativism has not only influenced thinking concerning history, but it has also pervaded the disciplines of both the social and natural sciences. In natural science, a utilitarian view known as "operationalism" has become common. "Operationalists" hold that science is true only in the sense that it provides us with formulas and operations that bring about certain results. Other theories and processes which work as well could be just as true even if they yield a different picture of things.

How deeply this spirit pervades our culture. We hear advice given constantly in regard to the issues of truth and right, put in terms of "If it makes you happy," or "If that's what you want," and even "Do your own thing." Hence, the issues of truth and morality are relegated to the level of personal preferences. There is no logical distinction between these preferences and other nonconsequential preferences, such as "I like chocolate cake." Today, even theories of law argue that law is a matter of the preferences of a particular society, with no transcendent basis.

Historicism is a movement based on the reaction of exposure to a variety of different cultures with their varying beliefs, moral standards, and traditions. It is based on the initial confusion of judgment that takes place upon facing the complexity of these cultural differences. Coupled with naturalistic theories of human origins (the theory of evolution extended as a philosophical theory of the meaning of life), historicism certainly has had a vast impact upon even popular thinking among the majority of Western people today. Historicism has, however, demonstrated the importance of the influence of culture on what people believe in philosophical, religious, and moral realms. God's revelation is certainly necessary to break us out of the prison of cultural relativism. However, historicists have been so influenced by a naturalistic world view (strangely this is the only area of truth claim that is really believed, even against the relativistic view itself.) that although they claim skepticism in religious truth issues, the thought of God breaking into our world order to reveal Himself is unthinkable to them. How many so-called skeptics, really in life and viewpoint, reflect a materialistic secular-humanist perspective.

THE CORRESPONDENCE THEORY OF TRUTH

In most realms, we could not function without a sense that we know the meaning of the word "truth." "It is true," we say, "that the #11 bus goes to the midtown bus terminal." "It is true that she is pregnant." "It is not true that this building is structurally sound; do not enter it." "I am truly in love." In countless ways, we show that we believe that we know the meaning of the truth. The question of truth raises a response in naive experience that is certainly reflective of a proper intuitive grasp of the situation. When it is asked, "Is that true?" what is being asked is, "Is the information conveyed in your statements the way things really are?" We can picture or understand the state of affairs reflected by language. Hence, we are asking if the state of affairs reflected in language is the way things really are in the world. This is the nature of what is usually meant by truth when we ask such questions as: "Is she pregnant?" "Does the bus stop here?" and even "Is the world a product of blind forces or the creation of an ordering consciousness?" This understanding of truth is known as the *correspondence theory of truth*.

Against the relativistic view of historicism, it holds there really is truth according to the way things really are. Actually, the historicist view is really contradictory. He claims that the view of cultural relativism is the correct way to look at reality. Yet there is no reason to be a cultural relativist, since this is just one view among others that is held because of cultural influences. The word "truth" never really loses the sense of correspondence to the way things really are. Hence, we hold to the correspondence theory, that *truth is the correspondence of a viewpoint to the way things really are.*

When Jesus used the word analogically and said, "I am the Truth," it included this element. He is the One through whom (by his teaching and his life) we understand the world properly and learn how to live rightly. To emphasize the correspondence dimension of truth with regard to the question of the existence of God, Francis Schaeffer entitled one of his books *The God who is There.* In other words, He is there apart from my subjective experience. It is the way things really are.

THE PRAGMATIC THEORY

Today there are other views of truth which absolutize one aspect of something connected to truth questions and reduce the meaning of truth to that level. Pragmatism holds that *the truth equals: whatever works.* Either this claim is itself not a truth claim about the nature of truth, and is only saying that what works is what works and therefore is saying nothing significant, *or* it is claiming that its definition of truth is *true* in some more significant sense. If it is claiming the latter, then it is contradictory. On the other hand, there is a truth in pragmatism. One of the great aspects of truth, especially scientific truth, is that it is very useful. A true theory will work. Yet the usefulness of truth does not exhaust its meaning. Not only can we know many useless things to be true (trivia), but usefulness itself must not be defined only in terms of scientific or material benefits. It might be very useful to know how to escape hell and attain to everlasting life with God.

Neither pragmatism nor radical relativism of the new consciousness (an Eastern view) provides any solution to the question of truth. Radical relativism defines truth as what we believe. In so doing we create our own world, which world is a part of our consciousness—a dangerous doctrine indeed. The world created by an LSD experience says that one can fly as Superman. However, launching forth from the tenth floor will prove fatal. Truth is not just my subjective perception but is an *intersubjective* (held in common among people or subjects) discernment.

Truth is something that is a subject of our experience, but it is also independent of us. Hence, the correspondence theory of truth surely is most adequately descriptive of the meaning of truth in human communication. Therefore, we conclude for our purposes in this book that *truth is the correspondence of a viewpoint to the way things really are.*

HOW SHALL WE DETERMINE THE TRUTH?

THE DEDUCTIVE APPROACH

The question of "What is truth" is a different question from the question of how to determine what the truth is. Traditional philosophies have tended to absolutize one dimension of truth testing and have sought to make that dimension all-encompassing. *Rationalism* in its traditional form thought that all truth was *deduced* logically from universally known basic truths. Deduction from universal to particular is reflected in the following simple syllogism:

> Premise #1: All men are mortal.
> Premise #2: Socrates is a man.
> Conclusion: Socrates is mortal.

We could ask, however, do we really know that all men are mortal from *a priori* (pre-experiential) knowledge? Or is the knowledge of human mortality a conclusion drawn from vast human experience? It is true that if we are to have truth, our statements must not violate the laws of logic. These laws are part of the structure of reality and the thinking process that expresses truth. Yet, for most people, the experiential dimension in the discovery of truth is undeniable.

Gordon Clark has sought to find a deductive method for apologetics. He begins with the premise that "Every word in the Bible is true." If this premise is true, then, since the Bible says that Jesus is the Son of God, we can know that this is true. That the world exists is also known to be true because the Bible says it exists. Although Clark demonstrates how important the knowledge of the Bible is for a proper understanding of reality, has he really disproved the importance of the experiential dimension simply by showing the contradictory aspects of many experientially derived philosophies? It is true that our knowledge of what the Bible says comes from its words which have a meaning for us as part of a *learned language*. Language is acquired by experience. If it is said that the Holy Spirit illumines the Bible, then He, at least, is experienced *before* we know. Rationalists have invalidly absolutized the logical dimension of knowledge and its deductive aspect. This is an important dimension, but is not in itself adequate.

THE INTUITIONIST APPROACH

Intuitionists have held that truth is known by a strong impression or intuition. We simply "know." That we know something is direct experience is much as the experience of the blue color of the blotter on the desk upon which I write. Certain things do seem to be known without either sensory experience or logical deduction. It seems to be just revealed. Augustine held that all knowledge, even if connected to logic and experience, is gained through revelation by the Holy Spirit. There are undeniable experiences in our lives of such an intuited nature. Such intuition is not emotion, but a direct knowing.

Once, when I was a youngster, my mother spoke of my sister, who was away, with alarm. She was sure my sister was injured. I passed this off as foolishness and sought to convince my mother that it was just a fearful idea with no basis. Later, in the evening, my sister returned home. She had been brushed by a car and injured. Since this time I have known many examples of such intuited knowledge. (We should also note the gifts of the Holy Spirit in this regard, gifts such as word of knowledge and wisdom in I Corinthians 12.) Through the prompting of the Holy Spirit, I have personally experienced knowledge of persons and events that I had no way of knowing. Those with special gifts point to people in audiences and say that they are being healed of particular diseases. There are too many accurate examples in my experience for me to deny them.

Most people come to faith by the preaching of the Gospel through an intuited certainty or conviction that it is true. We call this the convicting work of the Holy Spirit. Logic and the weighing of evidence play a very limited and hazy roll for many people who come to faith.

The scientist who discovered benzene's chemical pattern described the role of intuition in his discovery of truth. After repeated frustration in experimental trials, he decided to give up for awhile. He went to a room where he found his snake biting his tail. "That's it." he exclaimed. For those who are unfamiliar with organic chemistry, we note that benzene is a chemical that is best described as a hexagonal, circular ring in configuration. The snake formed a circle and the scientist intuited his answer.

Despite the crucial and mysterious aspect of intuition in gaining knowledge of the truth, is it alone adequate for deciding among truth-options? What happens when people claim opposing views on the basis of their intuitions? The scientist who discovered the chemical pattern of benzene went into his lab to test his viewpoint or theory. Einstein and his disciples tested his theory of relativity (an insight) by experiment. Indeed, Paul says, concerning prophetic intuitions in the Spirit, that we are to *prove or try* all things and to only hold fast that which is good (I Thess. 5:21). Evidently, the mind must use logic and compare prophetic insight to the truths already established.

THE EMPIRICIST APPROACH

Lastly, we have the views of the *empiricists*. Narrow empiricists limit knowledge to that which is acquired by the five senses. They tend to model knowledge on the scientific method of observation and verification. Narrow empiricism overlooks the extent to which experience is much greater than the five senses. We not only gain experience parallel to sight, smell, touch, taste, and hearing, but we experience much that transcends any sense or combination of sense experiences. Examples are the experiences of love, hate, guilt, shame, beauty, sadness, conviction, and a host of intuitive experiences. Narrow empiricism usually leads to materialism.

Broad empiricism recognizes the limits of narrow empiricism and is willing to define experience as that which human beings describe as their "lived-world" experience. The "lived world" includes not only sensory experience, but religious, moral, legal, romantic, and many other experiences. This "lived-world" concept of experience, which cannot be reduced to mere materialism, is a central theme of a movement of philosophy in Europe known as the *"Phenomenological Movement."*[3] The sensory dimensions of experience alone are inadequate. However, does even a broad empiricism adequately recognize the organizing function of logic as transcending our specific experiences? Logic seems to be rather a part of the *structure* of all knowledge and thought.

Actually, we find that logical, intuitive, and both empirical (narrow and broad) factors combine in our experience in the discovery and defense of truth.

Although intuition may play a crucial role in personal faith, for philosophical and apologetic purposes all factors are crucial. We therefore shall seek to describe how they are related.

THE CRITERIA (TESTS WE USE) FOR TRUTH

Human beings generally use three criteria for truth. These criteria are constantly used to test the truth value of ideas or propositions. Many are not even aware that they use these criteria. They are a part of our lives. We grow up with them, we value them and embrace them. We cannot but use them as first principles, for any proof of them uses them (even as Aristotle taught in Book X of his *Metaphysics*). We must either embrace them or deny them. They are part of the structure of our thinking. If they are acquired, they are acquired before we become self-reflective in consciousness. People who do not value them, and who deny them as Buddhist, still use them to get along in every day life. Even such Eastern thinkers as those who hold that the world is an illusion (*maya*) use them to operate in the world of so-called illusion. Some value them fully, some partially. Those who do not value them at all live in a different world; indeed, this is the world of the insane in psychiatric wards. These criteria give due respect to the rational-logical, the intuitive-creative, and the empirical dimensions of our existence. We here list and explain them.

1. *Consistency*: The first criterion is simply an affirmation of the basic laws of logic. Nothing that is contradictory is true. We use the criteria of non-contradiction or consistency all the time. We see this in the well-known syllogism:

> Premise #1:   All men are mortal.
> Premise #2:   Socrates is a man.
> Conclusion: Socrates is mortal.

We cannot deny the conclusion if we affirm the premises. So, in everyday life we discount as meaningless all statements that are of a contradictory nature. We would dismiss as nonsense the statement "I decided to vote for Ronald Reagan since he has been a good president, even though he has done a terrible job in both foreign and domestic affairs." This is a contradictory statement because foreign and domestic affairs encompass the whole of presidential responsibility. Although people do not maintain such obviously contradictory viewpoints, more subtle contradictions can often be found in the positions held by people. They are unaware that they hold as true two views, beliefs, or positions that cannot both be true. Exposing these contradictions may motivate them to change their view in various regards.

Sometimes it has been argued that truth can be contradictory. It is argued, for example, that light is described both by wave theory and by particle theory in physics. For some purposes we need to treat light as particles, for other purposes, as a wave. Is this really a contradiction? No, it is simply saying that light as a phenomena exhibits *partially* characteristics of both waves and particles. However, light as a phenomenon is distinct from both. Strange or paradoxical relationships are not contradictory.

By setting up problems in particular forms, ancient Greek and Hindu philosophers were fond of showing that reality was contradictory; hence this world was said to be an illusion. Usually these so-called contradictions arise from defining the phenomena of experience in invalid ways. Once these phenomena were invalidly defined, insoluble antimonies resulted. The problem is not in the phenomena, but in the invalid definition. Zeno defined motion as traversing an infinite number of points one at a time. Hence an object could never move at all, since any motion would require an infinite number of sub-movements that would take forever. All change and movement was seen as an illusion. This contradiction only proves the theory false. Motion is simply the movement of an object in a continuum of space. It can not be *reduced* to skipping between points.

The law of non-contradiction or consistency holds throughout human experience. In *seeming* contradictions we press for new insight to resolve the problem. The law of consistency implies the basic laws of logic.

2. *Coherence*: Oftentimes coherence is confused with consistency as a standard of truth. There is really a distinct criterion. *Coherence is the principle that any valid explanation must tie together that which it seeks to explain.* Coherence as a criterion stands between the logical and the empirical dimensions of truth testing. Incoherence is *not* necessarily a reflection of contradiction. This becomes clear in the simple example to follow:

> "Why did you go through the red light and crash into my
> police car?" asked officer Melton.
> "Because my Volkswagen is red and your police car is
> blue," answered Mary.

On the face of it, this explanation is incoherent. Although there is not an A = ~A contradiction, the explanation is clearly senseless. "Redness" and "blueness" are not the kinds of terms that explain accidents. However, if Mary answered, "Because my Volkswagen was unable to stop due to that patch of ice over there," we would note that ice and its ability to eliminate a great deal of friction are the kind of thing that thwarts the ability of cars to stop. This is a coherent explanation.

It is possible that an explanation that is on the surface incoherent can be shown to be coherent by the addition of new terms. Perhaps *colorblindness* could have something to do with making the first explanation sensible. However, as expressed without the additional term, it is not coherent.

Sometimes people have the illusion of having explained something because they place terms in an explanatory syntax or arrangement of phrases that is used in explanation. A closer examination reveals these terms to have no real coherence or explanatory value. The number of examples of incoherence can be multiplied without limit. For example, the statement "John slapped his girl across the face because Mayor Koch was a eating cheese sandwich" is incoherent. *Alice in Wonderland* is a book that not only exhibits inconsistency but also incoherence. This book is full of explanatory syntax being used in nonsensical ways.

We also find many examples of incoherence in philosophical explanation. Chief among them are proposed solutions to the mind-body problem (how the mind and the body are interrelated). When the mind and body are defined as two separate substances, one material and extended, the other nonmaterial and without extension, it is asked how they are related. It is said the mind and body interact on each other. How do they interact? Descartes, the noted early–seventeenth-century French philosopher, said that they interact through the pituitary gland, which is a substance between mind and body. It might be that the relationship of the mind and body is an insoluble mystery (although we do not think it is). However, once mind and body have been separately defined, positing the pituitary gland certainly does not give a coherent explanation of the relationship. Malebranche (after Descartes), on the other hand, posited a view called parallelism. He maintained that mind and body do not interact at all. Events parallel to those in the mind are ordained by God to occur in the body. These explanations do no make sense to us. It is possible that a reformulation of the problem could lead to a solution avoiding such incoherence. It is not our purpose here to discuss this, but we believe that some contemporary philosophers have given a more coherent account of the mind-body problem.

Life may present us with mysteries and seeming unexplainable phenomena. This we do not deny, yet no addition of incoherent terms of explanation to these phenomena clarifies anything. Better to leave the mystery than to give the illusion of explanation.

3. *Comprehensiveness.* Comprehensiveness is the criterion emphasizing empirical experience. This states that *the truth of a view or proposition is dependent upon its taking into account all of the relevant data of experience.* We may have a consistent and coherent explanation, but if it does not take into account all of the relevant evidence, it is an inadequate and perhaps even false explanation. For example, if someone stated that President Carter had been a poor president during his term of office, and upon questioning it was determined that the person making this claim was ignorant of Carter's policies and their effect on the American economy, and ignorant of his writings and speeches as well, we would have serious grounds to question this person's judgment, since he certainly did not take all of the relevant data into account or even take an adequate sampling before making his judgment. The person who dismisses the resurrection of Jesus before examining the primary source documents which testify to the event also violates this criterion. A person who believes in a materialistic explanation of reality, who holds that there is nothing outside of this world's sensory experience, errs greatly if he does not seek to seriously account for paranormal psychical phenomena such as are reported in G. N. Tyrell's *Science and Psychical Phenomena*, or Kurt Koch's *Christian Counseling and Occultism.*

We see the criterion of comprehensiveness constantly involved in the revisions and improvements in scientific theories. When scientists seek to determine various cancer-causing factors, they constantly stress the importance of taking into account all the relevant factors. Leaving something out might greatly distort or invalidate the conclusion. For example, one might isolate a factor in high correlation with cancer, such as coffee drinking. Coffee drinking could be then said to cause cancer. Upon further research, data could show that the cancer is rather caused by a physical, genetic lack in the person that causes tiredness and hence a greater desire for coffee in this group of people. Therefore, coffee is not the cause at all, but merely a response to the cause. Science must constantly be open to new data and theory-revision for progress to be possible. The refusal to take new data into account is *obscurantism,* the rejection of new evidence.

The same criterion was central in the acceptance of Einstein's *theory of relativity* in place of Newton's theory. Previous theory had posited the existence of ether, a very sparse substance said to permeate the whole universe. This ether would form into an "ether wind" caused by the rotation of the earth, a wind so slight that it was normally undetectable. Michaelson and Morely devised an experiment to measure the ether wind and its effect on light. This ether wind proved nonexistent. Yet it took another scientist, Albert Einstein, to come up with a total theory of space, time, movement, and light. This theory, the theory of relativity, replaced Newton's partly because it could explain the results of the Michaelson-Morely experiments whereas Newtonian theory could not. Many scientists clung to the old theory, refusing to adopt the new one. They questioned the experiments altogether. Finally, the evidence of new experiments that confirmed the original ones produced a weight of evidence which was adequate to convince the scientific community.

Biology, sociology, and philosophy all need to account for all the relevant data of experience. World-view thinking is often difficult since it needs to provide the *broadest* framework for all human experience. It must account for science, religious testimony, purported revelations, and more. However, much of the relevant information for world-view thinking is the same for every age and is not significantly changed by the addition of natural scientific data, which is of less significance in world-view philosophy than is the nature of human life and history. Human experience in every age exhibits love, guilt, faith, fear, courage, war, cruelty, and kindness. The evidence of history for believing in the Bible as God's revelation, for example, is largely the same today as in the second century. New archaeological and literary discoveries may be significant, but the basic evidence has not really changed.

It is a rule, in all science and philosophy, that only that theory or view that can account for all the relevant data that it seeks to explain or tie together is adequate. We must seek to choose the theory that does this best. *Therefore a theory is called true to the extent that it consistently ties together or explains (i.e., demonstrates coherence) all of the relevant experiential data (i.e., is comprehensive).* To the extent that it does not, it is falsified. We call the combination of tests using both deductive and inductive (empirical) criteria the "3 Cs";and we shall constantly refer to them: consistency, coherence, and comprehensiveness.

TRUTH TESTING AND VALUE COMMITMENTS

The limitations of these criteria are tied to the limits of persons: the extent of their experience, their openness to revelation as an experiential source of knowledge, their value commitments, and their prejudices. Weighing evidence in any area of knowledge is affected by these factors, but in world-view religious issues it is especially affected. No person is infinite in his experience but God. No person is without those mental and attitudinal filters which screen out and interpret data without allowing the data and evidence to speak in a challenging way. As Peter Berger has shown in *The Social Construction of Reality*, people and cultures have an unquestioned set of almost subconscious assumptions about life. What is admissible and inadmissible as evidence and perspective is predetermined by a cultural-mental grid. This is why, without reason, significant options are sometimes dismissed as unthinkable or absurd. Our only hope of transcending this bias is to seek to be aware of it, to question the almost universal assumptions of our particular culture and to seek to empathetically step into the shoes of those with wholly different perspectives. Then, by comparing perspectives and examining evidence, we move on, it is hoped, to hold views of greater comprehensiveness. Perspectives are part of us. They are reflective of our values and experiences. They are not simply the conclusions of weighing evidence, but are the filters of what is allowed to count as evidence. We could illustrate this by saying that every person's consciousness of the truth is colored by the mental glasses he or she wears. Some glasses let in more light, and some less; some distort more, and some less; some even give a false picture altogether. Today materialism, secularism, and *naturalistic-evolutionary* concepts of origins are so pervasive in some circles that any evidences or data that do not square with these cultural presuppositions are dismissed out of hand.

We can give many examples of this from common life and psychology. We once invited an older man to live with us. This man had been traumatized by difficult family relationships, a nervous breakdown, and very difficult experiences of self-rejection. Despite the great love lavished upon him by our family and our community, he simply could not rest in the truth of his being loved and cared for. Minor things were taken as major proofs of deep rejection. This was the way he actually saw existence. It was certainly reflected in his inability to believe in a God of love. How could one express an argument from the existence of love as to its origin in God to a man who did not *experience in his heart* the reality of love. While psychologists of atheistic persuasion are fond of explaining belief in God as only a reflection of psychological need, we can as well explain unbelief by psychological projection. A person who has experienced both the heights of love and the depths of tragedy has a fuller experience from which to judge life and its meaning. The person of limited experience does not realize that he is judging upon too limited an evidence base unless new experience breaks through these limits. Only thereby could he recognize past limits. It is not within his present experience to fulfill the criterion of comprehensiveness. *We all have to apply the "3 C's" within the limits of our own experience.*

One of the experiences of constant amazement to me is that people brought up without love and consistent discipline have an impossible time making judg-ments concerning whom they can trust. They tend to trust themselves to the untrustworthy and mistrust the trustworthy. The same problem would affect their ability to recognize the trustworthiness of Jesus revealed in Scripture. If we extend this, we know that a person in extreme paranoia really believes that everyone is out to get him. Every attempt to prove otherwise is looked at as fur-ther proof of deception.

Perhaps we could give an example of religious prejudice. Picture a super–right-wing fundamentalist Baptist. He believes that all who claim to be Chris-tians, but are not super–right-wing fundamentalist Baptists, are really the devil's deceivers in this world. They are all hell bound. Now imagine that this funda-mentalist meets a Presbyterian Evangelical who loves God with all his heart. The Presbyterian also seeks to love his neighbor as himself. Therefore he acts in love toward the Baptist, mowing his lawn when he is sick, sending financial help when the Baptist is in need, and quieting the neighborhood children so the Bap-tist can rest. When the Baptist finds out all that the Presbyterian has been doing he responds, "Why that social gospel-er, look at the lengths he is willing to go to deceive me, to draw me into compromising my doctrinal purity."

One day, however, after the Baptist has recovered, he slips and falls into a neighbor's pool. He can not swim. The Presbyterian hears his cry for help and jumps in to save him. At this point the Presbyterian sinks under the water in ex-haustion just as the Baptist reaches the pool deck. He drowns and gives up his life to rescue the Baptist. At this point, the Baptist could *see the light* and say to himself, "He really did love me; he really was a godly man." This could be a conversion experience that would greatly alter his life. His attitude to other Christians might radically change. Yet it is still possible that he could say, "Why, he was so perverse that he even risked his life to deceive me."

There are several conclusions to be drawn from this example. This is because religious knowledge is akin to personal knowledge (our knowledge of and rela-tionship to other persons). There is real evidence to be weighed, yet this evi-dence is *broadly* empirical, and not exactly like the evidence of a mathematical-scientific experiment. It is of the order of trusting persons. Concerning this evi-dence we can say:

1. A person's ability to weigh personal levels of evidence is limited by his per-sonal values, commitments, and prejudices.

2. Although there may be overwhelming and adequate evidence to convince some to a point beyond doubt, for others that evidence will not be allowed ad-

mission. Yet the one convinced sees himself to be more comprehensive in his evaluation of the evidence and may take confidence despite the fact that others are unconvinced.

3. Great evidence brings a person to a point of decision where either he may be in certain regards converted, or he may harden his heart. We saw both possibilities in the narrow-minded Baptist. It is similar in many other realms of life (political, moral, social, and religious). Our response to revelation in the religious realm is very much like a decision to trust a person. Our values greatly influence our viewpoints. For example, a solipsist believes that all life and all other persons are simply the creations of his own subjective ego. If one points out that he does not seem to be controlling events, he can respond that his subconscious is controlling them, but that his conscious ego and his subconscious are not yet adequately integrated. After all, he could say that he is no longer capable of controlling his dreams. We can certainly see that recourse to such argument is foolish; there is no way to invalidate the thesis of the solipsist if he wants to argue in this fashion. Rational argument will be inadequate. The reason is that the solipsist so dis-values other persons, regarding them as of no independent significance, that he has removed himself from the usual common ground of normal life, upon which basis most argument proceeds. His view of other persons is such that he is willing to make them only subjects of his imagination. A person who loves his neighbor as himself finds that this is not a real option. To love means the other person is valued as a distinct personality like ourselves with rights and significance not to be denied.

Imagine a rock-pounder, a person who has decided that the only thing worth living for is pounding rocks with a hammer. Yes, our society might put such a person in an institution. However, if a person has really come to this stance in life, can we necessarily and *rationally* argue him out of it? Even scientific and mathematical knowledge can be denied. There is a Flat Earth Society. However, when we move into the realm of the social sciences, philosophy, and religion, the ability of values, prejudice, human perversity, and human goodness to influence our knowing ability becomes great. Hence a Buddhist can claim that the world is illusion, that there is no soul, and that the end of human existence is the cessation of separate consciousness. This is a product of Buddha's response to suffering. The conscious life of separate individuals was not really desirable to him.

All argument, but especially argument beyond the mathematical and natural-science levels, proceeds only to the degree that there are common grounds of valuation, or at least openness to new ways of seeing by which the argument can convince the person(s) to whom the argument is presented. Argument reveals inconsistencies and incoherences and presents evidences that may lead a person on to a new viewpoint of greater comprehensiveness. The apologist needs to speak more of evidence and argument as providing a *disclosure* of new truth to the listener, just as the Presbyterian's drowning provided a *disclosure opportunity* to the Baptist. A person might decide that it does not make sense to value persons as of the highest worth if they are only chemical-physical arrangements of matter (if our origin is explained by chance), plus time.

This particular quality of knowledge I have called *the value pervasity of knowledge; that is, the knowing function is a function of the whole person, and a person's ability to know is inseparable from his values.*

It is my view that the evidence for the biblical faith is overwhelming. From where I stand, examining all the evidence I know of, I can not see it otherwise. But I do not thereby believe I can simply, by rational argument alone, convince another. Whole areas of prejudice, values, and even unrecognized philosophical influences and presuppositions may first have to be revealed. Therefore, prayer and the work of the Holy Spirit are the *essential factors* in the *opening-up process* in which evidence can be received with its full impact so that it might *disclose* new truth. *Value pervasity* is therefore a key and crucial point in understanding the doing of apologetics.

Any viewpoint that fails in fulfilling the "3 C's" test is invalid. Labeling other viewpoints false in regard to the "3 C's" test is part of an important process of elimination by which the case for the biblical faith is bolstered. Invalidation narrows down the options that can be wisely chosen. In principle, falsification is a key means of determining the validity of scientific viewpoints. In religious world-view matters the same falsification principle applies. However, the falsification principle in these realms must deal with the data of experience and evidence that do not provide the precision of test-tube knowledge.[6] Karl Popper has greatly expanded our understanding of the testing and verification of scientific theory through the falsification principle.[7] I believe that the same principle is significantly a part of testing religious views. Truth on religious levels is attained in part in apologetics by comparing world views.

Naturalism, pantheism, and biblical theism all must be tested upon the basis of which view best meets the criteria of consistency, coherence, and comprehensiveness. As views are compared, people are in dialogue seeking to transcend their value limitations to arrive at a more comprehensive viewpoint. No world view perfectly fulfills the criteria of testing, partly because of our own limits of expression. However, we believe that the biblical faith fulfills the criteria far better than any other viewpoint. We will also find that objections to the biblical faith are easily categorized as to whether it is claimed that our view is inconsistent, incoherent, or not comprehensive. We will not solve all mysteries. Still, by showing that these charges are not true, but are poorly founded, and by amassing philosophical and historical evidence, we believe we can put forth a case for the biblical faith which is convincing.

The student would do well to read Frederick Ferre's *Basic Modern Philosophy of Religion*. This book provides a section on the testing of religious world views that is similar to our own and is most satisfying.[8] A few years ago, a manuscript was sent to me by David L. Wolfe of Gordon College entitled *Epistemology: An Introductory Essay*.[9] This is now published for all to enjoy. This essay is the finest short piece I know which expounds and defends the basic viewpoint we have taken. Wolfe's thinking has had a formative influence on me. Arthur Holmes of Wheaton College has some excellent material as well in his *Faith Seeks Understanding*.[10]

By comparing our subjective viewpoints (intersubjectivity) we approach greater objectivity, since by so comparing we take into account a greater wealth of evidence and experience. Therefore we can respond to the objectivist and the subjectivist in apologetics by noting that they both emphasize aspects of the truth. We call our view the *intersubjective framework comparison approach*. We hold that objectivity (the way things really are) is approached by critically comparing viewpoints or frameworks. We will constantly see, in presenting evidence, where values limit the force of evidence for some. We will also see why a broader viewpoint, from our perspective, does lead one to see that the evidence strongly points to the truth of the biblical faith. Although we can force no one by the weight of the evidence, we can cause many to be aware of their value commitments. Apologetics can be a tool in the hands of the Spirit for conversion as well.

Arthur Holmes was fond of saying that an adequate Christian philosophy was "perspectival, pluralistic, dialogical, and redemptive."[10] First, we are limited and furthered by the perspective out of which we evaluate the meaning of life. Secondly, progress is made in a dialogue among persons of a plurality of different perspectives. This is a redemptive endeavor that allows for growth in understanding in the process.

CONCLUSION

The ability to apply a theory to more and more new evidence and experience without that theory being falsified, while other theories are falsified, provides verification for the theory sufficient to warrant our trust. This applies as well to religious knowledge, where trust includes the richer dimension of entering into a relationship with God. Our view of truth testing allows for the great richness of factors that are involved in personal decisions of commitment. It recognizes the importance of values, the work of the Holy Spirit, creative intuition in coming to know the truth, the importance of logic, and the central place of empirical evidence. New experience constantly confirms our faith. Yet only the Holy Spirit, not apologetic argument itself, can open the hearts of people to God's truth. Finally, whether or not one submits to God is more a matter of heart-condition than evidence. It is often the case that objections are only "smokescreens" hiding rebellion toward God. Therefore, the place of evidential apologetics is important but modest: helpful to the sincere searcher after truth, but of little use to the one who has decided to reject the God of the Bible.

CHAPTER 2: STUDY QUESTIONS

1. What is the criterion of coherence? Explain in your own words. How is it different from consistency?

2. What is the meaning of the criterion of comprehensiveness? Outline your understanding.

3. Explain the meaning of *value pervasity*. Clearly outline how values influence our ability to know.

PART TWO

HOW DOES RECENT CULTURE

POINT TO THE TRUTH OF

THE BIBLICAL WORLD VIEW?

INTRODUCTION TO PART TWO

The secular humanist has often promised a better life through man's self-efforts, through the application of science, and through improved political and social arrangements. The thought of man as merely a highly complex animal has gained wide acceptance. Secular-humanist perspectives can be seen in greatly diverse philosophies: from Marxism to the enlightened egoism of Ayn Rand, from Freudian psychology to the behavioral perspective of Harvard psychologist B. F. Skinner. Though amazingly diverse, these perspectives agree in their analysis of man. His origin is naturalistic, *and* all human behavior can be explained in purely this-worldly terms.

"Secular humanism" is a religion (as noted as part of a decision by the United States Supreme Court). A religion is a total belief system that structures a person's most basic values and commitments. Secular humanism is the dominant religion of both the communist world and the Western world. There are other religious influences in our culture beyond secular humanism, Judaism, and Christianity. They are mostly of Eastern origin and include Hinduism and Buddhism, usually in its Japanese Zen version or its parallel Mahayana school. Today's New Age movement is a primary vehicle of Eastern religion. Our secular culture tends to be relativistic in values and beliefs. Hence religious views and values are said to be matters of personal preference. New Age (Eastern) religious views are also relativistic.

Recently a group of thinkers has asked an important question, to wit: Do the prevalent relativistic religions, presently gaining favor in the West, provide a framework for life in which man can find fulfillment, satisfaction, and a lasting sense of purpose? To answer this question, this group of writers has turned to the artists and writers of our generation. Artists and writers often display a sensitivity to the implications of social trends and values before the population as a whole is aware of these implications. Therefore these thinkers ask, Do our art and literature reflect a view in which modern man's perspective really fits his "needs" as "man *qua* man"? Does the "mannishness of man," as the late Francis

Schaeffer expressed it, allow him to live comfortably within the frameworks of our new relativistic humanistic beliefs? Several writers have taken up this question, including Francis Schaeffer, the late Hans Rookmacher, Os Guiness, Stuart Barton Babbage, and C. S. Lewis.[1] We encourage the student to read these important works.

Before we present our own view on these matters, several comments are important for our apologetic task. Basically the argument from culture states the following (either implicitly or explicitly): *a correct world view should be one in which man finds a sense of fulfillment or satisfaction through living on the basis of it.* A world view should provide a knowledge of how man fits into the scheme of things. Furthermore, a man's life should be able to reflect a pattern that is basically consistent with the world view professed. If a man can not live consistently in line with his philosophy or live in a satisfied and fulfilled way on the basis of the world view he professes, then we have evidence that the world view is false, that man himself is other than what his world view professes him to be.

Schaeffer traces the origins of today's predominant secular world views to philosophers of recent centuries. He then seeks to show how the world-view perspective arising from these philosophers is reflected in modern theology, literature, and visual art.[2] Schaeffer sees many recent great artists as an intuitively insightful group of men and women who perceive the logical and practical results of secular world views. He argues that contemporary artists and writers clearly show that the modern secular world view is depressing and destructive to man. Also, man is not able to live consistently within this world view. To more accurately understand this argument, I summarize it as follows:

1. The true world view will enable man to live a fulfilling life by living consistently according to its teaching concerning his place in the scheme of things.

2. Modern art and culture reveal that man is not able to live consistently with fulfillment within this modern secular world view.

3. Therefore the conclusion is that the modern secular view is false.

4. The only significant alternative to this world view is the biblical world view.

5. The biblical world view both explains human life adequately and enables man to live a fulfilling life according to its teaching on his place in the scheme of things. This is reflected in biblically inspired artists.

6. *Therefore*, the biblical world view should be accepted as true.

It is obvious, however, that this argument only holds for the person who accepts the basic premise concerning the evidence of what would constitute a true world view. If the person does not value the criteria of truth outlined in the previous sections of this book, then this argument would hold little weight. Furthermore, if he holds that man absurdly does not fit into the scheme of things and that intense dissatisfaction, lack of fulfillment, and dehumanization reflect the nature of life, then these arguments will not persuade him. However, most people *do* hold to the above premises. They reflect basically held human values or orientations. Hence, when people embark upon a religious quest for truth, they are expecting to find a vision of reality that will enable them to live with purpose.

Basically, I believe that Schaeffer is headed in the right direction in his use of culture for apologetics. Even though I have adopted his scheme of the "upper and lower stories" for illustrating the wrong understanding of rationality and meaning in western thought, I do not wish to imply that no nonbiblical world view can be rational (consistent and coherent) within itself. Rather, some other rational world views (Islam, Ramanuja's version of Vedanta Hinduism) are, in my view, lacking in comprehensiveness in explaining all of the evidence. I do not believe that Schaeffer developed an adequate epistemology which would show the relationship between evidence, presuppositions, and logical criteria.

In addition, I note that while art can be evaluated by world-view implications, this is only one approach to art. Art is also to be approached according to its universality, beauty, and communicative power. Schaeffer at times gives the impression that art is primarily to be evaluated as rational philosophy. Some art reflects little world-view concern. There is literature which simply tells a good story, and there are paintings that simply reveal the nature of form and color. There is literature that reflects the human dimensions of life by God's common grace even though the artist is not a believer in the Bible. The artists chosen for our presentation are purposely selected because they illustrate the implications of some nonbiblical philosophies. The student should be forewarned that our selection would be a distortion if it were used to give an impression of the totality of the world of art and literature.

I believe that Schaeffer's insight into much of the intellectual world as dividing the rational-meaningless (personally) from the mystical-irrational-meaningful with its leaps of faith is brilliant and correct. However, not all nonbiblical world views fit this easy interpretation. Examples of rational but nonbiblical world views are John Macquarie's liberal *Systematic Theology*, Edgar Shetfield Brightman's *Personalism*, and Alfred North Whitehead's *Process and Reality*. It is too simple to believe that all nonbiblical philosophies are either irrational leaps to meaning or rationalistic reductions of life into matter in motion. My plan is to outline the roots of contemporary culture in a different way than Schaeffer, drawing from different sources and reinterpreting some of Schaeffer's sources. This will give us a significant exposure to the question of what contemporary culture has to say concerning the truth of the biblical world view.

Although our material reflects Schaeffer's insights, the perceptive reader will note differences. Our explanation of the mathematical roots of contemporary thought differs from Schaeffer's presentation He traced the problem of the divided field of knowledge to Thomas Aquinas' distinction between knowledge gained by natural means and knowledge gained by special revelation. Schaeffer's bent against natural theology, I believe, wrongly traces the origins of the problem in Western thought to Catholic natural theology. Leanne Payne's excellent book *The Healing Presence* gives an insightful analysis of the split between the rational and the meaningful in the West. Her explanation of the human psyche under this split is brilliant. Her understanding of the origins of this split are parallel and supplementary to my own analysis.

I wrestled with whether to use Schaeffer's scheme of the divided story. I chose to do so because it is an excellent teaching tool. On the other hand, I do not want the student to conclude that my apologetic method is the same as his.

Cultural apologetics can powerfully illustrate the human implications of some world views and give impetus toward seriously considering the biblical alternative.

THE ROOTS OF

CONTEMPORARY CULTURE

ANCIENT GREECE
THROUGH THE EIGHTEENTH CENTURY

Our study of contemporary culture's roots will make clear how important it is to carefully define the meaning of our terms, since many today use terms divorced from their traditional meanings. My desire is to avoid any unclarity in apologetic witness.

Western thought is influenced by two major streams of thought: Greek and biblical-Hebraic. Sometimes thinkers have sought to join these streams in incompatible syntheses. We do not want to so overemphasize the differences that the reader would conclude that there is no compatibility; both traditions held to a place for logical consistency in testing truth.[3] This alone can explain the biblical injunctions to test prophecy by its compatibility with earlier revelation (Deuteronomy 13, 18, Galatians 1, etc.). However, the logical dimension is more emphasized in Greek thought. Though it is a bit of an over-generalization, it is not far afield to say that Greek philosophy began as a rebellion against religious traditions and is a main root of modern secularism. This secularism denies belief in God and the grounding of human values in supernatural reality.

EARLY GREEK PHILOSOPHERS

The early Greek philosophers embarked on a quest for certainty in a world of flux. If the world constantly exhibits change and my senses are obviously fallible and part of changeable bodies in flux, how can anything be known with certainty? The Greek world was ever so much more stable than our own, yet the Greeks, as well as we, keenly sensed the impermanence of life. An examination of my home city of New York reveals incredible change. Buildings have been demolished, new skyscrapers have been built, people have died, and others have been born. If we and the objects of knowledge are always changing, can we know anything with permanence or certainty? As Heraclitus put it, "You can never step into the same river twice." He argued that all is relative; there is no absolute truth to be had.[4] Others could not abide by this conclusion. They looked for certainty in the world of logic and mathematics.

Pythagoras taught that the essence of everything is its specific number.[5] For Plato, that which was certain was the realm of eternal ideas.[6] The world of sensory existence could not be certainly known. Yet the idea of a thing remains ever the same. Although actual chairs can be destroyed and the material of which they were made can be used to make something else, the idea of a chair or of what constitutes "chairness" remains forever the same. The *ideas or forms* of a thing, Plato thought, had real existence in an eternal realm of the forms. Goodness, virtue, and beauty were also existent ideas in this eternal realm. We participate in eternity by the mind and hence can know the forms. We only recognize a thing to be a chair, for example, because our minds remember the form of the chair and are reminded of the form by a material manifestation. The soul itself, to Plato, is a form and knew all forms before its birth. This is why we can be reminded of the form by individual objects. All knowledge is remembering.

The later Plato greatly emphasized mathematics as a higher form of knowledge. It was a realm of greater idea-purity. The realm of the forms provided *certain* knowledge, as certain as two-plus-two-equals-four. However, the realm of sensory or empirical reality provided only opinion. *Rationalism* is the term used to describe such a philosophy, which denies the value of empirical experience for knowledge. The goal of existence, in Plato's view, is the escape of the soul from the body so that it might enjoy an unhindered vision of the forms in its eternal home.[7]

Although it is not directly pertinent to our apologetic purpose, the student may be questioning the reason why material things have forms which temporarily reflect the eternal ideas. Plato's solution is to posit a demiurge, a god-figure who stamps the form upon chaotic matter so that it temporarily takes its shape. Due to the work of the demiurge, the eternal chaos takes on a temporary form in *participation* with the eternal idea or concept. Yet the demiurge is not a God as is found in the Bible. He is only a functionary in the eternal scheme of things; He is not the creator of all, the highest Being in power and goodness. In Plato, the highest form is the form of the "good" which ties together all other forms. We emphasize again, however, that for the later Plato, mathematics provides a higher form of knowledge and certainty than the more unclear ideas of other forms. Mathematics was *knowledge indeed*; empirical knowledge was mere opinion. The quest for certainty and security in our knowing process rested in the fixity of mathematics. Thus Plato solved the problem of the flux and impermanence of Heraclitus.

Aristotle did not accept the rationalism of Plato. Instead he came up with a new approach to the forms and empirical reality. For Aristotle, the forms did not exist in some trans-empirical realm, but were within the various individual objects of matter. The universal "chairness" only exists in chairs. The mind has the ability to perceive the universals within material things. This view is called *hylomorphism*. In Aristotle, the soul is the form of the body; they must exist together. Yet for Aristotle as well there is a strong emphasis on the importance of mathematical knowledge, measurement, and logic. In Aristotle, we find the crucial beginnings of classification in scientific study. Just as an aside, we might note that Aristotle was famous for his concept of the *"Unmoved Mover,"* the source in the universe of all motion and secondary causation. This concept of a first "uncaused cause" was the basis for later arguments for the existence of God in the most famous Catholic thinker, St. Thomas Aquinas.

We mention these philosophers because they are central in understanding the basis of modern culture, which is traceable to the fourteenth to sixteenth centuries. We do not discount the importance of philosophers and theologians between the time of Aristotle and Thomas Aquinas, but are tracing the key roots of modern thought which happen to be in Greek thought.

HEBREW THOUGHT

Hebrew thought, in contrast to Greek thought, is less abstract and more functional. Hebrew thought is rooted in the realm of empirical time. It is concrete and describes life and reality in the terms of common human experience. Philosophically, we could say it is *phenomenological*, a term used for philosophies that base themselves on the *lived world* rather than upon abstract thinking. Relationship with God, revelation, miracle, love, pain, death, battles for God, a coming Messianic Age, moral sin, goodness, and the Law of God are the subjects of

Hebrew thought. This contrasts with forms, mathematics, abstract arguments for God's existence, and schemes of classification. Hebrew thought is *essentially religious*, whereas Greek thought is a reaction to the religious myths of Greek religion. Greek thought has a *secularizing* impact. This contrasts with Eastern thought, which is both religious and abstract. More will be said about this later.

THE REDISCOVERY OF ARISTOTLE

During the Dark Ages, social, economic, and political upheavals disrupted the dissemination of manuscripts for learning. Monasteries became centers of preservation, but much was temporarily lost to many circles of learning. The rediscovery of manuscripts and the delving into ancient Greek sources intensified at the end of the Middle Ages.[8] (Some manuscripts had never been recovered.)

Aristotle, the successor of Plato, was rediscovered first. He had already influenced Islamic thought. Islamic scholars were a great influence in science, math, and philosophy. They preserved and translated Aristotle. The work of Thomas Aquinas in the thirteenth century drew upon this source of learning. His rational arguments for the existence of God based upon a first cause for material motion, design, and morality were squarely based on the logic and argument of Aristotle. Although Aristotle was more empirically oriented compared to Plato, the heavy emphasis on an almost *"mathematical proof type of argument"* became greatly influential in Western thought. It is also well to note Aristotle's influence on what came to be known as *natural theology*.

In Thomas Aquinas there is a strong distinction between what can be known by natural reason, even in unregenerate men, and what can be known by revelation. Yet, seven hundred years after Aquinas, we find that natural man does not come to common convictions. This distinction was a means of preserving his high regard for the views of the Greeks and giving a rationale for how non-Christians could discover such amazing truth. Unfortunately, this produced a Western tradition where man was seen as autonomously able to achieve greatness without regard to God whatsoever. It added to the ascendancy of an independent spirit, intellectual pride, and a sense of autonomous ability in the intellectual community.

How fantastically different and more biblical was the view of Augustine, that all knowledge is illumination by God's Spirit. In *common grace*, even fallen man, because he is created in God's image, can be given the revelation of partial truth. However, to the extent that the effects of the fall take root in society, to that extent are knowledge and truth eclipsed. The criteria of truth testing can be applied to the whole of a world and life view. The biblical world and life view can be presented in all of its force intellectually. Yet without the Holy Spirit's illumination even the criteria of truth themselves can be rejected, as well as all other dimensions of knowledge. Hence, apologetics aims to be the most forceful "world view"–ish presentation of the biblical faith as a tool for the Spirit in illumination. It is akin to preaching the Good News.

We can distinguish common grace (which enables all people to receive some levels of knowledge and understanding) from the special grace and knowledge given in regeneration through the work of the Holy Spirit. However, we cannot separate any area of knowledge and culture as independent of God's Lordship and of God's grace as its means of reception. Man is dependent on God for all knowledge and value.

THE FLORENTINE ACADEMY

The next great wave of learning can be traced in part to the circle of scholars and students who gathered at the Florentine Academy.[9] The Florentine Academy centered its philosophical study on the rediscovery of Plato. This rediscovery was of the later Plato, with his emphasis on the higher value of *mathematical knowledge*. The mathematical aspect or mode (as Dooyweerd would put it) was absolutized as a higher more certain form of knowledge, the basic way to understand reality. *Also, from Plato, Jewish and Christian theologians understood the realm of heaven and the place of God's dwelling as an eternal, timeless, fixed sphere with the forms as archetypes or ideas in the eternal mind of God.* This timeless God differed greatly from the God of the Bible.

Once it was accepted that God was beyond all time and sense, all biblical concepts about God loving, mourning, changing his mind in response to human behavior, judging and intervening had to be taken as only metaphorical or analogical ways of talking about God. These terms were seen as more correctly interpreted by philosophical abstract terms. Human language was not seen as directly applying to God. We are not too far afield in seeing this development tending to later skepticism in which there is doubt as to whether or not one can meaningfully speak about the divine at all[10]

How can human time-related words refer to a timeless deity? In Scripture, the God of the Bible creates the world. The world of his creation is reflective of his life, thought, and heavenly abode. There is no unbridgeable gap between time and eternity.[11] Although God relates to the whole universe beyond our limits of spatial location on this earth, time-related words which speak of his

intervention in the world, of his forgiving those who repent, of his love and judgment, etc., do directly or adequately refer to Him. The most basic dimension of
time-relatedness, *before and after*, appropriately refers to God without any great
qualification. The divine is best spoken of in personal terms (love, judgment,
forgiveness, anger, etc.) rather than in the abstract terms of Greek philosophy.

Unfortunately, the gulf between Hebrew and Greek modes of thinking was
not perceived. For the Hebrew, the personal and relational dimensions were the
most basic and real, even though knowledge in this realm was not amenable to
mathematical certainty. "I trust you" is more central and important than the
knowledge that "3 x 7=21." Knowledge built from the model of personal trust
was the model for all knowing, rather than knowledge built from mathematical
models of deductive reasoning.[11]

The sixteenth-century French philosopher Descartes did not understand this
gulf. Directly influenced by the Florentine Academy, Descartes was the father
of modern European philosophy. This thinker sought to prove the existence of
God in a mathematical way. Like Plato, Descartes saw sensory or empirical
knowledge as so subject to error that he sought religious certainty in innate (un-
learned) ideas in the mind. These ideas were clear and distinct, indubitable. All
other certain knowledge had to be deduced from these clear and distinct ideas
just as mathematics proceeds by deducing new relationships from basically held
premises. Those clear and distinct ideas, according to Descartes, upon which we
can rest secure are mathematical and geometrical truths, premises, postulates,
and theorems.

How then do we get from mathematics to God? This comes in the form of
what is known as Descartes' *ontological argument* for God's existence. An ontological proof proceeds by *deduction* from an idea that is innate in the mind. It is
not inductively learned by reflecting on empirical experience. Descartes says he
has an idea of a "most perfect being" in his mind, and he reasons accordingly:

P#1: There is an idea of a Most Perfect Being in my mind.

P#2: A Most Perfect Being must have existence to be perfect.

P#3: This idea is not gained by any knowledge of the imperfect

───────────── objects of empirical experience.

C: Therefore God must exist

Descartes begins his discourse by doubting all knowledge. However, he cannot doubt his own existence: "I think, therefore I am." Furthermore, he can not
doubt the clear and distinct ideas of math or the reality of God. Because God is
good, he can assume that He causes his empirical knowledge of the world to be

real and basically trustworthy. The world is real, for God would not delude him. This style of reasoning is known as *rationalism*. The most real and important knowledge is deduced from innate ideas.

Although our contemporaries reject Descartes' rationalism, aspects of his thought still influence us all. This includes the idea that *more certain* and *even important knowledge* is based on mathematics at least as applied to *measurement* and *scientific* formulae that have a mathematical base. Number, measurement, equations, frequencies, etc., still have ascendancy in the learning of Western culture. Pythagoras' statement "everything has a number" parallels our day.

THE TURN TO SCIENCE

The Florentine Academy had a direct influence on Galileo and an indirect influence on Newton. Although these early scientists were empiricists, there were points of amazing similarity with rationalists. To summarize then, empiricists are those who seek to gain knowledge from the world of experience. Rationalists are those who believe knowledge is gained from the innate ideas in the mind. The rationalists, including Plato and Descartes, gave a high priority to mathematical knowledge as a higher type of knowledge. These "clear and distinct ideas" are certain knowledge.

The early empiricists such as Galileo distinguished between primary and secondary qualities. The primary qualities of objects were those which could be quantified. They included length, spatial relationship, speeds, velocities, accelerations, etc. — all aspects of reality that can be described in mathematical formulae (quantified). Hence the empiricists gave priority to mathematics, calling such properties *primary* as opposed to *secondary* qualities. Color, smell, taste, and sound would come under this category of secondary qualities. These distinctions were preparation for the impetus in modern thought to quantify all experience.

A radical form of this empiricism can be found in a twentieth-century philosophy known as *logical positivism*. In logical positivism, objective knowledge was defined as that which was scientifically observable or mathematically measurable. Truth became defined as that which was capable of scientific-observation or measurement types of proof. All else was consigned to the subjective, emotive, and nonimportant dimensions of life. Experiences such as intuition, color perception, love, hate, and inner consciousness all had to be either dismissed as unimportant or capable of being translated into *observation measurement statements*. Under this framework of reasoning, "I love you" as a phenomenon could be fully accounted for by measuring and formulating the chemical reactions in the brain (chemical reactions being the relationships between those small objects known as molecules, made up of atoms of neutrons, protons, and electrons). Life was *reducible* to physics and chemistry. For example, the experience of "green" was reducible to measurable wave lengths of light.

The quest for certainty caused a devaluing of common human experience, which was disparaged as merely subjective. We might *see* all colors differently, but the *measures* of the wave lengths of color are objectively the same. The roots of this kind of thinking can be traced to the primary- and secondary-quality distinction of Galileo and Newton, though they never would have come to the radical conclusions of positivism. Both were biblical theists.

PRIMITIVE WORLD VIEW

This modern objectivism contrasts greatly with other significant approaches to knowledge and truth. A critique of such thinking is certainly in order. Our critique will trace a line of thought parallel to this *objectification-certainty* preoccupation. The *primitive world view*, reflected in both the Bible and *other religious viewpoints*, stands in sharp contrast to these trends. The writings of Mircea Eliade are fruitful in this regard.[14]

When primitive man thought about his world, it was more in terms of spiritual meanings, both negative and positive. Mathematical relations were secondary. For example, when a primitive tribe set up its camp, it would place its temple or religious shrine at the center of the camp. This then, in their conception, became the center of the universe. In other words, the center of the universe is where the gods are. This concept of center is not mathematical.

In ancient Israel, Jerusalem was considered the center of the world because this was where the presence of God was to be found: in the temple. If the tribe moved, the universe was conceived to be in chaos, without a center, until the new spiritual center was established. Though I view primitive religions as aberrations from God's truth, they do preserve the fact that relationship to the supernatural is the center of life.

In all primitive world views the earth was the center of creation. Man was seen as the most important part of creation because he was the apex of all which was upon the earth. That the earth was the center was less a statement about scientific astronomy than a statement about the locus of meaning and importance. In this world view it was easier to believe that God was concerned for man, since man was viewed as significant in the creation. This conception came into conflict with later scientific conceptions of the center of the universe because recognition was not given to the fact that the scientific and religious points of view were speaking from completely different referents of meaning. These two views were not necessarily in conflict unless the scientific was given a superiority.

THE SCIENTIFIC CONCEPTION, 1600–1900

The scientific study of astronomy has shattered this primitive conception. This shattering was without real validity. When mathematics was looked at as the basic way to see reality and meaning, a false premise gained influence over Western thought that was bound to destroy the concept of man's significance in the scheme of things. The astronomer Ptolemy had worked out the mathematical relationships of the planets and stars from the viewpoint of a geocentric (earth-centered) conception of the universe. It was so well constructed that accurate predictions could be marvelously made. However, the mathematics was extraordinarily complex. The astronomer Copernicus discovered that by positing the sun at the center of the solar system, he could make the same predictions with much greater mathematical simplicity. It was assumed that simpler equations that performed the same function were *truer*; Copernicus concluded that the sun was the center of the solar system. Believing that the universe was an aesthetically balanced creation, he assumed that planetary orbits must be circular. Circular motion was also seen as perfect. This, unfortunately, proved to be mathematically false, and Kepler discovered the elliptical nature of planetary orbits. The conception of a heliocentric (sun-centered) solar system with elliptical orbits was given great confirmation in the work of Galileo.

The Roman Catholic Church, usually scorned and mocked for its opposition to the sun-centered concept of the solar system, *rightly* sensed a danger in this conception. However, it fought the battle on the wrong grounds. Unfortunately, the Catholic divines accepted the concept that a mathematical relationship determined meaning. They reasoned that if the sun was the center of the universe, man and the world were no longer central in meaning to God. Instead, the Church should have argued that mathematical relationships of space, time, and distance are *totally irrelevant to religious significance*. The Church should have opposed the misconception that mathematical knowledge was a higher form of understanding and certainty. This misconception alone could lead to the false conclusion that the heliocentric view was a danger to religion. This false conception of the centrality of mathematical meaning led to technological advances but impoverished the human spirit.[15] The Church should have argued that the earth was the center of the universe for spiritual purposes in a nonmathematical way. Once we note how unfounded assumptions called religious meaning into question, it amazes us to note how these assumptions have dominated and continue to dominate Western thought. This is because the application of the scientific method to the world greatly advances technology and physical understanding. Western progress in science deludes us into ignoring more important but unchanging aspects of personal existence. *The basis of man's spiritual centrality (significance) cannot be in any way determined by mathematical relationships among objects in space.*

TWENTIETH-CENTURY SCIENCE AND ASTRONOMY

I look with great humor upon the rethinking of science and math in the twentieth century. Most people still conceive of the universe in pre–twentieth-century terms. Yet the work of Albert Einstein, in his theory of relativity[16] has revolutionized our conceptions with such thoughts as:

1. The universe is finite.

2. Space is curved, so that unlimited travel will bring a return to the starting point.

3. Time slows down as speed increases.

4. All mathematical relationships in space are relative to the object chosen as the point of reference.

If these conceptions seem strange to you, perhaps you can see that Einstein was seeing a very different universe from the integrated machine-universe in the science of Isaac Newton. Our common understanding is usually Newtonian. For example, in common speech we usually conceive of the earth as a fixed reference point when a train moves upon the face of the earth. However, we could *mathematically conceive of it* by making the train the fixed reference point. When we press the throttle, the earth moves underneath a fixed train. That which we choose as a fixed reference point is a matter of convenience, or of what works more easily for us. Yet from the view of mathematical truth, which object we choose as a fixed reference point is *relative*. This is the case with all objects in space and their interrelationship. This theory is called the *theory of relativity*.

Einsteinian theory is well established. Calculations based on it are used in sending out distant space probes. (This would not be possible by the use of pre-Einsteinian theories.) Einstein even went so far as to say that it is not "truer" to say that the sun is the center of solar system rather than the earth. The mathematics can be worked out in either way. It is all a matter of which view is more convenient to the scientist in regard to the operations he seeks to perform. Simpler math is more convenient but not truer. Sun-centered views are mathematically simpler but not truer. Every school child is taught that the sun is the center of the solar system in some absolute truth sense. Yet we can say that the earth is the center of the universe in many ways. What are these ways?

1. *From the view of our common experience:* From our phenomenological, everyday speech, the earth is our fixed reference point. We walk upon the earth, we say the sun rises and sets. This speech is convenient, adequate, useful, and true within its own sphere of usage. Our reference point is the earth in relationship to our common experience.

2. *From the viewpoint of religious meaning:* God created the world and sent his Son the Messiah to die for man, earth's highest being created in God's image. The earth is therefore central.

3. *From the viewpoint of relativity theory in science:* We can make the earth our fixed reference point from which we make all calculations. It may not be convenient for all scientific operations, but it is no less true than other reference points.

AN EVALUATION FROM HEIDEGGER

The great twentieth-century German philosopher Martin Heidegger[17] made some devastating comments in his writings concerning the priority of measurement and mathematics in determining human meaning. First Heidegger argued that the most direct and real source of meaning is the world of everyday experience, the "life-world" or *Lebenswelt*. Scientific meaning is an abstraction from the "life-world" that aids us as a tool for using the objects of reality. Yet these abstractions are *not the meaning* of reality. For example, the meaning of red is the *common experience of the color in human life* which we *trust* is the same for most human beings. We can also scientifically say that red has a mathematical equation of wave lengths per second connected to it that can be measured by a light meter. Yet red is not *reducible* to the mathematical measure of light waves. The meaning of red is simply red as a perceptual experience of human beings. It is the same as with all human experiences: love, hate, guilt, smells, sounds, etc. Significant mathematical, chemical, and spatial relationships may be connected to these experiences, but these experiences can not be reduced to scientific meanings.

C. E. M. Joad well stated that science alone leaves us with a tasteless, color-less, and meaningless world.[18] Not only so, but scientific abstractions *depend* on life-world meanings for their identification and use. For example, let us say that a scientist desires to identify the chemical reactions in the brain connected with love. The subject is wired for the experiment, and his wife walks in; his heart beats faster for the joy of her presence. He says, "I feel love." At that moment, the scientist gets a reading on the chemicals. Yet if the subject did not first iden-tify his experience as the experience of love, the chemical connection would not be discovered. Scientific meanings depend upon life-world meanings for their very existence. They are dependent upon the "prima facia" reality and value of life-world meanings. Only by experiencing love can the chemical reaction be dis-covered. Love can not be *reduced* to chemical reactions. This is true for all other life-world experiences: colors, sounds, smells, tastes, and love, hate, and guilt.

To seek to reduce life-world meaning to scientific meaning is to saw off the limb upon which scientific meaning sits. This is a philosophical error known as the *"fallacy of reductionism." Scientific meaning is an abstraction from the life-world; it is not the whole of meaning or truth. It is a partial aspect of the world that serves as a tool for human control and understanding in the material realm.*

By the same token, we can understand other issues of the relationship of science to faith. Some people are overwhelmed by the huge numbers measuring the distances of space and the ages of our universe. These numbers cause them to think that human beings are insignificant. Yet mathematical measures again have no direct relationship to personal meaning and significance. Space and time are a matter of mathematical measures which are mere conventions of the human mind for use in science. Our minds are greater than the large sums of numbers within them. We only dwarf ourselves in the face of these large num-bers by giving them quasi-poetical meanings that these numbers do not objec-tively possess. It is all a matter of perspective. Man feels small because he is so small in size compared to the size of the universe. However, he can also be seen as very large in stature because he is so much larger than microscopic life. Actu-ally, man is, according to the teaching of Pascal, halfway between the size of a galaxy and a molecule. So much for math determining meaning.

The modern movement in European philosophy known as *phenomenology*[19] is helpful in the areas we have been discussing. The tremendous pre-eminence of seeing meaning through mathematical measure must be broken; it is a bondage over the human spirit; it robs man of the sense of his significance and makes the concept of God's love for man seem foolish. The Bible notes that with God a thousand years is a day. Time measures are projected according to how we sub-jectively experience them. To the evolutionist, the ages of evolution may seem long but they also may be seen as short periods in God's experience for man was not yet on the scene to give greater meaning to time and creation. Man projects *his experience of time* back into history and gives this subjective projection of experience a significant meaning; yet this projection of meaning is not objectively valid.

WESTERN PHILOSOPHY:

SIGNIFICANT ASPECTS, 16th–18th CENTURIES

Western philosophy after the Renaissance (the sixteenth century) continued to move down mistaken paths. Thomas Hobbes (seventeenth century) built up-on mathematical and materialistic models to produce a godless philosophy. All was composed of atoms moving in spatial relationships. This was the only basic, lasting reality. This philosophy was as old as the ancient Greeks, who also had atomists among them (e.g., Epicurus). Although John Locke rejected Hobbes' basic atheism, he perpetuated several of the misconceptions already present in Western thought. His concept of primary and secondary qualities was an exten-sion of past thought. He also developed a concept of a basic material substratum underlying all the objects of experience.

Why choose to believe in a material substratum rather than an ultimately spiritual substratum, or no substratum at all? This questions has been a continual source of debate in philosophy and has led some to the conclusion that the material-substratum view has no real foundation. Nevertheless, the view that there is a material substratum does tend to lend credence to materialism. Locke wrote an apologetics book in defense of the biblical faith, including arguments from fulfilled prophecy and miracles.[20] In spite of his positive attempt to de-fend the faith, he perpetuated concepts which undercut human significance.

As scientific progress confirmed the great usefulness of math and measure-ment, God, personality, salvation, and the mystery of life were lessened in sig-nificance. This is seen in the perspective of the men of the eighteenth-century Enlightenment. Successful material applications of scientific knowledge caused many to evaluate other types of knowledge to be of lesser significance or un-important. God was a distant first cause of the material order that ran on its own according to material laws. He was not considered a necessary and involved party to the process of nature and human society. This philosophy was called *deism*. Only the theory of evolution was needed to provide a fully materialistic conception of human origins.

The philosophy of Immanuel Kant, the great German philosopher, is the root of much modern thought. After reading the skeptical philosophy of David Hume from England, Kant sought to explain how knowledge was possible. Although most of Kant's work contained brilliant insights, one dimension of his work would perpetuate skepticism. Kant held that we have no actual knowledge of reality itself (the noumena), but only a secondary knowledge of the contents of our own minds (the phenomena).[21] The very structure of our mind and senses filters and organizes this knowledge. Whether or not our knowledge is at all parallel to the *real* is a matter of faith. We can never get beyond the phenomena to the real (noumena) realm of being. In his *Critique of Practical Knowledge*[22] Kant argued that God, freedom, and immortality are not knowable or provable realities, but are postulates of human ethical existence. Freedom is a postulate of the meaningful-ness of moral speech concerning right and wrong. If I am not free, I cannot be held accountable for my behavior. God and immortality give impetus to moral behavior, since these two postulates imply that good behavior will be rewarded and evil behavior will be punished after death. Without God and immortality there is no possibility of there being just compensation according to what we deserve. This life alone does not fairly recompense man according to his morality.

Knowing was thus limited in scope to the organization of sensory experience through the logical capacities of the mind. Religious realities became postulates of ethics. Yet for a religious person, God was known as certainly and directly as other persons. Rather than seeing God as a postulate of ethics, the true believer sees his ethical behavior as a product of his *relationship with God*. Only this relationship motivates real moral behavior without self-righteousness. Only a love relationship issues in a humble life of obedience to the Law of God. God is not a postulate of reason but is the sum and source of all existence. As proverbs stated, "the fear of the Lord is the beginning of wisdom" and knowledge and understanding (Proverbs 1:8). It is not the weak conclusion of a postulate.

In his *Religion Within the Limits of Reason Alone*, Kant extended his concepts to dismiss the central concepts of the Bible: substitutionary atonement, the pervasive nature of sin due to the fall, and the cross and resurrection as the basis for right standing before God. There was no room within his limited concept of reason for revelation.

In this climate, humanistic religion gained ground over against a truly biblical faith. Friedrich Schleiermacher wrote of religion as a feeling of *absolute dependence*. As a feeling, religion was emptied of significant doctrinal content.

The way was now open for man to dismiss religious realities as insignificant. Sensory knowledge was at least producing the progress of science. Why be concerned with the unknowable ultimate reality (the noumena)? Why not just better man's knowledge by a more accurate application of sensory knowledge? We can now see the beginnings of what Francis Schaeffer called the divided field of knowledge. A lower story of rational sensory knowledge unintegrated with an upper story of nonrational religious myths which man can choose to be a part of by an irrational leap of faith.

Leap of	Religious realities	Noumena
faith	The Ultimate, the really real	The upper
postulate	meaning, significance, purpose	story
Gap between		Gap between upper
upper and		meaning, and lower
lower stories		religion and rational

The World of Sensory Experience,
Mathematics, measurement, scientific organization

The rational world becomes a meaningless empty world void of religious significance. It is made up of the measurements and mathematical organizations of material things. The religious world is not integrated with regard to the rational. It is participated in merely by an inexpressible feeling, by a leap of faith, or by making a postulate.

The Bible still had great sway in Western culture; therefore, the realities of religion were not yet relegated to the ephemeral realm of the upper story. People still saw the world through the Bible and integrated their learning by its basic teaching. Yet the impetus from philosophy and science was gaining ground for the view that the really real and knowable was tied to the sensory, the measurable, and the mathematical. In popular misunderstandings of Kant, it was held that the phenomena constituted the only real world of importance with which we have to deal. Of course, in Kant the phenomenal world is the world of our experience, but it is not the really real since it is filtered through our categories of understanding.

How could one account for human personality and nature without reference to the Creator revealed in the Bible? The mid-nineteenth century provided the secular humanists with an answer to enable them to believe they could account for the world without reference to God. The ancient idea of evolutionary materialism would now be given quasi-scientific credibility. Until then, there was no alternative in the West to the concept of creation, despite the materialistic bent or drift of post-Enlightenment thought as we have outlined it.

CHAPTER THREE: STUDY QUESTIONS

1. Generally, how does an argument from culture logically work?

2. How does the later Plato still impact contemporary approaches to meaning?

3. Compare and contrast primitive and scientifically influenced approaches to meaning.

4. Explain the critique of scientific-mathematic approaches to meaning by M. Heidegger and C. E. M. Joad.

THE NINETEENTH AND TWENTIETH CENTURIES, PHILOSOPHY AND THEOLOGY

HEGEL, MARX, AND DARWIN: THE ROOTS OF EVOLUTIONARY MATERIALSIM

GEORGE FRIEDRICH W. HEGEL provided a comprehensive world view that captured universities in both his native Germany and in Europe and America. Hegel's central idea was the evolution of *Divine Spirit*, or *the Absolute*.[1] Hegel saw both history and philosophy in terms of a logical outworking of basic principles. This logical outworking was called *dialectic*. Dialectical thought seeks to tie together all of the dimensions of human existence by finding conceptual bridges between opposing ideas and aspects of reality. For example, in Hegel, the opposites of matter and mind can be tied together by the larger concept of Spirit. All of reality can be seen in terms of such opposites being tied together by larger integrative concepts.

History as well proceeds by the progress of opposite historical movements and stages being united by a new stage where the opposites are united. The movement both of thought and history followed a dialectical progress of *thesis, antithesis, and synthesis*. For example, we could look at the present system in the United States in which free-market capitalism (thesis) and socialism (antithesis) have been merged into a synthesis of democratic liberalism which includes aspects of both. (Hegel would not have chosen such an example, but it is a helpful illustration for students today.) The progress of history and thought moves toward these larger syntheses. The new synthesis becomes a new thesis with a new opposing antithesis which is integrated into an even larger synthesis.

This movement or *progress* in history and thought is part of the progressive self-realization of an Absolute Spirit that pervades the universe. The god of Hegel is, of course, a humanistic god who is far removed from the God of the Bible. Yet in the nineteenth century, scholars of even Jewish and Christian seminaries sought to accommodate the Bible to Hegelian thought. Of crucial note is the widespread acceptance of the concepts of evolutionary development that began to pervade universities and seminaries. The sense of progress in science gave impetus to this concept of progressive social development in history as well.

Karl Marx, a student of Hegel, is said to have turned Hegel on his head. Marx saw a dialectical moment in history, too. It was not the progress of an Absolute Spirit, but was rather the progress of material forces in history. Marx's philosophy, the basis of Communist thought, was called *dialectical materialism.*[2] In Marx, the progress of history, determined by materialistic economic forces (*economic determinism*), moved through the stages of thesis, antithesis, and synthesis with inevitability. Feudalism and its antithesis, monarchy, led to a new synthesis in capitalism. Capitalism struggles with the dictatorship of the proletariat, eventually leading to the ultimate synthesis and end of historical process in a classless utopian communist society. Though there was no pantheistic spirit guiding or moving the historical process toward this desirable end, it was accepted that the material forces of human societies were moving them to this wonderful goal.

As profound and brilliant as Hegel and Marx were, it is astonishing to note how subjective their organization of history is. Choices for what constitutes a thesis and its antithesis seem coherent within the context of their thought. However, when one questions the basic premises of their thought and their choices for their thesis and antithesis, their choices reveal themselves as arbitrary. Unfortunately, ideas gain credence through *cultural acceptance*, not necessarily through their validity. It is well to note that the concept of history moving toward a goal is really, at root, a biblical idea and is based upon biblical theism. Pantheism and, especially, materialism in no way supply the concept or implication that history moves toward a goal, even a desirable goal. These philosophies are really perversions of an originally biblical idea.[3] Because men and women flee from the living God and seek to resist his will, they construct systems of apostate thought to enable them to more easily hide from God. Deception makes rebellion easier to maintain; a seemingly coherent philosophical system justifies the rebellion. These evolutionary philosophies prepared the ground of society to receive a *quasi-scientific* philosophy which has dominated the world for over one hundred years. This is the *Darwinian theory of evolution*. The central problem with evolution is *not* the issue of whether or not present life forms on earth came after the appearance of myriad other life forms which antedated the present life forms on earth; nor is it that these previous life forms were ordered in time such that later forms more closely approximated today's forms; nor is it that simpler, less developed forms preceded present forms. Whether or not such a natural history is correct is determined by comparing both the evidence of the historical record of fossils (geology) and the biblical record properly understood. The *real issue* is whether or not life forms on earth can be *fully accounted for* on the basis of *material causation*. Can the concepts of chance, mutations, and natural selection fully account for vegetable, animal, and even human life on earth?

Darwinism gave a rationale for atheism by providing a system of explanation to account for creation on a solely materialistic basis. Yet this explanation is a delusion. The concepts of time plus chance plus matter can never account for the order and complexity of creation or for the capacities and qualities of human life. Nevertheless, Darwinism gained great acceptability and provided a model of explanation in the nonbiological fields of philosophy, science, history, and sociology as well.

Evolution as a basic root concept for explaining all dimensions of existence pervaded nineteenth- and early–twentieth-century teaching. The issue of its scientific adequacy will be handled when we compare the adequacy of various world views in a later chapter. For now we desire to note how evolutionary concepts were invalidly transposed to understand world history (Hegelian and Marxist historiography), but especially religious history.

EVOLUTIONARY CONCEPTS APPLIED TO THE BIBLE

Despite the great thrust of evolutionary concepts, one great bulwark always remained to ward off the ascendancy of nonbiblical philosophies; it was the Bible itself. Western culture was tied to biblical roots. Far too many people saw the supernatural revelatory character of the Bible as proof enough to preclude them from wholly adopting these new evolutionary philosophies. The Bible evidenced a moral character and a quality of credibility through fulfilled prophecy and the evidence of the resurrection of Jesus the Messiah. Its effect for good on society and its power to change individual lives were important as well. However, a skeptical spirit began to influence academic institutions. People in these institutions began to approach the Scriptures with a destructive critical bias coupled with an evolutionary mentality. This was not a healthy, humble questioning by which truth is discovered. It was rather an attitude of arrogance. If all of life naturalistically evolved from simple to complex, from primitive to advanced, they reasoned, we should expect this to be the case with the history of religion. Indeed, it was thought, Hegel's philosophy is the highest evolution of human understanding. Therefore, we should expect to see history progress in understanding from primitive times unto our own advanced understanding.

This reasoning was also applied to the Bible. Since the Bible developed over centuries, we should see this evolution within its own development. Destructive critics with Hegelian-evolutionary presuppositions approached the Bible to show how it was a natural product of human religious evolution rather than the product of divine revelation. These critics held that the Old Testament underwent many phases of re-editing, adding materials, and reformulation. They taught that, as one looked at the text, one could see primitive strands of material and strands of more advanced material. This was especially emphasized in regard to what had been traditionally regarded as the Mosaic writings.[4] The attribution of the first five books of the Bible to Moses was seen as legendary. Rather, these books were seen as the products of story-telling, embellishments and myths within the history of Israel.

Four basic strands were discerned. "J" material was the oldest and reflected a more primitive concept of God. This material calls God by the name Jahweh and pictures God in visible manifestations like unto a man relating personally to His people. This material was dated in the ninth century B.C., hundreds of years after the period of Moses. "E" material, the second strand, was intertwined with the "J" material during the period from the eighth to the seventh centuries. This material calls God Elohim and reflects a higher concept of God. The third strand, the "D" material, includes material from Deuteronomy through II Kings. (Some held that its influence on the earlier material could also be discerned.) This material was said to show a higher concept of God and social justice. It was dated during the time of King Josiah at 609 B.C. The book of Leviticus and other very complex ritual material were dated in the fifth century B.C. and were called the "P" material.

Fulfilled prophecy was discounted as well. Prophecy was seen as written after the events it purported to predict. It was explained that this was done in order to give credibility to the writing as if it had come from ancient times and from significant legendary persons.

Archaeological evidence since the time of the origination of these theories has seriously undercut the credibility of these theories (called variously the documentary hypothesis, the JEDP theory, and the Graf-Wellhausen theory, named after its first founders). The balance of new evidence supports the traditional views of the authorship and dates of the biblical books as well as the supernatural character of the Bible.[5] William Foxwell Albright, the renowned archaeologist and father of modern archaeology used his weighty pen to disprove the "prophecy-after-the-event theory."[6] Yet, just as in the development of human life, now the concept of evolution was used to show that the Bible was merely a human book. Liberal thinkers professed to hold a high regard for the Bible because it sometimes came close, in their view, to Hegel's view of Absolute Spirit. However, in liberal thought of the nineteenth century, the best of the Bible was still reflective of merely creative human insight concerning Absolute Spirit, not God's revelation breaking into the world of human culture.

These evolutionary ideas were also applied to the New Testament. The miraculous was discounted. The evolution of New Testament theology was seen in terms of Hegel's thesis, antithesis, and synthesis. Peter's stance represented the Jewish-Christian stance; his antithesis was Paul's anti-law stance. These opposing views were said to be synthesized in Luke's writings (Luke and Acts).

Reginald Fuller develops criteria for what was authentically from Jesus in his *Foundations of New Testament Christology*. Basically, only that which is greatly at odds with and transcends the contemporary culture of Jesus can be known to be authentic. By this a person supposedly can see the higher stage of development brought by Jesus.

This approach to the New Testament continues today in the Jesus Seminar. A group of liberal scholars comes together to vote on which material in the Gospels should be received as authentically from Jesus. Therefore, through the democratic vote of radical scholars, we can rediscover what Jesus really taught as opposed to the what the later Church attributed to Him. Critical presuppositions abound. A new red-letter edition can now be produced with much that is from Jesus expunged. What is or isn't from Jesus changes from year to year according to the annual vote supposedly based on the "progress" of new scholarly discovery. Perhaps conservative biblical scholars should attend and out-vote the liberals to prove that Jesus really said and did what the Gospels attribute to Him. (This is tongue in cheek, of course.)

Two views thus gained credence. First was the atheism or agnosticism which claimed that modern scientific criticism had vanquished, once and for all, belief in God and the Bible. The other was liberal religion that saw the Bible as a significant stage in the evolution of the human spirit and its understanding of divine reality. For both, religion evolved from animism to polytheism to crude theism, to theism and finally to Hegel's Absolute idealism, a semi-pantheistic philosophy. For the atheist or agnostic, this was the latest stage of human myth-making. For the Absolute idealist, it was the highest stage of human insight. These viewpoints first swept German universities and seminaries and then spread to other countries. Most American seminaries had succumbed to these ideas by the 1920s. Only Presbyterian Princeton and the Southern Baptist seminaries remained committed to the traditional view of the Bible among Protestants. Catholics also maintained traditional views until midcentury. Most non-orthodox Jewish institutions also adopted the new views of the evolution of biblical religion. In the transition, some tried to salvage what they could of biblical faith. Attempts were made to synthesize some key biblical doctrines with a more human understanding of the origins of the biblical books (as a product of human development). One could still believe in the resurrection of Jesus; a personal God was there and had guided the evolution of human understanding which reached its apex in the teaching and example of Jesus. To this day, we can still find exponents of a variety of viewpoints spanning a spectrum from the traditional view of the Bible and biblical faith to the most radical reformulation and rejection.

The attempts to hold to destructive criticism and yet maintain some aspects of biblical faith achieved inadequate success. Most Protestant denominations began to drift into a more secular humanistic understanding of life and of the role of religious institutions. Liberal Judaism paralleled liberal Protestantism in its development. Today, liberal Catholicism has joined in these perspectives. Without a confidence in the Bible as the Word of God, insufficient conviction was maintained to avoid reinterpreting faith so as to support the spirit of the age. To this day, these evolutionary concepts of the Bible are found within liberal theology text books.

RESULTS IN CULTURE

The results of all of this, as one looks over the past hundred years, was a steady erosion of faith and of the influence of Judaism and Christianity. The faith and life of the Bible cannot long be maintained apart from the concept of the revelation of God to man. Unless the Bible *is* what it *seems* to be—the record of and inspired interpretation of God's intervention for mankind and God's instruction through men moved by his Spirit—the ground and basis for our faith and life are destroyed.

From the biblical revelation, the Western world gained the understanding of man as created in the image of God. Reverence for life, the sanctity of the family, the rule of law, and right over might and tyranny—all are products of the Bible's influence over Western culture. Yet, since the seventeenth century, an opposing influence exalted man apart from God. This was enlightenment thinking or secular humanism. This thinking only gained ascendancy, however, through the acceptance of evolutionary ideas. What have been the results for human life?

It was no accident that Germany was the scene of the Holocaust. Six million Jews and millions of others as well were destroyed because the concept of the sanctity of life based on the Bible had been undercut. The German universities were most successful in the nineteenth century in propagating the destructive criticism of the Bible. The connection is clear. Even though anti-Semitism had been part of institutional Christianity (though truly inconsistent with Scripture), it required the removal of biblical belief to treat human beings as disposable organisms. The vacuum created by destructive criticism was filled by *the evolutionary views* of National Socialism and its concept of furthering evolution through the survival of the strong in war and by human breeding programs.

It was no accident that the Soviet Union and other Communist countries could show such incredible disregard for the human individual. Those with opposing political viewpoints were institutionalized in psychiatric hospitals and injected with excruciatingly painful drugs to destroy their independence. Chemicals causing horrible deaths were sprayed on Asian villages; religious groups were persecuted severely and their leaders were tortured.

Marxist evolution simply provides no rationale for faith in human dignity. The dignity of the individual is religiously based. It is a biblical idea. The very worst religion-based abuses in Western history, such as the Inquisition, cannot compare with the wholesale slaughter of millions which was found to be consistent with the new evolutionary philosophies.

We in the Western world are also seeing an erosion of human dignity through the influence of the same secular humanism. The proliferation of divorce, adultery, pornography, extraordinary venereal diseases, and, above all else, the wanton destruction of human life in abortion reflect the loss of belief in the sanctity of human life. Western civilization has been disintegrating for the better part of half a century.

Only the recovery of biblical faith can stop the disintegration of society. Truly man in his rebellion and unbelief suppresses the truth (Romans 1). His anti-biblical philosophies are means for him to maintain this suppression of the truth.

REFLECTIONS ON THE TWENTIETH CENTURY

The twentieth century has seen the worldwide extension of science and technology. This, of course, brings both benefit and detriment. Yet, the spread of Western science has been accompanied by the *mathematical quantification assumption*, as though math and measurement are the most adequate way to understand all the dimensions of existence. That which is real and rational is defined by what can be measured, predicted, and controlled.

This was especially the case in the philosophy of *logical positivism*. A. J. Ayer, in his classic book *Language, Truth, and Logic*, stated that truth is a concept only applicable to statements which are either mathematical or scientifically verifiable (subject to sensory observation).[7] All other statements were said to be meaningless as concerning truth. This relegated religious and ethical speech to meaninglessness or mere emotive speech. Many have pointed out that this theory, called the verification theory of truth, *would by its own standard be meaningless*. This definition of truth is neither scientifically verifiable or capable of being shaped as an observation statement.[8] Logical positivism, though an abysmally incoherent philosophy, marvelously puts into words the spirit of the age and its predominant delusion—that the "really real" is the scientifically measured. Despite the value of science, scientific knowledge is only a fraction of what must be considered in developing a comprehensive world view which encompasses all the dimensions of human experience.

In psychology, behaviorism has provided a theory of human behavior that is compatible with logical positivism. For B. F. Skinner, human behavior is fully capable of being understood within the boundaries of scientific-mathematical statements. External observation and measurement, in terms of the stimulus of an organism and its response, provide adequate understanding. Chemical and physical constituents of the human organism provide another dimension of our understanding. Love, hate, guilt, joy, sorrow, courage, fear, and the whole gamut of personal terms are thought to be capable of explanation in terms of the external behavioral response of the organism to stimuli.

The German philosopher Martin Heidegger produced a brilliant critique of this kind of thinking in his classic *Being and Time*. Heidegger noted that all meaning is based on personally shared experience in what he called the "life-world." The "life-world" and its basic concepts of personal experience and personalistic language are intuitively grasped and are real in the context of a common human community of shared experiences (*intersubjectivity*). Trust, faith, guilt, hate, fear of death, and dread are shared human dimensions of experience and cannot be comprehended by or reduced to the materialistic concepts of science. Heidegger goes on further to demonstrate that scientific language is an *abstraction* from the "life-world" and depends upon an acceptance of the reality and meaning of "life-world" concepts as generally understood.[9]

Love, for example, is not a chemical reaction in the brain. One must know love as an experience to testify to the scientist who identifies chemical patterns that are present when love is experienced. Love can never be the pattern; it is always *more than* the chemical pattern. Bright fire-engine red is not the mathematical wave lengths that accompany the phenomena.

C. E. M. Joad stated that the scientific world is a world of numbers, waves, particles, electrons and formulas. It is a tasteless, colorless, odorless, and loveless world. This world gives helpful added information for technology, but it is not the whole of the world, nor the really real and true picture of the world. It is an abstraction from the real and is only one dimension of it. Hence we can see with full force Dooyweerd's critique that non-Christian philosophies absolutize one modal aspect of experience and seek to explain all of creation through this limited modal aspect. They seek to squeeze all of reality through a funnel through which it can never fit.[10] Yet, the delusion persists and erodes faith in the human and religious dimensions of existence. Michael Polanyi, in his Gifford lectures, published as *Personal Knowledge*, brilliantly shows the humanness of the scientific enterprise itself. This enterprise depends on human qualities of patience, honesty, ethical integrity, a desire for truth, *creativity, intuitions, and hunches* which can not be reduced in meaning to statements of scientific measurement.[11]

Man at the end of the twentieth century finds himself adrift. He doubts his own meaning in the scheme of things, looks at himself as a complex biological machine, and is thoroughly puzzled as to how he can derive ethical direction from his own world view. He, of course, is holding to a world view which lacks coherence and comprehensiveness. He cannot live within this barren world view. Since he has been taught that the rational is the scientifically measurable,

he concludes that rational knowledge is barren and gives no meaning to life.
Thus he lives with a false understanding of rationality. He reacts and seeks to
find meaning in the totally irrational: drugs, mystical experience beyond language, and sexual experimentation. Even Christian irrationalists quote Tertul-
lian,[12] "I believe because it is absurd," and say that one can only be a follower of
Jesus if you take an *irrational* "leap of faith," as spoken of by Christian philosopher Søren Kierkegaard.

This state of affairs is accurately portrayed in the writings of Francis Schaeffer. Schaeffer in his book *The God who is There* speaks of the divided line of
knowledge. It can be diagrammed as follows:

UPPER STORY	Existential experience, final experience, mysticism, drugs, free speech, do your own thing, modern sadism, sex, irrational religious experience	IRRATIONAL EXPERIENCE

L I N E   O F   D I V I S I O N

LOWER STORY	Man is matter in motion; man is a machine—a stimulus- response organism; no purpose, no meaning, particular objects	LEVEL OF SO-CALLED RATIONAL

In the lower story, we find so-called rationality. It is a world of particulars
where man is reduced to a machine. There is no purpose to existence on the
plane of modern rationality. Totally apart from this realm, and un-ntegrated
with it, man looks for some kind of experience to authenticate his purpose. He
therefore blindly strikes out in a search for pleasure, love, mystical religion, or
even sadism, sex, and obscene speech. There are no absolutes or universal standards to guide his experience, for the religious and ethical is not thought to be
rational. Schaeffer's view is not a scheme that accurately describes the conscious
position of most modern unbelievers. It is rather a brilliant and helpful simplifi-
cation to portray the drift and implication of much of modern culture.

This explains the reason for the turn to the East among so many Western
youth. Some Eastern philosophers held that the world was irrational and that
ultimate meaning was to be found in experiences beyond sense, rationality, and
human speech.[13] Those who found the twentieth-century view of a mechanical
world to be meaningless could rejoice at the Eastern dictum that the physical
world of common human experience was an illusion (*maya*).

We must, beyond this, acknowledge that the Jewish and evangelical world has also fallen into its own dimensions of irrationality due to a reaction against meaningless rationality. Hence we find fanaticism, mindlessness, and even the thought that humble thinking is suspect and contrary to faith. Platonic views of world denial (despising the physical world) that are contrary to the biblical view can be found. Some see God as a timeless being, closer to Aristotle's concept of the unmoved mover, rather than perceiving God as the One who is involved with his world. People hope for the soul's escape from the body rather than for the resurrection of the body taught in Scripture. False concepts of faith and rationality pervade Christian culture.

The only solution is a return to a true wholistic rationality, the piety of humble and prayerful thinking, and a biblically based world view that adequately fulfills the criteria of consistency, coherence, and comprehensiveness. When the Bible appears to speak against rationality, it is crucial to realize that it is not speaking against the mind or thinking *per se*, but against the false thinking of the unrenewed mind, the unspiritual man who produces the very false concepts of which we have been speaking. A humble biblical rationality is not reductionalistic; it does not reduce life's varied meanings to any one of its experiential aspects.

CULTURAL REFLECTIONS ON THE DIVISION OF THE RATIONAL AND PERSONALLY MEANINGFUL (THE TWO-STORY PROBLEM)

THE UPPER AND LOWER STORIES IN PHILOSOPHY

One can see the results of the division between the rational and the meaningful, previously discussed, in many departments of human culture. This is no less true in philosophy, which traditionally was an integrative discipline for all the other disciplines of the university. Philosophy has mostly lost this larger integrative role. Our summary is not to be taken to imply that modern philosophy does not provide significant insights. Rather, we are noting a tendency that strongly reflects our analysis up to this point.

The Anglo-American world reflected the great influence of positivism. As noted above, positivism defines the mathematical and the narrowly empirical as alone having a connection to truth. If a statement is not capable of being phrased in observation form, so that it may be empirically checked, or put in scientific terms, so that it may be verified, it is said not to be meaningful in regard to truth and falsehood. This *verification principle*, of course, defines meaning and truth in terms of empirical measurement and reflects the preoccupation of Western culture with the material progress of applied science. In positivism, statements about God, creation, the afterlife, etc., are all curious verbal babbling without any truth value. A. J. Ayer's *Language, Truth, and Logic* makes no apologies for boldly proclaiming this viewpoint.[14]

One can see the reflection of this in the work of C. L. Stevenson of Yale. In his *Ethics and Language*[15] Stevenson sought to explain ethical statements on a positivistic basis. Ethical statements in themselves are not true or false, but are reflections of individual and cultural preferences held so deeply that we seek to influence others to adopt our preferences. As a statement, "Killing is wrong" is neither true or false. Yet it reflects two other statements that lie behind it. The first is "I do not like killing." This statement is subject to truth or falsehood by *observing* the *external behavior* of the one who makes it. If he is honest, he will not kill and will seek to prevent killing. However, "Killing is wrong" also includes the urging of the other to adopt a similar stance and behavior: "I urge you to not like it too." Ethical statements are not logically different from statements such as "I hate cabbage," though ethical preferences are held with greater intensity and cultural backing. Ultimately, Stevenson's position leaves us with ethical relativism, "nothing is either *truly* right or wrong but thinking (preference) makes it so."[16] Positivism relegates moral and religious statements to the junk heap of linguistic meaninglessness, at least insofar as having truth-value in their traditionally understood form.

Positivism was not limited to Anglo-American philosophy, but had its root in the Vienna circle thinkers in the 1920s. However, the greatest influence of positivism was in philosophy departments in Anglo-American universities. Because positivism is essentially inconsistent (e.g., the verification rule itself is not verifiable under the rules it sets out) and limited, Anglo-American philosophy has mostly moved beyond positivism to language analysis in a program broadly known as *analytic philosophy*. Analytic philosophy has not fully overcome its positivistic roots but is making strides toward discussing more traditional philosophical issues as more than verbal curiosities.

In seeking to understand language and meaning in terms of usage, there is at least a crack in the door for more fruitful dialogue. Positivism itself was a hardened dogmatism. We can see that the tendency of Anglo-American philosophy has been to stay within Schaeffer's lower story in the level of the so-called rational, which is defined in terms of the limits of the mathematical and the external-sensory.

Continental European philosophy also was influenced by the concept that the rational-empirical or scientific level of description left man as a mere machine. Skepticism concerning religious truth and values was influential as well. Yet in *existentialism* (a philosophy concerned with human existence) and in *phenomenology* (a philosophy which seeks to describe human phenomena or experience), the two major Continental philosophical movements, philosophers sought to describe human life in more than mechanistic ways. For these philosophers, an intuitive and careful description of human existence would provide us with a fuller and richer understanding of man. These descriptions would give full weight to man's experiences in the "life-world": love, death, striving, fear, success, guilt, etc.—human meanings that are not reducible to the merely empirical-mathematical levels of experience.

At this point, we would say, "So far, so good." However, when these philosophers sought to give a meaning to the human existence they described, a meaning to protect man from the dehumanization of positivistic views of man, their views became amazingly irrational. This is because the loss of biblical revelation as a foundation for their understanding resulted in the loss of a basis for a rational and humane understanding of creation. The biblical revelation is the true basis for human significance. Instead of a rational-biblical world view as a solution to the riddle of human existence, there is a leap of faith into irrational meanings to give worth to life. In Karl Jaspers, this is found in a mystical, incommunicable *final experience*. In Martin Heidegger (earlier writings) it is in facing one's own death honestly and in living in the light of the fact that all of human life is a "being towards death." By not ignoring this reality, but allowing its full force in human consciousness, one lives *authentically*. In the later Heidegger, meaning is found by experiencing language, poetry, and art in a kind of *language mysticism*. In Jean-Paul Sartre, human existence is seen from a philosophical viewpoint to be an accidental *surd* (in mathematics, an irrationality). Man is radically free and may choose dozens of alternatives for living morally, politically, and socially. The key is *to choose*. If I choose and hold my choice to be of universal significance for all, then I *authenticate* and *give meaning* to a basically meaningless world. Why is the world meaningless? Because we know from science that man is simply the product of time, plus chance, plus matter.

In Albert Camus, life is *absurd*. Yet meaning comes from choosing to rebel in the face of this absurdity. This creates meaning in the face of absurdity. The more religious philosophers found meaning by participating in Christian symbols beyond a merely rational understanding (e.g., Gabriel Marcel, Paul Ricoeur). Despite brilliant insights into human existence in the writings of many of these philosophers, they certainly confirm the basic thrust of Schaeffer's concept of the divided story of knowledge in Western thought.

Because significance is found through nonrational mystical experiences, according to these philosophies, when Schaeffer met students who claimed to have had a final self-authenticating experience, he sat in silence. They were convinced he understood. However, he would completely shake them when he would say that he had had a final experience too, but that it was rational and communicable.

THE DIVIDED STORY AND 20TH-CENTURY PHILOSOPHY

EUROPEAN EXISTENTIALISM

Irrational leaps of faith to attempt to give meaning to human life	Jasper's "final experience"; Heidegger's "facing one's own death," "listening to language"; Sartre's "making an authentic free choice"; Camus' "rebellion against absurdity"; Religious existentialism's "mystical participation in religious symbols"

UPPER STORY

LOWER STORY

EUROPEAN EXISTENTIALISM

Human meaninglessness, rationality, or no great significance to man	Man is absurd; life is absurd; man is a product of chance, time and matter—yet human life must be described as more than scientific terms

ANGLO-AMERICAN PHILOSOPHY

Logical positivism—religious and ethical statements have no truth value; analytic philosophy-religious questions unproductive

Because man finds his own analysis of human origins (evolutionary materialism) and destiny (ultimate cessation of personal life) to be dissatisfying, he leaps to seek to find satisfaction beyond his rationality. As Schaeffer puts it, man cannot live within the structure of his own world view. His "mannishness" rebels against it. He must take a leap of faith to escape the meaningless of being merely a biological machine.

THE UPPER AND LOWER STORIES IN THEOLOGY

It should not be surprising that contemporary theology reflects the same bifurcation between the emptiness of the empirical-scientific world and the irrationality of that which gives personal significance. Old-line liberalism accepted a critical view of the Scriptures. No longer was the Bible seen as an infallible revelation from God. It was rather a product of the evolution of Israelite thought and culture, a culture seen as often in continuity with its Near Eastern surroundings. Yet mainstream liberalism sought to save various classical meanings despite the loss of biblical revelation. Human reason and natural theology affirmed the existence of God, life after death, and other significant insights to be found in the biblical revelation. In spite of liberalism's discounting of the miraculous as pre-scientific mythology, other classical religious concepts were still maintained.[17]

Unfortunately, the classical liberal did not recognize that the same critical perspective and false understanding of the implications of science, those which led to the rejection of the miraculous and of the Bible as revelation, implied the overturning of those basic religious conceptions dear to his heart. God and creation, life after death for the individual, and other beliefs would be rejected by the following generation of liberals as also mythological, meaningless for modern man, or pre-scientific. Thus religion was only a source of cultural richness and memory devoid of spiritual power. Churches and synagogues maintained religious symbols for their emotional value in stirring people to social action. The purpose of religious bodies changed. Religious institutions were to be agents of change to motivate people to effect secular-humanist ideals.

Neo-orthodoxy, spurred by the brilliant work of Karl Barth, recoiled in horror at liberalism's capitulation to secular humanism. For Barth, the Scripture as a tool of the Holy Spirit became the Word of God for man. Only its basic conceptions of God, creation, the fall of man, and redemption from sin by the death and resurrection of Jesus could provide a true solution to the human situation and give adequate significance for living. Yet the acceptance of these biblical concepts was based on the witness of the Spirit of God to the human heart in a totally subjective way. Barth brilliantly exposited biblical truth, but he did not hold that the Bible, in an *objective sense,* was the Word. Parts of it become the Word to us when given to our hearts by the Spirit of God. As a human book, the Bible was, to Barth, full of scientific and historical errors. The realm of history (*historie*) could never confirm biblical salvation-events. These events are in a category that transcends the tools of historical research. Historical research can not discover the parting of the Red Sea or the resurrection. These events are known only by faith and are part of history (*Geschichte*). However, this makes religious knowledge wholly based upon subjective choice or experience.

Despite Barth's great respect for the apostolic witness ("we cannot look over their shoulders and correct their notebooks"), his understanding of biblical authority was inadequate to keep his students from drifting back into liberalism.[18] Indeed, the way was open for them to say that the parts of the Bible that the Spirit of God made to be revelation to Barth were not made to be revelation to them. Hence Barth's student Emil Brunner could teach that Jesus' body rotted in the grave, but that He rose spiritually and is still alive today. Why? Because according to science, dead bodies stay dead. However, on the plane of the Spirit, we can hold to continued existence and survival by faith. Miracles are thus not events of history, but are events of faith. For Barth, the miracles of the Bible could be events of history but cannot be established by a scientific historical method.

When we come to the work of Rudolph Bultmann and Paul Tillich, we find that some of Barth's disciples drifted almost totally back to liberal-humanism. Bultmann accepted a rigid mechanistic concept of the universe based on his misunderstanding of the implications of science. As he stated, "For people who turn electric lights on and off, there can be no such thing as a resurrection."[19] Biblical miracles are mythological. For modern men, he taught, we must demythologize the Bible to get at its valid continuing meaning. What is this meaning? It is the *affirmation of life in the face of tragedy*. This is the demythologized meaning of the resurrection: that the disciples joyously affirmed life after the cross.

Paul Tillich came up with a different approach. It was to recognize the miracle stories as mythological. However, beyond their literal meaning they have symbolic value. As long as we recognize that we can no longer literally believe the content of the Bible, we can participate religiously in the symbols. As long as we recognize them as broken symbols in this way, we can participate in a transcending meaning that is communicated by these myths and symbols. However, that transcendent meaning cannot be literally expressed outside of the symbols.[20]

These theological leaders of mainstream European and American Protestantism have only recently died. They had allies in Catholic and Jewish circles.[21] Mordecai Kaplan, for example, often reads like a combination of Harry Emerson Fosdick and Paul Tillich. Since the time of their passing, the disciples of these theologians have given us an amazing array of theologies, including the *death-of-God theology*[22] (either God is a dead concept in the twentieth century, or God has literally died); *The Secular City*[23] theology of Harvey Cox, in which we celebrate man's coming of age in the new secular city; and even new Marxist reinterpretations of Christianity in the more left-wing *liberation theologies*. Yet they all find meaning in the symbol of "Jesus" either as a "man for others," the representative of "authentic humanness," the "true radical," or the "truly self-actualized man."[24] They are all excited about "Jesus," but *which* Jesus?

It should therefore come as no surprise that the number and power of liberal churches and synagogues are declining. The average person simply does not see adequate enough meaning in these theologies to motivate them to continued involvement.

What is the root of these theologies? Once again, it is the acceptance of the spirit and concepts of this age in which scientific-mathematical models of knowledge and rationality reign supreme. Jesus has to be recreated to fit the ideals of a modern secularized, scientific age. Furthermore, the "death of God" theologians found that they did not have a sufficient bulwark in the biblical revelation to stave off doubts about classical liberal affirmations about a good and benevolent God and the immortality of the soul. Only the Bible's concepts of the fall, sin, judgment, and redemption fit the wide possibilities of good and evil in human societies. The liberal image of God as a benevolent grandfatherlike being did not square with the horrors of war, evil, famine, and plague. Furthermore, these thinkers had no knowledge of the substantial weight of evidence behind the Bible as God's authoritative revelation. Therefore, they pathetically concluded that God was dead but affirmed "Jesus" as an ideal human.

We can also diagram this theology according to Schaeffer's divided field of knowledge. In the lower story are found several concepts from these theologians: the Bible is full of error; dead bodies do not rise from the dead; miracles are not historical; the Bible must be demythologized; the biblical symbols must not in any sense be taken as literal; and even God is dead. In the upper story we find irrational mystical sources of meaning. This is the subjective-leap-of-faith realm. We should note in deference to Barth that he did not deny that the resurrection and other miracles really occurred. Yet his removal of these events as proper subjects for historical inquiry and testimony opened the way for others to deny them.

Barth's theology is often superb, but his theory of historical knowledge (historical epistemology) is woefully inadequate. Barth did not overcome Lessing's ditch, but instead succumbed to it. Lessing said that historical research can not bridge the chasm between historical evidence and the certitude of faith. It is true that faith as a walk with God is more firm than any of the probable evidences of history. Faith is held with conviction far beyond the tentative convictions of probability in empirical research. Yet to overcome the divided stories, we must hold that probablistic evidence should confirm the truths held by faith whenever there is an intersection of the biblical account with archaeological and other documentary evidence (if we are interpreting this evidence correctly).

Subjective choice for irrational participation in faith chosen;	*Radical God is Dead* - Jesus is the "man for others," the "authentic human" or the "ideal human," or the "true revolutionary."
Spiritual words or symbols taken from the Bible but emptied of traditional content;	*Tillich* - Reaffirm and participate In transcending meaning of myths and symbols
	Bultmann - affirm life (resurrection) in the face of tragedy
Irrational world of symbol, or word mysticism, or life affirmation;	*Barth* - The Bible becomes revelation by the Spirit; Jesus is Lord and rose on the plane of trans-history

Upper story leap of faith

to bridge the chasm

Scientific empirical world;	*Radical Theology* or *God is Dead*— We can no longer believe in a loving, personal God.
No significance for human life;	*Tillich* - Bible stories are symbols and myths, not to be taken literally.
Meaningless plane of scientific human history.	*Bultmann* - Dead men do not rise bodily from the grave; demythologize the Bible.
	Brunner - Jesus' body is in the grave.
	Barth - The Bible is full of errors; miracles can not be discovered by normal historical research.

THEOLOGY 1970–1990

Recent trends in the liberal Christian world reflect a continuing relativizing of Christianity. However, there has been an amazing growth in varieties of evangelical Christianity (charismatic, Jesus movements, Presbyterian, and others). This has especially been seen in Latin America, the Third World, Asia, and Russia.

In liberal church circles, the growth in relativism is especially manifest in movements toward homosexual rights (even to the point of ordaining practicing homosexuals) and a redefinition of what constitutes ethical sexual expression. Christian symbols are still mystically valued. However, biblical authority is without significance. The commission of the Presbyterian Church, U.S.A., on human sexuality (whose report was rejected by the General Assembly) clearly calls for accepting homosexual relationships of fidelity. The report also argues that extramarital sexual expression can be good if it is in a context of caring and giving. An excellent critique of these trends was given in the December 1990 *Journal of Presbyterians for Biblical Renewal*.

Once a rational biblical foundation for theology and ethics is eliminated, the church becomes an institution which merely baptizes as "Christian" whatever seems to be the new trends in society. Unthinking acceptance of change as progress often accompanies these directions, as argued in James Hannigan's *Homosexuality*. John S. Spong, Bishop of Newark, argues for ordaining practicing homosexuals. The apostle Paul is interpreted as a mentally tortured person because of conflicts over homosexuality. Yet Paul testified that freedom from sexual desire was a special gift which he had from God. A very sensitive orthodox Jewish conscience can be very troubled by imperfections that are not at all related to gross sexual lust. Whatever is the latest trend in "new morality" will be affirmed as "Christian" by someone.

Liberal theology is also willing to relativize Christianity itself. It is said that Christianity is simply our tradition, but not distinctly superior to other religions. The differences are seen as merely symbolic preferences. The overall religious philosophy then becomes similar to New Age religion (see section on the New Age). As in the New Age, the world view becomes pantheistic. God and the afterlife are vaguely defined. Ethics also becomes loose and relativistic. The values of meditation and human self-actualization take the place of prayer to a supernatural personal God. Christian language is thus redefined to fit this new world view and its acceptance of most religions.

Hans Kung, in *Eternal Life*, questions these trends and their compatibility with Christian concepts. However, without a significant spiritual revival, we will continue to see the members of liberal denominations turning in these directions. Presbyterians and Methodists will practice yoga and adopt reincarnationist ideas while ordaining practicing homosexual clergy.

Liberation theology is another trend of note. While it is important for biblical people to apply the Scriptures to the issues of poverty, wealth, ecology, and a host of other issues, this must be done in a context of biblical authority. Out of Scripture itself will come creative, Holy Spirit–inspired ideas for dealing with modern issues. The solutions will be biblically compatible. Among many Latin American Liberation thinkers, a Marxist approach is truly the basis for thought. Marxism is then found to have support in Jesus and his identification with the poor. Certainly the fall of Communism in Eastern Europe has somewhat discredited these theologies, but there are still proponents. Does Scripture really support the orientation toward state centralization, Marxist patterns of economic development, and armed revolution? An excellent evaluation of liberation theology has been given by Michael Novak in *Will it Liberate?* Once again, an overaccommodation to a nonbiblical viewpoint has taken place in such thinkers as Gustavo Gutierrez, Enrique Dussel, Juan Luis Segundo, and Jose Miguez Bonino.

The power of prayer and godly action is replaced by an acceptance of an "ends justifies the means" approach to armed violence. The levels of ideology that sustain proponents and the lack of clear evidence to sustain Marxist analysis are amazing. Yet much of Marx is baptized as "Christian" by these theologians.

CONCLUSION

Recent theology, outside of evangelical and conservative Catholic or orthodox contexts, seems to be only refinements of perspectives predating 1970. We have already noted the Jesus Seminar in this regard. The rejuvenation of evangelical thinking is not without note as well. Wolfhart Pannenburg, who teaches at the centers of radical German liberalism, argues for a rational theology and puts forth the evidence for the resurrection. Evangelical bible schools and seminaries have proliferated. In the December 1991 issue of *Newsweek* we read that the evangelicals (used in a broad sense to include charismatic varieties) have for the first time since the nineteenth century become the majority Protestants in America. In the major mission fields of Africa, Latin America, and Asia, there is little competition. Biblical

Christianity is the only real force with the name "Christian." While denominational liberalism declines in numbers, biblical denominations and associations grow. Among the Jewish people, Orthodoxy is the fastest growing branch of Judaism. It appears that the major culture clash of the future will be between biblical movements and relativistic religious movements.

CHAPTER 4: STUDY QUESTIONS

1. Trace the roots of Darwin's evolutionary views to the philosophic climate in Western Europe.

2. How were evolutionary views applied to biblical interpretation?

3. How did logical positivism give conceptualization to the new scientific attitude toward meaning?

4. Heidegger and Polanyi provide a critique of the measurement preoccupation of Western thought. Explain.

5. What are the roots that give impetus to liberal theology? What are mystical directions for meaning in liberal theology?

6. Why is Einsteinian science important in questioning past conclusions on the insignificance of the earth and man's place in the universe?

THE ARTS AND THE
TWENTIETH CENTURY

REFLECTIONS ON MODERN LITERATURE

THE SECULARIST PERSPECTIVE ROBS MAN OF HOPE, personal dignity, and self-esteem. Modern literature vividly reflects the loss of faith in human worth. It is important that we note the limits of our analysis of modern art. Our goal is to briefly describe the "world view"–ish dimensions reflected in modern literature and art. We have no intention of giving the impression that art is to be solely judged on the basis of the world view it reflects. This is only one dimension of understanding. Some art does not clearly reflect any world view. Every work of art is the result of a cognitive project on the part of its creator. A judgment may be made on how well the artist carries out the intended goal of his project (if such a project is either professed or discernable).

Secondly, we may judge the worth of his project goal: is it a worthwhile undertaking? Thirdly, we may analyze the message of the work of art as well as judge its message (if it has such a message) in regard to truth. Beyond all of this, there are judgments of literary quality and artistic execution. Does the work reflect classical standards of beauty or other standards; is it a metaphorical statement on some aspect of life? Those works which are truly great have a universal quality and are judged highly by generation after generation. I am limiting myself primarily to art that reflects or interprets the world view implications of the scientific-mathematical method as the foundation of rational knowledge. With these comments in mind, we can turn to our survey of literature.

Jean-Paul Sartre had the distinction of writing both philosophy and literature. His plays reflect a stark world with characters who discover the tragic realities of life without transcendent meaning. His play *No Exit* describes a group of people who are sentenced to hell. There are no flames and no external instruments of torture. This is a puzzle to all until they realize that hell is their consignment to be with each other forever. Hell is other people. Hell is that dimension of alienation from others that is an inextricable part of our human condition. There is no solution.

Albert Camus is the greatest writer of existential literature. His essay "The Rebel" depicts life as basically absurd. The only meaning that can be given to life is to rebel against this absurdity. "The Myth of Sisyphus" reflects the nature of human life. Sisyphus is a character in ancient Greek literature who is condemned by the gods to an eternal punishment. The punishment consists of rolling a stone up a mountain, but just before the goal of the top of the mountain is reached, the stone rolls to the bottom. Sisyphus must start all over again and again, ad infinitum. Camus uses Sisyphus in his essay to provide a type of the nature of all human life.

For Camus and for Sartre we can only find meaning in an irrational choice of radical freedom in the face of meaninglessness. *The Plague* is probably Camus' most famous novel. It describes a city in the horror of bubonic plague. The plague itself mirrors the absurdity of evil. Evil and suffering strike indiscriminately with no rational explanation. It cannot be explained as a punishment for evil as the religious leadership would have the people to believe. It is an absurd and cruel world. The best we can do is fight this cruelty. Many respect the human compassion reflected in *The Plague*. Yet what is to motivate us to the sacrifice necessary to fight evil and human suffering? Camus offers a bleak, dignity-destroying, and tragic view of human life.

Finally, we are left with the unconvincing joy of *The Stranger*. The stranger has committed a crime and sits in his cell reflecting on the absurdity of life. He finds joy in looking at the stars in the midst of absurdity. That there was no rationale to the stranger's crime also fits the surd nature of existence.

Ernest Hemingway's works also reflect the meaningless of existence. Even his style has been described as a staccato style of short syllables and sentences. This reflects an *atomistic* view of life—life without any transcendent divine origin. *For Whom the Bell Tolls* presents his view of life through the horrors of the time of war. The tragedy that concludes the book is the one thing that gives meaning: a loved and valued person dies in the closing scene. The hero pleads, "Please don't die," over and over again, but the one he loves dies. The sense of the tragic nature of life is also reflected in Hemingway's *The Old Man and the*

Sea. The hero rebels at the sea, at the meaninglessness of life.

There is an amazing unity to much of this literature. Despite the view that there is no transcendent source of values, morals, and ethics, and no absolute standard of right and wrong, we find such literary figures taking stands on political and social issues with passionate commitment. They inconsistently act as though there were standards by which to judge human behavior. For example, Sartre judges social systems by Marxist values. Marxism is a world view with its one set of absolutes from which human behavior and social reality are judged. Yet Sartre's view of radical freedom allows for neither Marxist determinism or absolute values. Sartre argues that the radical free man simply authenticates himself by value choices. However, once he chooses, that life might have seriousness—he must live as though this choice was a universal standard for all. (He must act according to what is not so.)

In Archibald MacLeish's *J.B.*, the biblical character of Job is recreated in a contemporary setting. However, the conclusion of the play is quite other than the biblical epic. Tragedy strikes the family of J.B. just as it did the biblical family. As in the biblical account, God's justice and goodness are questioned. The Devil summarizes the dilemma.

> "If God is good he is not God (omnipotent)."
> "If God is God (omnipotent) He is not good."

Either God is so weak we can not put our trust in Him for deliverance, or He is not good and loving. The conclusion of *J.B.* is that there is no answer; we are left with skepticism concerning divine realities.

The writers of the "Theater of the Absurd" seek to creatively make similar statements. In Samuel Beckett's *Waiting for Godot*, the characters wait for Godot (God), but Godot never comes, intervenes, or shows himself. Other plays, like those of Ionesco, produce dialogue that is at times incoherent in order to reflect the absurdity of existence.

The playwright Edward Albee is less easy to classify. The sense of emptiness, however, does profoundly come through his works. His play *The American Dream* is aptly named to reflect a character who is supposed to be the "American Dream." Yet, this character is shallow, without any qualities of sustaining depth. *Who's Afraid of Virginia Wolff?* reflects the inability of people to maintain intimacy. It shows us a modern American couple, George and Martha, who verbally cut each other with cruel and biting interchanges while they still remain together to play the games of human cynicism. They are held together by a mutually compatible sickness. *Everything in the Garden* also exposes the meaningless-ness of modern American affluence and materialistic commitments. The typical American housewife sells herself in prostitution to fund her suburban lifestyle. *Tiny Alice* brings us a play in which a model dollhouse becomes a real world. The boundary between reality and fantasy is lost and a delusion of meaning is exposed through a dialogue that speaks in Tillichian terms of the God beyond God.

Albee wants man to *authentically* face reality: to break out of these illusions and look stark existence in the face and build a society from such a base of honesty. Yet, can such a basis provide motivation and direction for living? Can it give man a sense of dignity and self-worth to sustain him in the ups and downs of life?

Other writers reflect the same themes or seek to find a sense of meaning in a mystical or nonrational experience of transcendence. Henry Miller's plays reflect the destructive dimensions of sex and love, yet leap to a mysticism beyond words for meaning in entering into the stream of life.

John Osborne's play *Luther* reflects the uncertainty of all values. The play paints a portrait of a Martin Luther who lacks courage and doubts the rightness of the whole Reformation. Nothing is certain. The reader is reminded of C. S. Lewis' comment in the *Abolition of Man* that we have produced a generation of men without chests, people without moral conviction. Lewis comments that humility was never meant to imply convictionlessness.

There is also the *Elegy* of Dylan Thomas, "Head downward, legs upward, he tumbles into the bottomless from which he came." Man is portrayed as dead. William Golding in *The Lord of the Flies* portrays the innate barbarism in man through a group of stranded choirboys. Cruelty and self-preservation take over, for these are the roots of human life. Man has not escaped from his basically animal nature; it has only been thinly covered. In *1984*, by George Orwell, we are introduced to a world of dehumanization in which all values and truths are relativized to serve the ends of the totalitarian state, represented by and known as "Big Brother." Aldous Huxley in *Brave New World* introduces us to a sterile world of total scientific planning and control. However, it is a world without the normal human qualities that make life worth living. Huxley found meaning later in his life through the mystical higher consciousness obtainable through drugs.[1] We could easily continue to cite examples but for the limits of the scope of this paper.

The final loss of all standards and meaning is reflected in Hans Arp and the Dada Movement. Since chance and absurdity reign supreme, literature and art can best reflect reality by being full of chance incoherence.

Not all of modern literature reflects such a tragic view of life. It can easily be said, however, that the predominant view of "serious" literature from 1930 to 1970 that is cut off from a biblical base of values is a literature that portrays man as an absurd, sad creature destined for nothing. Even those who portray such a tragic view of man find it difficult to live within their own view. They stab at an irrational something to give meaning to life. Modern literature reflects that same basic division into upper and lower stories that was discovered in philosophy and theology.

The lower story in literature is a reflection of the view of man that arises from modern secular humanism. It leaves us with no transcendent (divine realm) source of values or purpose. Man is a product of time, plus chance and matter. Life is absurd. Yet, in the upper story, one finds the mannishness of man rebelling against this mechanistic view to latch on to something to give meaning to life even if that something is woefully inadequate.

	Sartre - Self-authenticating choice
UPPER STORY	Camus - rebellion re absurd
of irrational choices	A. Huxley - mystical mind, consciousness-
to give meaning	raising experiences

Leap of		
Faith to	------------------------ Line of Despair-----------------------------
bridge chasm	

	Camus - There is no meaning, life is absurd.
LOWER STORY	Sartre - There is no Exit, Theater of the
Man is a machine-less	Absurd; no meaning.
mathematical	A. Huxley - Rationality reveals
improbability	sterile scientific world.

Once again we find clear evidence that the contemporary secular world views are inadequate to provide a sense of "fit" or meaning for human life. These are not views that man can truly live with. Art and literature often reveal the implications of a culture that would not otherwise be recognized.

LITERATURE FROM 1970-1990

Much of the literature of the last twenty years has tended toward a broad variety. Most of the literature I have chosen to illustrate this point was purposely selected to reflect the twin themes of the pessimistic conclusions of secular humanism and the irrational leap toward meaning in drugs and Eastern mysticism. The events of the '70s and '80s have brought a trend away from the domination of anti-war, socialist, and leftist themes. There are also new plays and novels that are simply entertaining, some that show forth aspects of human behavior and life, and others which still reflect social commentary. There is work that promotes empathy for and the legitimacy of homosexuality and other social trends of deterioration.

Serious commentary is not lacking. Czech playwright Vaclav Havel depicts the oppression and tensions of totalitarian society in the his play which opened on Broadway in 1986, *The Perfect Party*. The state's psychological pressure erodes the self. However, the pressure to risk life to oppose the state also brings anxiety. Amazingly, Havel became the leader of Czechoslovakia. The failure of Communism to produce material and spiritual well-being and the fall of Communism in Eastern Europe certainly has discredited much of the literature of the Left. Writers like Havel and Alexander Solzhenitsyn point the way toward seeing human existence in more biblically compatible terms.

Plays are not lacking which promote radical feminism and moral decline. However, some plays reflect both reservations and modern lifestyles. Jane Wagner in her book *The Search for Intelligent Life in the Universe* depicts the negative pressures, raised expectations, disappointments, and frustrations that accompany feminism. The women's movement promised much, but produced mixed fruit.

In spite of radical social trends, Western people in many cities were amazingly receptive to the musical production of *Les Miserables* and its depiction of such religious values as deliverance from hatred, the forgiveness of sin, and compassionate life motivation. Even life after death in heaven is portrayed. This nineteenth-century novel appeals in its twentieth-century form.

Recent literature reflects no great unifying themes or trends. It is as if there is a shying away from the more deeply philosophical trends of earlier years.

MUSIC OF RECENT TIMES

For music, only a few recent examples will be covered. These examples reflect the same themes. We will look at both popular and "serious" musicians.

Pierre Schaeffer's "Music Concrete" is a significant example. There is a distortion of music, a machine-like sound. His follower Pierre Henry, in "Greek Voice," depicts a voice and chance sounds. Eventually the voice falls apart in destruction, chance triumphing over order. Truly this is music below the *line of despair*.

The music of John Cage is the music of chance, truly reflecting the view of the surd character of the universe and human life. Cage goes so far as to pick notes at random from a hat to write a music truly representative of the essence of the modern secular perspective.

Beyond this music, which is in my view below the line of despair, are attempts to transcend the meaningless-ness of life through finding something of transcendent worth. In the "Kaddish Symphony" of Leonard Bernstein, the musician's creativity is a god. The Kaddish is a traditional Jewish prayer of praise especially to be prayed during a time of mourning. Yet, Bernstein, unlike Bach, cannot really write music in praise of the God of the Bible because he has accepted modern destructive conclusions about life. Popular music as well reflects the same division between that which reflects the tragic absurd dimension of human existence and that which offers mystical leaps to grasp at something worth living for. There is the despair of John Lennon who sings, "I don't believe in Jesus . . . Buddha . . . Kennedy," etc. There is mockery as well over the socialistic ideal of the worker in "A Working Class Hero." Herein we find despair itself viewed as the existential experience that gives meaning to life. Previous to these musical compositions, the later Beatles as a group also displayed despair and cynicism concerning political and social solutions to the human dilemma. In "Sergeant Pepper" we find a portrayal of the emptiness of modern secularism and its consumption and greed. In "She's Leaving Home" there is a poignant representation of how houses, cars, and other material things do not satisfy. In "Lucy in the Sky With Diamonds" there is a hidden message in which drugs (LSD.) provide escape. Certainly this is seen in one song whose message is "I get high with a little help from my friends." The last Beatles album continues in this vein of despair and cynicism. The album pokes fun at both Communism and other ideologies.

Despair and tragedy also found their way into the songs of Simon and Garfunkel. In their song "Patterns" man is represented according to behavioral psychology "Like a rat in a maze . . . the pattern never alters until the rat dies." Human conversation is seen as an empty expression of our empty human involvements in "Dangling Conversations." "You read your Emily Dickenson and I my Robert Frost . . . Is analysis worthwhile . . . Is the theater really dead?"

Who cannot but realize the same trends in the more recent types of music among our young people. We have had acid rock, punk rock, other forms of sexual rock, and violent rock. The music of our youth reflects the poverty of our culture.

This music is not lacking in upper-story mystical leaps to find a base for human meaning, value, and purpose. The mannishness of man requires something to live for. Hence, former Beatle George Harrison looks to the East and proclaims that in "Chanting the names of the gods" we are free. The gods may be variously Vishnu, Buddha, and Jesus. The Moody Blues also reflected the turn to the irrational mysticism of the East and experience that can only be had, not expressed in rational propositions. They repeat the Eastern word "OM" to achieve mystical transcendence and balance. This is the message of their "Journey In and Journey Out." Space again does not permit extensive descriptions of many other artists such as Jethro Tull and his iconoclastic antisocial music or Mick Jagger and the Rolling Stones with their rude and violent music and drug-type atmosphere. These artists rebel against the hypocrisy of those who held to traditional moral norms when these norms have no basis in today's humanistic theories of human origins and destiny.

It is in this light that we note those artists of significant fame who also integrated their music with the revelation of the Bible. Their new music now reflects a biblical base for human meaning and purpose. For a time, Bob Dylan wrote out of this perspective. Dylan certainly has been considered the most prominent influence in modern folk music. His songs reflected cynicism, despair, confusion, compassion, war protest, and a desire for peace. During a period of biblical orientation however, Dylan found peace in faith in Jesus and a return to traditional Jewish roots. His lyrics reflected the many facets of the biblical record. Since that time he has entered into a period of questioning concerning the biblical faith.

We can also look with joy upon the witness of Noel Paul Stookey (formerly of Peter, Paul, and Mary). One significant example is "The Wedding Song." In this simple and beautiful song, often heard at today's weddings, Stookey points to the meaning of love and marriage as having its source in the Creator. "Whenever two or more are gathered in His name . . . there is Love."

Modern man has been so imbued with the secular-humanist perspective that there has not often been a fair hearing for those musicians who write from a biblical perspective or who refuse to mimic modern rock styles. The message of these musicians seems unauthentic, antiquated, and no longer believable because so many operate within the hopeless perspective of irreligion. However, we are seeing a turning of many artists in the West to biblical verities and the beginnings of a new artistry to represent this turning. Only time will tell if Western culture will turn from despair and upper-story leaps to an integrated biblical framework. We can diagram much of recent musical culture as other aspects of culture.

UPPER STORY LEAPS FOR MEANING	Drugs and Eastern Religious leap of faith; Harrison, Moody Blues
	--------------------------------
LOWER STORY PURPOSELESS UNIVERSE	P. Schaeffer - Music Concrete J. Cage - Chance music; Beatles: John Lennon - cynicism, despair; Garfunkel

MUSICAL TRENDS: 1975-1990

The amazing longevity of the rock medium continues into the nineties. Space does not permit more than a few brief words concerning popular culture during this period. Decadence is greatly in evidence in today's rock culture. There is continuing social commentary such as in Bruce Springsteen's "Born in the U.S.A." However, the social commentary so prominent in late '60s rock has receded and the exaltation of hedonism is pronounced. The music of Prince advocates sexual perversion to such an extent that I am not at liberty in conscience to quote lyrics. He is one of the early '90s most popular artists with youth. Madonna's MTV productions and much of video rock are full of blatantly seductive images.

So also, the rap music of 2 Live Crew exalts violence and promotes sexual abusiveness toward women. Few would argue that 2 Live crew produces significant art. The reason we include comment on it is the importance of its exemplifying the difficulty our society has in enforcing any standards. The lyrics of 2 Live Crew are clearly pornographic and led to a trial in Broward County, Florida. In a section on recent social trends, I will note the incredible confusion of pornographic literature, music, and art as expressions of free speech to be protected by law.

Of course, there are good songs and unobjectionable music. Some Christian artists have even produced hits (Amy Grant, Debbie Boone, Michael W. Smith, U-2). Amy Grant has several "top of the chart" songs. Her music reflects biblical themes and celebrates aspects of human life and creation from a biblical point of view. In spite of these examples, the most predominant trend is still the drift of our society in its allowance of much that is decadent. Social breakdown is a product of our permissive society. It results from a departure from

Judeo-Christian values. The results of this departure have been devastating to the quality of human life. Family breakdown, venereal disease, and abortion are clear manifestations. Increased poverty in our cities is, to a significant extent, a product of family breakdown. Much of popular music encourages these trends.

REFLECTIONS ON VISUAL ARTS

To an amazing degree, the visual arts portray the history of modern Western culture. Claude Monet serves as a good starting point for analysis. Monet's paintings are truly beautiful, creative, and brilliantly executed. Yet a philosophy of the nature of existence is also reflected. For *impressionism* (the school of Monet's style), the sensory level of existence is seen as the really real. There is an attempt to get beyond the mentally integrated images of meaning, which are part of human experience, to that dimension of raw sensation itself. Reality is only known with the eyes or senses. Traditional painting was more thematic, reflecting the great issues of good, evil, redemption, and the beauty of God's creation. In impressionism, *any subject matter* can be a source of discovering the base of reality. Heated discussion marked the impressionist movement. Are we losing painting as an interpretive and vast undertaking that depicts the *universal* dimension of existence? This was the great question.

In impressionism the subject, sensation, and pictorial object are identical. The final dissolution of reality into the flux of sense impressions, of nothing perceived by no one, was a dimension of this painting. The ideal of science should also be noted as having influence, for the really real is not understood as experience in a broad sense, but is solely the limited sensory aspect of experience. We see this in Seurat's pointillist revival of impressionism. Atomistic sensory impressions are scientifically and meticulously planned out; this makes up the world of his canvas. In summary then, we are left with sensory flux alone and universal meaning is lost.

In Van Gogh and Gauguin there is a search for new universals or standards by which we can see the truly valuable, the real nature and meaning of man. Van Gogh sought to respond to the problem raised by the impressionism of the late nineteenth century by expressing his experience when confronted with reality. He sought therefore to touch deeper more general truths. The artist's work will somehow tap these levels.

Gauguin sought as well to paint not a representation of nature, but of the human reaction, feeling, and experience. Hence, the painting would not depict an animal but the human fear of the animal. There was a desire to recapture the human dimension lost in positivism and to find meaning in man's experience of nature. There was more to life than impressions. To recover a more basic experience of reality, Gauguin sought to return to the primitive, to human experience before the loss of innocence. He traveled to Tahiti to discover it. This universal perspective held that primitive life was good, pure, and natural before it was corrupted by civilization. We might think of Michener's novel *Hawaii*, in which the natives are pictured as being in a kind of Utopia until the Westerners invade. This was the ideal of the noble savage depicted in such Gauguin paintings as *The Day of God* and *Why Are You Angry*.

Yet as Gauguin become more acquainted with primitive life in Tahiti, he became disillusioned. The universal human ideals were not to be found in primitive styles of existence. He explains his painting *What, Whence, and Wither* in a letter. On the right side of the canvas is the sensuous beauty of the noble savage, a beautiful Tahitian woman. On the left, however, we see death, aging, and deterioration. There is also a strange, stupid bird sitting by incongruously, as if mocking. There is no counterpart in nature for this bird. There is the sick and bizarre. After this painting and the letter of interpretation, Gauguin tried to commit suicide. Was an adequate universal meaning for human life to be found in primitive human existence, an existence closer to nature? No, the natural, intuitive, noble savage failed as an ideal for Gauguin. Although Gauguin sought to value human life and response, he could not find an adequate basis for believing in man thorough this merely humanistic ideal.

Impressionism and naturalism led to a reaction in still another movement to find a more universal basis for life; this was the *cubist* movement. The cubist movement may be seen as an attempt to save rational structure as real, not only sense data. The real as rational became represented in mathematical measure or structure. The cube, as a most basic geometric form, inspired paintings of intersecting planes. This can be seen in the early work of Paul Cezanne, as in *Anvers Village Panorama*.

Nature and life appeared as a thin diaphragm spread over geographic forms. This was part of his quest to discover a lasting structure in a landscape. In so doing, he sought to add his understanding, a rational structure, or "our reason," as part of what is seen. There is more concern to paint the structure of reality, the universal as seen with human rationality rather than the fleeting impressions of sight. As art historian Hans Rookmaaker states:

They had to escape from the principle that there is nothing
more than what the eye can see at any given moment, that
there is nothing there but the individual, the specific, things
just as they can be *seen* and no more. It was a problem arising
from the positivist and impressionist principle that there are
no laws that govern reality, that only experimental facts can be
called true and certain. So these four post-impressionists tried
to depict something that is more than what the momentary,
fleeting impression can make us understand. They looked for
a way to find something of the true values and lasting principles of reality, the deeper universal.[2]

We can see influences from both natural primitivism (noble savage) and the
cubist movement in the early work of Picasso. In *Les Demoiselles d'Avignon* we
notice greater abstraction. There is a loss of the distinctively human. The universal is seen in terms of the mathematical. An *individual* reflecting humanness
is lost in such abstraction. *Les Demoiselles* may be all women or everything. In
the Bible, the universal is seen as the particular in the person of the Messiah.
However, we here see the attempt to find the universal in abstraction—
abstracting universals from particulars. This is more apparent in *Nude Under a
Pear Tree*, and *Man with a Pipe*. The trend finds its logical end in painting in
which there is no clue to the meaning of the painting in what you look at. You
decide what you see, but there is a lack of commonality in communication
between painter and audience, and a lack of common understanding among the
observers.

We can certainly see a reflection in this art of the inability to find rational coherent meaning to give life purpose or a reason for living. We see the later
Picasso as a mixture of many trends. There is the horror of war in his painting
Guernica based on the Spanish Civil War. This is a *nihilistic* painting, for it gives
no hope. Yet Picasso leaps to find meaning in romantic love and can say, "I love
Eva." The later Picasso enters into a mode of free expression. Later nudes are
truly empty; there is a preoccupation with genitals. Some have argued that Picasso's later paintings are a joke on humanity. He trades upon his famous name;
his drawings and paintings sell for much, but he knows that they are not of real
worth. This was the impression of many in viewing a mid-Seventies presentation
of Picasso's later drawings at the Chicago Art Institute. Some have interpreted
Picasso's abstract sculpture at the Chicago Civic Center in a similar vein. What
is it? Is it his hound dog from a front view? Is it just an interesting conjunction
of geometrical figures? No one can give an answer for sure. However, gone is

any great presentation of truth, meaning, or beauty.

Mondrian is known for excellent designs, architectural forms, and abstract balance. This is seen in his *Diagonal Composition*. Yet, in this abstract art there is no place for man; abstract geometry leaves no room.

In the art of H. Matisse, on the other hand, one can perceive a wild cry to get to the human beyond the traditions of nineteenth-century science. His nudes in *Bathers by a River* represent a humanistic quest. Rookmacher calls his early painting "the dream of high humanity conveyed by the metaphor of nudes."[3] The attempt evidences a desire to show subjective emotion on canvas. One critic called this painting wild, *fauve*. Matisse's later work shows less and less of the humanistic element and more and more of the abstract decorative. There is more and more of a loss of any personal quality.

The trends discussed so far paved the way for the movement of *expressionism*, a movement of the spiritual and imaginative—away from the natural. In Kandinsky, in the early twentieth century, we find a chief exponent of this view. He stated:

> The artist must express himself, the times in which he lives, and the "eternal," what belongs to all times and to all cultures. This, the objective, what I have called the universal, has to be shown by means of the subjective. . . . The strife of colors, the sense of balance, unexpected assaults, great questions . . . , useless striving, storm and tempest, broken chains, oppositions, and contradictions, these make up our harmony.[4]

However, this also landed Kandinsky in abstract art and the loss of any subject matter. Yet again, as with the cubists, it was hoped that abstract art should reveal the deeper cosmic laws of nature, the universal law of reality. Art becomes a tool in the quest, a revelation of a new mysticism, a religious life of the spirit. This is an Eastern way of religious thinking. In the art of Mark, a significant figure of the same movement, this Eastern mysticism and world denial is complete.

> I found man to be ugly, animals are much more beautiful . . . but in them too I discovered so much that I felt to be appalling and ugly that my representations of them instinctively, out of inner necessity, became increasingly more schematic, more abstract. Each year trees, flowers, the earth, everything showed me aspects that were more hateful, more repulsive, until I came at last to a full realization of the ugliness, the uncleanness of nature . . . . The longing for indivisible Being, for lib-

eration from the sense deception of an ephemeral life is the
main objection of all art.[5]

The view of the world as illusion, *maya*, and the pantheistic concept of indivisible being is exactly parallel to the irrational mysticism of some forms of Vedanta Hinduism. This mystical quest is found as well in Paul Klee. The later Heidegger in philosophy hopes for the universe to push through and speak through the poet. In Paul Klee, the canvas is like a ouija board which the universe will push through and speak. However, there is no one there to speak. Line, surface, and space are used to depict that which is beneath change and destruction. Yet, there is no God in this cosmic mysticism. In the paintings *Schoolhouse* and *Dancing Girl* there is a sense of both wit and tragedy. There is a ghostliness in this art, as if there is a magic force from man who knows about the absurd. These paintings are given irrational, enigmatic titles after they are finished, reminiscent of the language mysticism of Heidegger.

Surrealism provides a different solution to the quest for meaning. It seeks to find meaning in the subconscious—in ideas, feelings, and sentiments. It reacts against the rationalistic-mathematical planes of the cubists to depict fear, agony, despair, and the revolt against all strictures—the bourgeois, God, and reason. Freud, de Sade, Marx, and Nietzsche are philosophical parallels and inspirations. In their quest is another type of mystical experience to give meaning, the mysticism of the subconscious. Surrealism is revolutionary and destructive. Some of the surrealists were against personality, conscience, beauty as a goal, talent, and even the will to live. In this view of life and art there was an interest in long-forgotten mysticism, gnosticism, and the primitive. The goal was to liberate many, but what a strange liberation.

In this world, bombs explode into flowers. The eerie sense of the irrational conjunctions, the hatred of logic (since logic was seen to be totally mathematical and inhuman), overt and concealed eroticism, sadism, and alienation—all are depicted. In the art of de Chirico, there is a portrayal of deserted and haunted places, and a depiction of alienated men as human puppets. He is a displaced object in a estranged world.

We see similar dimensions in the works of Yves Tanguy (e.g., *Rapidity of Sleep*) and A. Gottlieb's *Primeval*. Such trends are clearly visible as well in the work of Salvador Dali in his mystic images of the past. His *St. John of the Cross* depicts a mystical, surreal Christ. He never touches the world and humanity. He is a gnostic Christ, beyond suffering, beyond good and evil. In the strange, abnormal world of surrealism, we are awakened to the question "Isn't our world strange, or abnormal?"

The amazing dimension of modern art reflects how puzzled artists are about the meaning of life. The *Dada* movement saw the world as chance absurdity. Here is art to break all taboos, all norms of art, and all sacred and nonsacred traditions. This is true nihilism—a reflection of life as meaningless. In the art of one of Dada's leading exponents, Marcel Duchamp, one finds work which states that life is absurd. All values, norms, forms, and traditions in Western culture have lost their meaning. He embraces anarchism. Duchamp's work spans most of the twentieth century. His painting *Nude Descending a Staircase* is in the cubist style. One can see no woman or any of the tantalizing or titillating elements men would look for. This is also the case with *King and Queen Surrounded by Swift Nudes* and *Bride Being Undressed by Her Bachelors*. There are no queen, king, nudes, bachelors, or brides. All are anarchistically destroyed in black humor.

This was well depicted in the 1969 display of Machine Art at the Museum of Modern Art in New York. Man, in many pictures, was an engine with a clumsy addition of some human organs. The whole atmosphere was utterly depressing. Duchamp's work was displayed as well. His work was more destructive than the rest. Those who attended could watch and see the effect of his titles. The onlookers only saw cubes as they searched in vain for the content of the title. They were turned into voyeurs and made dirty. People whispered to each other and pointed out a possible breast or sexual organ. Yet, it was not really in the picture—only in their imaginations. To have watched this process was amazing. Duchamp wanted to kill the idea of high art as a representation of more traditional human values.

Other artists also radically reflect the meaninglessness of human life. Since the world is a product of chance meaninglessness, Jackson Pollack's canvas also is a product of chance. He devised various methods to drop paint on canvas in a totally random way. This shows the absurd nature of the world.

Also of note is *pop art*, a rebellion against great artistic themes and scenes. Here we have the painting of cheap objects. Pop art at times celebrates the positive dimensions of that which is common. At other times it reflects, as in some of Andy Warhol's work, the absurdity, the cheapness, and even the tearing down of things previously valued. What else did modern art bring us? There has been *op art*, basically interesting forms and configurations; there has been *self-mutilation art*, the ultimate nihilism. Photographs of the mutilated are considered artistic. These types of art steer clear of wrestling with human problems and solutions. In this context of modern art, we can understand the *happenings* of the late '60s. The art work did not last, but people turned off and tuned into drugs for their artistic experiences.

The nature of modern art largely reflects the tragic view of life. Perhaps the work of F. Bacon sums up the horror of world views that reject the God of the Bible. Bacon gives us macabre images of despair, a preoccupation with sickness, the decadent, the horrid. The alienation is well portrayed in his painting *The Scream*. Other paintings show us a world of paralytics, neurotics, and schizoids in cages. They are lost in a void.

Bacon remarks, "Also man now realizes that he is an accident, that he is a completely futile being, that he has to play out the game without reason."[6] Art, he goes on to say, is a game, a distraction to keep us living.

These sentiments are reflected in the existential anguish of the films of Ingmar Bergmann. In *The Seventh Seal*, the horror of judgment without God is perceived. In Antonioni (*Blow Up*) there is murder without guilt and love without morals.

How shall we evaluate the basic trends of twentieth-century art? We would certainly be foolish to not see brilliance in the artists' ability to use form, color, texture, and light to portray their views of life. Certainly there are reflections of keen insight into the plight of man without God in many of these works. Yet we see artistic expression at an impasse. The failure of various approaches to find values, universals, and human purpose have placed much recent art in the category of the trite. Alfred Neimeyer of the Metropolitan Museum of Art even goes so far as to say that modern art is dead unless it can move to a new view of and source of inspiration.[7]

Since our purpose is apologetics and not artistic criticism, we must limit our comments. Artists are often intuitively brilliant people who perceive the implications of the direction of a society, long before the population at large perceives it. Hence modern art is at its best in depicting the dilemmas faced by 20th twentieth-century people for whom religious verities seem unconvincing. The tragic, hopeless, despairing dimensions of modern art are often a reflection of man's creation in the image of God and his reaction to a world view that does not accept God as the source of human life. As Schaeffer puts it, the "mannishness of man" recoils in dread at the prospects of life without God. This mannishness also strives to find an adequate meaning for life, one not provided by materialistic interpretations of man's origin and destiny. Cut off from biblical roots, modern art shows fitful, sometimes chaotic stabs at a meaning for life, whether in an Eastern mysticism, in a nameless reality that speaks through art, in the universals to be gained by the subconscious and, finally, in the act of embracing nihilism or nothingness as a value in itself to give meaning. None of these solutions provides an adequate meaning or purpose to the "mannishness of man."

From a biblical point of view, where the basic world view perspectives are reflected in modern art, they are false viewpoints. This does not mean that there is no beauty, truth, or creativity of value in modern art. Modern art has made us aware of the *truth* of the negative implications of the direction of twentieth-century societies cut off from biblical roots. Modern art has revealed the contradictions in man's own conscious and subconscious life; it has even shown the beauty in the mundane and in forms and colors. Yet modern art, in reflecting philosophies of life, has clearly revealed the severity of the human dilemma when life is lived without God. It has not provided significant solutions, or even positive hints at solutions, in the human quest for meaning and purpose.

Modern art—as in the case of modern literature, philosophy, music, and theology—reflects the dilemma of twentieth-century secular life with an upper and lower story division.

UPPER STORY	Mystical solutions;
mystical,	Gauguin—art as meaning "noble savage" ideal;
nonrational	S. Dali—Gnostic mysticism;
solutions	Other Eastern viewpoints

LINE OF DESPAIR	-----------------------------

LOWER STORY	Machine art, man is a machine;
man without	Rejection of traditional values;
purpose or	Surrealism, sensory alone real;
meaningpurpose or	Impressionism;
meaning	Chance, absurd nature of life; Dadaism

ART TRENDS: 1975–1990

Two trends are discernable in the art world. One is a continuation of unbelievable decadence. The other is a return to art as a depiction of beauty and an enhancement of life. The first reflects the end point of man outside of a biblical world view. The second is a return to more traditional values of beauty. The mannishness of man can not live in the world implied by the absence of the

God of the Bible.

Artists have often formed a society of their own that uses art as a cover for immorality. In this, art is given a value that frees the artist and his work from moral restrictions. Those who would bring art under any moral restriction are looked at as hopelessly puritanical and violating freedom of expression. Some artists have valued radical freedom above all else. To censor pornographic art or to judge it morally, after the manner of Victorian critic John Ruskin, is seen as antiquated. Biblically, the moral tone of a society is a supreme value. Freedom has limits. Artists influenced by the Reformation eschewed the humanistic ideals of the immoral art culture. Nudity in painting (with models stripping for artists) was proscribed in societies under Puritan sway. The culture of the artists involved much immorality.

The implications of radical artistic freedom of expression are nowhere more fully revealed than in the recent debate (which continues into the 1990s) on the funding practices of the National Endowment of the Arts. Artists are not only arguing over their right to express themselves in crude and immoral ways. Indeed, they are arguing for their right to equal government funding no matter the moral content of the art.

This is especially seen in three artists. First is the work of Karen Findley, which claims to be social commentary concerning male domination. Stripping herself of clothing, she pours chocolate sauce on herself and sprouts. This is a representation of semen. According to news reports, she then pretends to engage in masturbation. The message is anti–male chauvinism.

The second artist, J. Flek, urinates as part of his act. Amazingly, the NEA peer-review panel recommended funding his work. The bankruptcy of secular humanism and its inability to restrict anything is manifest here with extreme clarity.

It later came to light that NEA funds were used in funding the exhibits of the works of the late Robert Mapplethorpe. A jury in Cincinnati was asked to decide if his homoerotic pictures were art and should be allowed or banned. Mapplethorpe's exhibit included photos of children in erotic poses and even a picture of bull whip protruding out of the artist's rear end. The jury decided that they could not restrict freedom of artistic expression, and though they did not like his pictures, they deemed it art. The question is not "What is art?" The question is rather "Are some artistic expressions so immoral that they must be precluded?" or "Are some artistic expressions to be precluded as immoral even if they are brilliantly executed?" High artistic quality can make immoral artistic expression even more dangerous. An X-rated film that is well produced and has a "redeeming social message" is even more dangerous because it attracts more people, especially the young, into immorality. Some pornographic magazines have excellent photography.

It boils down to the question, Does a society have the right and responsibility to safeguard a basic moral climate as necessary to the social fabric or social stability? My answer is, clearly, yes. Our nation and the Western world, until recently, has answered yes.

The NEA and the jury in Cincinnati, with some misdirection from Supreme Court decisions, were both befuddled because they asked the wrong question. A biblically informed Jewish scholar, Jacob Neusner, asked more correct questions and voted against funding this immoral art. The implications are again highlighted by the 1990 case of a nude bar owner in Fort Wayne, Indiana, who asked why can't his dancers be seen as engaging in valid artistic expression. If those in high culture can have their nudes, why can't "Joe Sixpack" have his variety of nude artistic expression? This is an airtight argument based on the assumptions of a secular-humanist society.

On the other hand, some artists have returned to a more traditional ideal of enhancing life with beautiful art. Marc Chagall often fulfilled this role in his many works with beautiful mystic themes which included biblical and Jewish symbolism. His form of expressionism certainly went against the trends of his contemporaries. He found positive religious meanings. Hilton Kramer has dubbed a return to painting with subjects and more realistic dimensions "The Revenge of the Philistines." The "avant-guard" art world looked with disdain upon the tastes of the middle class, calling it "Philistine." Yet how many, except those who sought to be "in" with the trendsetters really and deeply enjoyed much of the "art as the subject of art" found in highly abstract modernism and in the loss of the human in painting and sculpture.

Composition has and always will be important to art. Man does in some way seek to celebrate the glories of creation, and composition has its place in this. Even if his world view does not encourage it, he will sometimes unintentionally celebrate the work of The Greatest Artist.

For example, Fairfield Porter never fit the constraints of modern abstraction. Though approaching composition and form with seriousness, his paintings celebrate the human and the creation in pictures with family, friends, houses, flowers, and landscapes. (Porter died in 1975.)

Jack Beal's style of painting is termed social realism. In *The History of Labor*, a mural for the Department of Labor Building in Washington, there is again an affirmation of human themes in painting. So also in *The Farm* and *The Harvest*, two recent paintings which some see as an overly romantic view of the goodness of agricultural life. On the other hand, there are in the memories of children and adults greatly enjoyable experiences in nature. Sometimes our experience is so enjoyable that it seems almost ideal.

Thematic art reaches a high point in Jacob Lawrence's paintings, which chronicle Afro-American history. Alex Katz's paintings are filled with acute observations of dress, personality, and manners. Formal concerns are still important. Neil Weilliven's landscapes evidence an intense and long devotion to *subject matter*.

Artists in the movements of *photo realism* and *super-realism*, in a controversial departure, take their return to realism to an extreme. Many do not see this as good art. Examples of super-realists are Duane Hanson and William Bailey.

Malcolm Morley, another contemporary artist, combines subject matter with formalistic concerns in expressionistic flourishes. Neo-expressionism seeks to give room for many levels of emotional expression. Julian Schnabel is a controversial representative of this art.

Thus we find a return to realism in a postmodern context, a return to the emotional quality of expressionism and other combinations (even a new surrealism).

There is also not lacking those who want art to serve the cause of political and social change, especially among leftist and Marxist artists. Painting that does not serve the political and social cause is seen as irresponsible. That painting must serve the women's movement, Latin American revolution, and environmental concerns is argued by such artists as Lucy R. Lippard, Nancy Spiro, and F. Torres. The aesthetic quality of much of this art is doubted by many art critics. That art has served and does serve as a vehicle for values, and hence religious, social, and political ideals, can hardly be doubted.

The extraordinary aspect of art over the last twenty years is the breakdown of any principle of dominating orthodoxy. We are not in a period where an artistic school or elite is dictating what constitutes valid art for our time. In the past, various orthodoxies such as impressionism, surrealism, expressionism, cubism, and abstract modernism dominated. This may be a good thing and open a door for the rejuvenation of biblically inspired art in a broad sense. These artists can produce varieties of works that can celebrate the many aspects of creation, speak the truth of God, and show forth the beauty and wisdom of our Creator. Artistic culture for the past 150 years has been amazingly proud and arrogant. The present situation is probably good for art and good for truth and beauty.

A FEW WORDS ON RECENT MOVIES

Film is an extremely powerful medium. The American film industry is still capable of producing extraordinarily good films with significant character development and tender reflections on the truths of human life. Greatly differing examples would be *Henry V* and *Driving Miss Daisy*. For great adventure and the battle of good triumphing over evil in a classical way, the *Star Wars* series is noteworthy.

However, more and more films promote, depict, and titillate toward sexual immorality. In the 1990s the preoccupation of the film industry with sex and violence is almost unbelievable. Appropriate films for family entertainment are few indeed. A recent edition of *The Movie Guide* for 1990 noted films promoting or reflecting every perversion. The great majority of films were not recommended by this biblically informed guide. Although it is a Christian guide, the reviewers are not Victorian prudes.

Secondly, more and more films reflect aspects of New Age religion. As fine a film series as the *Star Wars* series is, it depicts a nebulous god called "the Force." The Force has a good and a dark side. This is New Age pantheism. Yet many of the values in the series are clearly more compatible with a biblical perspective. This includes the ideals of truth, justice, and good portrayed in the film. Unfortunately, some of the values of New Age relativism are fostered, too. Talented filmmakers like George Lucas and Steven Spielberg do have a New Age perspective, but these stories do reflect the great fairy tale with the triumph of good over evil. J. R. R. Tolkien noted that such themes are a reflection of the biblical themes of creation, fall, and redemption.

From *E.T.* to *Ghosts* to many other space-based, extra-terrestrial, and occult themes, many movies reflect New Age thinking. This is because, apart from biblical faith, New Age themes at least provide a more exciting artistic vision and deliver the viewer from the bland world of secular humanism.

New Age thinking is devoid of clear ethical and religious concepts, although there is a New Age value structure of sorts. Its emphasis is on environmentalism, health, meditation, and mental self-control.

It is noteworthy that Hollywood can combine such New Age themes with crass perversion. Does the New Age provide moral norms to halt the erosion of Western morality? It is quite doubtful. Everything that is helpful in transcending secular humanism in the New Age view is in biblical Christianity. The latter has the ultimate victory of good over evil with none of the dangers of New Age relativism and occultism.

RECENT TRENDS IN SOCIETY

The last twenty years has seen a decline of secular humanism and the ascendancy of New Age religion on a large scale. This is not to say that secular humanism is not still important in our society; it continues to be an influence in schools, courts, and halls of government. However, New Age is more subtle as a religion. It invades our society and overcomes the separation of church and state more easily than the direct and clear perspective of biblical faith. In my evaluation, New Age is at least equal to secular humanism as an anti-biblical influence in society. Our society has seen a continual erosion of moral standards. These trends should wake us up to the ultimately destructive nature of nonbiblical philosophies. Furthermore, the media elite are generally sympathetic to liberalizing directions which foster this moral breakdown.

One important manifestation already mentioned is the debate on the nature of free expression. The Supreme Court rightly argued that community standards could be taken into account in defining and precluding pornography. However, the Supreme Court's guidance is so vague that it is very difficult to prosecute. The expression must primarily appeal to prurient interests and be devoid of significant dimensions of redeeming social or artistic value. Pornographers are therefore careful to include something that could be argued by their lawyers as having this artistic value. There will not be lacking someone to find redeeming social value in anything that is produced. Thus, as before noted, the Mapplethorpe homoerotic art was found to have redeemable value and to not be pornographic. Previously, law simply precluded nudity, erotic behavior, and explicit descriptions of sexual experience as pornography. These more objective laws were far easier for juries to uphold.

We have become a pornographic society. The media of film, television, and advertising are so filled with sexual innuendo and enticement that young people (and many others) find resistance difficult. This has been a major force in family breakdown and social disintegration. The traveling husband and father finds "soft-porn" piped into his hotel room in every city. The message is clear: "Cheat on your wife—illicit sex is normal, good, and desirable." Promiscuity has become a way of life in spite of horrible venereal diseases and many negative social consequences.

A second and related force is the pro-abortion movement. When sex is divorced from marriage and family, there is a strong motive to see that the product of sexual relations (the baby) be eliminated. Despite all the information on birth control, unwed pregnancies among teens accelerate. Teens will take chances no matter how well educated or informed. Free love can only be totally free if there is freedom from birth control. This thinking requires the allowance that an "accidentally" produced baby can be aborted. The denial of the sacredness of human pre-born life is an extraordinary departure from biblically informed Western ethics. Life has become cheap. The true joys of sexual fidelity are lost as modern people sell their birthright of monogamy for a pot of porridge. The 1973 Supreme Court decision on abortion unleashed destruction beyond anyone's wildest dreams as we approach thirty million aborted babies in the United States.

Radical feminism also is part of the destructive trend. Surely women are entitled to better treatment and opportunity in society. Yet, radical feminism sees marriage as bondage and abortion as necessary to sexual equality. They define worth in terms of worldly success. Anger and bitterness are not far from the surface. Thus, equality is seen as even better served by lesbianism. Lesbianism can provide a transcendence of male-female sexual interdependence. All of this culminates in the gay rights movement. After great political pressure, the American Psychiatric Association removed homosexuality from its list of psychiatric illnesses. The celebration of homosexual marriages and the acceptance of patterns of promiscuous male homosexuality would have been considered unthinkable a mere twenty-five years ago.

No society can survive the full triumph of these destructive trends. The importance of monogamous marriage, stable family life, sexual mores, and a limit to pornographic expression makes them essential to stability and liberty in society. The nature of these movements and destructive trends are brilliantly described in two recent books, *Men and Marriage* by George Gilder and *Enemies of Eros* by Margie Galliger. These trends and movements certainly confirm the proposition that the biblical world view provides the best context for social stability and human fulfillment.

NEW AGE RELIGION

A society with low moral standards will seek comfort in religious conceptions with low moral or ethical demands. Secular humanism does not give most people a sufficient sense of meaning and purpose. Human beings innately seek some reason for hope beyond the grave and a divine sense of purpose.

The New Age movement is filling the vacuum of religious meaning for many and may be the most significant social trend at the end of the twentieth century. For presentations of the New Age movement from within, the reader is encouraged to read Marilyn Furgeson's *The Aquarian Conspiracy* and Frijhof Copra's *The Turning Point*. The latter is a physicist and New Age philosopher. An excellent presentation and criticism of the New Age movement and perspective is given in Elliot Miller's *A Crash Course on the New Age*. The last book is a non-hysterical, balanced critique.

The New Age movement is not really a new point of view. The New Age world view is essentially pantheistic. All of the sections on pantheism in its "pan-everythingism" form apply to the New Age movement, especially since the New Age movement is essentially the acceptance of Eastern religious ideas in the West.

The New Age projects an unbelievable confusion in concepts as if it were profundity. By a trick of the mind, using words in ambiguous ways can appear to be profound. This is the case with the basic New Age concept of the self. At times the self appears to be just what we mean in ordinary language, the personal identity that all self-conscious individuals possess. However, often the self is used as interchangeable with the concept of "the Self," the absolute base of existence. In New Age reason the real self of every individual is God, and God is the inner Self. This is very similar to the concept of ancient Vedanta Hinduism taught by Sankara. Therefore, a person may say that in the deepest core of his being he is God. At other times, language seems to project that the God in us is a being distinct from us. This gives good religious feelings, but the New Age certainly does not believe this more biblical understanding of the presence of God in the believer. Because language about the ultimate is said to be ultimately futile and woefully inadequate, cosmic oneness is to be experienced beyond words. However, by this claim of futility, muddled language can be defended as the most profound way to get at this reality.

The New Age adds to this Eastern irrationalism (which amazingly is taken by its followers as more rational and enlightened than biblical faith) a heavy dose of occult experience and spiritism. New Agers often uncritically accept, at face value, the information from spirit guides, out-of-body experiences, and memories of previous existences. New Agers often have a dramatic conversion experience that convinces them that "All is One" and they are "One with the All."

Reincarnation is an important part of New Age thinking. Of course, according to the biblical conception, this is a world filled with deceptive spirits as well as angels. Many are the spirits which can provide deceptive experiences leading one to believe they had had a former life. With the New Age espousing evolution, ethical relativism, and toleration for all religions that do not make absolutist claims, it becomes the perfect deception to fill the vacuum left from the Western abandonment of biblical faith. This vacuum was created through the influence of the false concepts of secular humanism.

The New Age movement is another example of Francis Schaeffer's mystical leap of faith in a society that cannot quite live with the emptiness of scientific materialism. Although the New Age movement does put forth some concepts of ecological preservation as a key value, since all is God or part of God, the distinctions in value between man in the image of God and other creatures is often lost. All of the criticisms of Eastern viewpoints in this text apply without qualification to the New Age movement except that New Age formulations are frequently just simplified perversions of Eastern views tailored for Western consumption. Hans Kung's *Eternal Life* raises perceptive comparisons between biblical perspectives and the reincarnationist relativism of the New Age.

The New Age movement must be taken seriously. It has influential advocates, from Prince Charles of England to actress Shirley MacLaine. Because its doctrines are nebulous, it can be taught as nonreligious exercises to our children in public schools. Yet it is profoundly religious. It is grossly deceptive to claim otherwise and to then claim that one believes in the separation of church and state. Many were the practitioners of transcendental meditation who were solicited under the claim that TM was nonreligious.

The New Age faith may possibly be more dangerous than any other present trend. Since it is eclectic, it can incorporate into its broad symbol system into all but an absolutist faith like biblical Christianity. The psychology of Jung can provide further impetus. In the writings of Carl Jung, good and evil are both parts of one divine reality. Perverted images can be part of his god too. The dangers of this, even in Jungian influences in "Christian" healing movements, are excellently documented in Leanne Payne's *The Healing Presence*. Jungian psychology is New Age in basic flavor and conception.

In New Age thought, a human being can be deified. If my higher "Self" is

God, why would it be wrong to worship me as God? Indeed, in a pantheistic world view, since all is God, wouldn't it make sense to worship the head of state as especially a manifestation of God? There have been, in New Age thought, many incarnations (*gurus*); we in another sense are all incarnations. The potential for New Age religion to be used by an antichrist, or even *the* Antichrist, to achieve a higher mystical authority is awesome. If the emperor of Rome was a divinity, why not the head of a "new world order" of toleration, peace, ethical relativism, ecological balance, and all of the other New Age emphases? Yet, this easily can become a delusion that does not face the deterioration and destruction of society brought by a relativistic value system. It is not as though Scripture does not support ecology and peace. It does, but in an absolute ethical framework where we are to be judged by a personal God in whom there is *no darkness* at all.

New Age toleration and ethical relativism can easily turn to hate for those who are not "with the program." Christian author Dave Hunt points out that Hitler was a great fan of many concepts that are part of New Age thought. New Age ethics is ill defined; and its worship of self can easily lead to tyranny. What are the New Age concepts of marriage, family, male-female relationships, democracy, human sexual morality, gay rights, etc.? There is no New Age consensus. Would a dictator be needed to force the people into higher consciousness? Would this especially be possible if major economic dislocations and hardship took place? Would the dictator be worshipped as God?

The gullibility of New Agers to channels (mediums) who give messages from ascended masters is itself uncanny. A true analysis of the dangers of channeling is found in Kurt Koch's *Christian Counseling and Occultism*. On the other hand, as both Koch and Elliot Miller (*A Crash Course on the New Age*) document, there is evidence of real supernatural manifestations in New Age experiences of channeling, seances, out-of-body experiences, and visions. What these supernatural experiences imply is determined by the context of one's world view, which gives an interpretive framework. Do the memories of past lives prove that the person really had a past life? Or does it reveal demonic telepathic communication which is mistaken for one's own memory? Does reincarnation really explain injustices and inequalities as manifestations of judgments for past lives (*karma*)? Or is the biblical view—that we live once and after this there is judgment—the true view? The caste system in India, an example of a society in the grip of reincarnation belief, is oppressive beyond anything in Western society. We must not, it is thought, interfere with the workings of karma. Leave the destitute in their state. Biblical concepts of corporate judgment from generation to generation are equally powerful as explanations of inequality among nations, groups, and individuals. Sin against groups also deprive them of opportunity. The power of the Gospel breaks the cycles of inherited sickness, poverty, and sin.

When all of the evidence is in, it is clear that the source of New Age revelation is demonic (evil spirits). It is also clear that New Age concepts do not have sufficient clarity to provide a just and stable social order. We should remember that Satan masquerades as an angel of light. Many of the channeled spirits give out philosophy that is amazing for its shallowness.

Because in New Age practice one invites spirits to be involved with the person, to inhabit and speak, there is great danger of direct satanic control. It is an invitation to occult bondage and demonic possession. One of the great evidences for the biblical faith is to see such spirits cast out in the name of Jesus. People fall to ground, scream, and speak in other voices during deliverance prayer. I have personally witnessed such deliverances.

New Agers are very difficult to convince by argument. The broad toleration of humanistic love looks for what is thought to be a view that is superior when compared to narrow-minded biblical concepts. All is reinterpreted by the amorphous concepts of the New Age. Only the power of prayer can bring a revelation of Jesus to the New Ager. The Holy Spirit is the key in breaking through the New Age spirit.

SUMMARY OF CULTURE AND APOLOGETICS

Twentieth-century culture has shown, more than the culture of any other age, the logical implications of the rejection of the biblical world and life viewpoint. Naturalism and the views of a so-called rational or scientific understanding of man's origin and destiny lead to misery and despair. The universe and all life-forms on earth are conceived as merely the product of time plus chance plus matter. The world view which leads to despair is suspect since most would agree that:

> 1. Man should be able to feel at home in that which is his true base and environment, just as a fish is at home in water.
> 2. Any world view in which man can not live in peace, that is so against his nature that it leads to despair, is not a correct explanation of his origin and destiny.

Of course, not all artists created pessimistic and despairing images in their writing, music, and painting. Yet, those few which were optimistic during the first three-quarters of the twentieth century seemed to not face the facts of the secular view they held.

It is a shallow utopianism that suppresses the force of modern despair. Certainly, modern culture lends great credence to the biblical world and life view by showing that its alternatives either lead to despair or are not adequate to foster a vision of human life that can, for most people over the long term, inspire a positive hopeful existence. This is not only reflected in artistic culture but in the disintegration of Western society to the extent that it has turned its back on its biblical roots. The condition of the family, divorces, poorly adjusted children, crime, and selfishness are the results of our secular humanism.

We do, however, need to note the limits of this evidence. For those who refuse to allow the truth of our above premise, that a true world view will provide a basis for a positive purpose for living, our argument will not make a significant difference. A person can choose to deny the logical implications of the rejection of the God of the Bible, although culture shouts out these implications. A person can choose to remain nihilistic and say that man is tragic and out of kilter with the whole universe, which is bent on his destruction. Bertrand Russell professed that the basis of his own view was the full acceptance of the destruction of the solar system and all humanity. All great human works and acts would be finally destroyed and forgotten.[8] It is possible to hold such a view. However, I hold that the premise of man *fitting* in the universe and *being at home* in the true world view is an "intuitively perceived-as-correct" premise by most of mankind. This is evidence to be taken into account by any world view. The biblical world view sees man as created in the image of God and created for fellowship with God and other people. God has placed eternity in man's heart so that man desires to never die. This would explain the disintegration of our society through its rejection of the Bible and would also explain the despair of modern art.

This evidence can be of great value in what Schaeffer calls pre-evangelism. It can help us to listen with compassion and understanding. Additionally, the message of salvation can be convincingly spoken into the context of the lives of those who are most acutely showing the implications of secular humanism. It is important to show the point of tension in their world view which causes their "mannishness" to rebel against the implications of meaninglessness in their own viewpoints. This rebellion is expressed in mystical leaps of desperation to find some irrational source of meaning. The false view of the rational as yielding a mathematical materialism leads to a divorce between the rational and the meaningful. How amazing it is that man can not live within the implications of this viewpoint. Camus never gave up hope, although there was no basis for it. Sartre spoke on political issues (e.g., his protest of the French-Algerian War) as though there were absolute moral and social standards of right and wrong. Pointing out these inconsistencies under the leading of the Spirit can lead many to question and even to seek solutions in the Bible. The behaviorist must use personal language in expressing love and friendship. His world view does not leave room for the irreducibility of the personal, but in his living he must admit what his world view does not allow.

Those who have chosen inadequate solutions can often be shown the flimsiness of their solutions. The new left could have been shown the evidence of fallen human nature as certain to thwart any humanly created utopia. Certainly in a chance universe we should not expect to overcome. Perhaps one in despair will hear other evidences as well. We need to be those who will unmask false gods, the quest for affluence, scientific progress, or even human love as adequate to sustain humanity. The death of a loved one will come; what then? Material acquisitions can be lost. Those who have lived for wealth have reaped a tremendous sense of emptiness.[9]

Edward Albee's *The Zoo Story* shows an attempt by a beatnik to rip the mask off a complacent, middle-class businessman. He has defenses by which he refuses to squarely face pain, misery, and tragedy. He lives an unauthentic life. Finally the beatnik in frustration begins to physically draw this man into a fight. He hands him a knife and runs upon it, killing himself. Finally the defenses fall; reality in all its starkness and horror hits him as the beatnik dies. He cries, "Oh the horror." Perhaps we as Albee need to use modern culture to reveal the horror of life without God to create a hunger for Him in those who have suppressed facing the issues of life. *Only the Holy Spirit can enable this to be effective.* In the work of Francis Schaeffer, this has been amazingly and supernaturally effective as many intellectuals and students have come into a personal relationship with God.

In all of this we need to clearly define our terms so that we are not perceived as just offering one more mystical-leap solution. We are presenting the Messiah, not simply to give people peace or a better life, but because He is *the truth*. A person is responsible to obey the truth. However, in our presentation, let us find that unique need and point of contact for every person.

In presenting the biblical world and life view, we are presenting not just a philosophy but a relationship with a person.   We are also, however, desirous of pointing out that the biblical world view provides us with a solution to the upper- and lower-story division of modern culture. For in the Scriptures we find a world view that is rational (coherent) and meaningful. It gives an adequate purpose for human life and a clear direction for living. It also provides a point of integration in which science and art have a proper and valued place that is properly understood.   Let us note that the Bible gives us a unified and integrated vision to tie together all the dimensions of life and culture. Let us as followers of Jesus be involved in understanding culture and in transforming culture on a biblical basis. Too often, the followers of Jesus have opted out of significant cultural dialogue which can provide a context by which the gospel can be communicated with great authenticity.

CHAPTER 5: STUDY QUESTIONS

1. How conclusive is the evidence from modern culture for the truth of the biblical world view?

2. How do the writings of Albert Camus reflect the depressing conclusions of a secular-humanist perspective?

3. How does modern literature reflect upper- and lower-story division in human experience?

4. Why is John Cage's music such an apt reflection on modern skepticism?

5. How does expressionism attempt to find meaning?

6. Explain the implications of Dada in art?

7. Why is reincarnation important in New Age thinking?

PART THREE

OBJECTIONS TO THE

BIBLICAL WORLD VIEW

OBJECTIONS TO THE BIBLICAL WORLD VIEW BASED ON THE PROBLEM OF EVIL

The problem of evil has been traditionally put forth as the greatest objection to the biblical faith. If God is truly loving and good, how can we account for the massive amount of evil and suffering among his children? Is it consistent with goodness and love to allow a holocaust in which six million Jews are murdered with unspeakable torture and suffering? If God is all-powerful, the creator of all as the Bible teaches, then He is able to stop such suffering. Why does He not do so? So great is the inconsistency, according to the skeptic, that in no way can we accept the Bible as true.

This objection is reflected in the history of both philosophy and literature. In the play *J. B.* by Archibald MacLeish, the Devil puts the objection of the problem of evil into syllogistic form. He says, "If God is good, He is not God (omnipotent, all-powerful), and if God is God (omnipotent, all-powerful), He is not good." This play, built upon the story of Job, clearly presents the dilemma.

> P#1: An omnipotent God *can* prevent evil.
> P#2: A Good God *would* prevent evil.
> P#3: God is good and omnipotent.
> ------------------------------
> C#1: Therefore evil must not exist, if P1-P3 are true.
> P#4: But evil does exist.
> ------------------------------
> C#2: Therefore God is either not good or powerful (or does not exist);
>   or a good and omnipotent God did not create the world.

This objection is not at all new, although sometimes modern writers seem to present their view as if they were the discoverers of evil. In Camus' *The Plague*, the horrors of suffering and death show that the world is absurd; there is no God. The cruelty of life in Ingmar Bergmann's film *The Seventh Seal* leads to the same conclusion. In the nineteenth century several others powerfully presented the objection. In Dostoevsky's *The Brothers Karamazov*, the Devil makes his case against God in the famous chapter known as the "Grand Inquisitor." He accuses God of evil in his harsh treatment of man and his unrealistic expectations from this poor, frail creature. Indeed, another part of the novel brings this to bear with existential power. Ivan Karamazov recounts the story of a child who was playfully throwing stones. He accidentally injures the dog of a noble master. In revenge, this noble strips the child bare and makes the mother watch as he sics his dogs on the child. The mother watches in horror as the child is torn to shreds. Ivan then says that nothing in eternity can ever compensate this mother's pain; it is irredeemable. Hence, there is such evil that the Bible must not be true. This powerful statement comes from a writer who was a Bible-believer. His main character Alyosha demonstrates the value of faith in spite of the objection.

The French writer Voltaire mockingly caricatured religion because of the problem of evil. In *Candide*, he clearly reflected the position that the horrors of the Lisbon earthquake, which killed the innocent and the guilty alike, made religious faith absurd.

Analytic philosophy as well has entered the ancient debate. Antony Flew[1] believes that the statement "God is good" is meaningless. He says we know what it means to say an earthly father loves his son. He describes a child dying of cancer in excruciating pain. His earthly father is frantic to help this child, yet his heavenly father, who supposedly *can* help him, does nothing. This comparative analysis of the meaning of love disproves religious faith in Flew's view.

Richard Rubinstein, Jewish chaplain at the University of Pittsburgh, echoes these themes, too. God is dead. A world of indiscriminate natural disasters, mongoloids, and concentration camps is a world in which we can no longer believe in God. If God is loving and powerful, He certainly would prevent such evils.[2]

The above-cited examples adequately outline the problem of reconciling the fact of evil with a good God. It is at this point that we turn to representative solutions.

SOLUTIONS WHICH CHANGE
THE DEFINITION OF GOODNESS

THE CALVINISM OF GORDON CLARK

The Calvinism of Gordon Clark provides a solution that is not unique, but his is a clear representation of this view. Clark is a determinist and holds that all behavior is the product of God's will or causation. To Clark, there is no problem of evil since *whatever God does is good by definition*. Goodness must be redefined as behavior that is according to God's law for man. However, since there is no higher authority or appeal for a standard than God, no one can call God anything but good. Goodness then is also defined as whatever God does. To Clark, we must derive our *proper* use of the word good by this method of understanding. In Clark's book *Religion, Reason, and Revelation* he states that if God chooses to put a child through torturous pain it must be good, since God does it.[3]

Certainly Clark's solution eliminates the logical contradiction dimension of the problem of evil, but can we really be satisfied with this view? When a person says that God is good, he is seemingly making a statement that adds cognitive content to our understanding of God. To claim that God is good means that God *has a quality* that accords, in some way, with the usual sense of the common use of the word "goodness." The meaning of goodness may have to be altered by a better understanding, but if our use of the term is totally apart from common understanding, then to talk of God being good is either deceptive or noncommunicative. Actually, in Clark, the statement "God is good" is void of content for it adds nothing in content to the statement "God is God." If goodness is defined as what God does, why not eliminate the confusion and not use the term "goodness." Simply say that God does what God does; He is all powerful; He is the final authority. Basically this solution eliminates significant content for the word "good" when applied to God. This is a serious objection to this solution.

THE CLASSICAL SOLUTION OF LEIBNITZ

This objection also applies to the classical answer of eighteenth-century philosopher G. Leibnitz, who argues that this world is the "best of all possible worlds" since it is the product of God. God is the author of the best since He is good. All evil is only evil if not seen in the context of the whole, which is not only good but the best. It is all determined by God.[4] Leibnitz, like Clark, does not at all defend the goodness of God in the sense in which people raise the issue.

A more serious objection to this solution is its incompatibility with the Bible's own portrayal of goodness. The Bible defines God's goodness in terms of compassion, justice for the poor and needy, and the releasing of those in the bondage of disease and oppression. The Bible states that "God is love." This is the only quality that is so identified as the highest essential quality of God, more than justice and even power. In hyper-Calvinism God's "will" is the predominant feature. This has been described as a "voluntaristic" concept of God. God has a loving, compassionate side and a vengeful, angry side that seeks justice. He chooses to love some but to pour wrath on others. Hence, the Bible's statements on God's compassion are in reference to those times when God chooses to display this quality.

In Scripture, God always acts according to the totality of his character. His will always reflects both his love and justice which are compatible or one and the same. It is not loving for God to be unjust. God is a person of character-constancy, not just an intelligent, creation-organizing power principle.

In Leibnitz, evil is acceptable because of the balance it brings to the total picture of creation. The whole painting is what is good. This defense subsumes God's moral quality under an aesthetic ideal derived from painting. Shadows may be necessary to bring out contrast with light, but this does not mean that evil is necessary to show up goodness in such a way that the whole can be said to be good.

In summary, when we say God is good we mean to ascribe characteristics to God that are reflected in the world of our human experience and concepts which are corrected by the biblical picture of God. Certainly, our sinful distortions of the meaning of goodness may need correction, but not in such a drastic fashion that we completely abdicate any position of commonality with the language use of the rest of mankind. Of course, a hyper-Calvinist does not believe there is common ground between the believer and the unbeliever. We cannot accept this view.

SUB-BIBLICAL SOLUTIONS

The defense of theism in the writings of F. R. Tennant[5] is commendable in many respects. In Tennant, evil is explained as a necessary ingredient in moral development. Such evil produces a depth of solid character in the one who responds rightly. There are important elements in his teaching explaining how some dimensions of evil are really used for a higher good and are not ultimately evil. Yet, his view does not adequately explain the necessity of the horrible evils; Auschwitz, monstrous deformities, and the surd nature of the visitation of evil with such great inequality.

Frederick Sontag explains evil as God's irresponsible love. Sontag's solution would be one variety of *the Finite God Solution*. God loves so much that it hurts us and causes pain, for in his love God acts without foreseeing the painful consequences. The Finite God Solution was given great exposure by the well-known philosopher of the Boston Personalist School of thinkers, Edgar Sheffield Brightman. His student, Peter Bertocchi, carried on this viewpoint. It was recently re-popularized by a New England rabbi, Harold Kushner, in responding to the tragic loss of his son.[7] The solution is really quite simple. It chooses to believe in a good God *rather than* an all-powerful God, and thereby solves the problem of the syllogism with which we began our discussion. The inconsistency is solved by denying that God is omnipotent. In this view God is a powerful and loving creator, but not powerful enough to stop the evil that is an accidental byproduct of his creation. God created and God loves, but his creation is imperfect. God could not help it. Human freedom and natural disasters are occurrences beyond God's control.

On the surface it looks as if this view provides a solution, but it is both philosophically unsatisfying and incompatible with the Bible. Some finitists talk as if for some reason God can not intervene in the world; others as if God's intervention is severely limited. Yet, if God is our maker, even if He is not all powerful, it would seem that He is powerful enough to do much more than He is doing. Could not God at least have destroyed the Nazi rail system transporting Jews to concentration camps, or assured the success of attempts on Hitler's life? Or could not God heal a cancer? For argument's sake, grant the proposition that God cannot do everything, but there seems to be no intervention at all in the midst of some of the most crucial evils. Could there not have been at least a mark of supernatural intervention that would have saved a million, if not all six million? This would have shown that God was working for good.

Actually, the Finite God Solution only works if God is so powerless that there is no reason to hope in his providence or salvation. If its implications are seen, it is destructive to religious faith. Either God is too weak for faith, or, as in Deism, He does not intervene in the world of his creation. A God who does not intervene does not care.

Finitism is incompatible with the Bible because the Bible portrays God as being someone who intervenes. He splits the sea for the Israelites to cross over, sends hail and plague against the oppressor, and brings conquering armies into battle and defeats them (Isaiah 45, Daniel 2). Through Divine power Jesus heals all sickness and raises the dead; on the third day, after His own death, is raised from the dead. The finite God of philosophy is not the God of the Bible. He is so weak in this view that we can not rest our faith in Him. Let us turn then to a more biblical solution.

A BIBLICALLY COMPATIBLE SOLUTION

It is our contention that the nature of evil in the world is actually an evidence for the truth of the biblical world and life view. Properly understood, evil is not an insuperable difficulty at all. Rather, the criteria of truth—consistency, coherence, and comprehensiveness—when applied to the basic biblical concepts of explanation, show that evil is explained better in the biblical world view than in any other. This assumes that we have a clear understanding of the meaning of "omnipotence" or the all-powerful nature of God. When we say that God is "omnipotent," we mean that God is the creator of all that is; He brought this universe into existence and can annihilate it. Since it is all a product of his creation, He can intervene in it in any way He pleases. Yet, this "any way" has two qualifications. He can only do that which is *logically possible*, or not contradictory. Secondly, He can only do that which is compatible with his moral nature of love and justice. God cannot act so as to violate his own character; this character is revealed in Scripture. In other words, although God is all powerful, He is *self-limited* by his promises, by the law of sowing and reaping, and by his own faithfulness to his principles which are a part of creation.

Evil itself must be comprehended under those most basic categories of explanation derived from the Bible. All aspects of life are tied together by these concepts. They are: *creation, fall, and redemption.* These are the final ultimate concepts of explanation in our world view. They explain all else and are not themselves explained by any higher categories.

By creation, we mean that we understand that the world was brought into being and ordered by one great intelligent personal God (Hebrews 11:1ff.). All things exist through Him. The understanding of evil, and the compatibility of the presence of evil in a world created by a good and omnipotent God, is understood under the concepts of the fall and redemption.

In nonbiblical religions there is no clear explanation of evil or goodness. Nor is there any explanation in secular humanism. No one can explain why human acts of evil are so far beyond the instinctive behavior of animals: so far beyond naturalistic explanation. Animal behavior is quite lawful; it follows clearly defined paths of behavior. Human behavior often exhibits a refusal to be rational: a behavior that produces an endemic (seemingly intractable) evil. In his later years C. E. M. Joad, the noted British philosopher, was converted from atheism to biblical faith partly because he could find no adequate explanation for the qualities of earthly evil in secular humanism. His books, *The Recovery of Belief* and *God and Evil*, make fascinating reading. Joad concluded that the biblical world view accounted for this evil whereas the secular view did not.

Understanding evil requires an understanding of the biblical concept of the fall and of redemption as well. The fall is a key concept for classical apologists as far back as ancient Jewish sources. It found its classical Christian form in the writings of St. Augustine.

This classical defense holds that God created a perfect world. However, due to the free choice of moral beings, sin was brought into existence. Sin is the breaking of God's law, the disobeying of His will. Through the choice of sin, Scripture says, "death entered into the world" (Romans 5). The evil and suffering of this world order is therefore attributed to *the fall*, that is, man's fall into sin. In classical thought, based on the Scriptures, we note that the fall had several consequences. First, this became a world under the judgment of God. This judgment included our being subject to the destructive works of that archenemy of God, Satan or the Devil. Due to the fall, man lost many of the greater abilities whereby he could have avoided natural disasters, sickness, and death. His knowledge, his intuitive powers, and his ability to choose good over evil were greatly damaged. Even the animal creation, because it was under man's dominion, suffered change and deterioration.

It is therefore crucial to note that the fall is the *solution to natural evil*, not only the moral evil that man does to one another. It is difficult for us fallen humans to conceive of the awesome powers of an unfallen race of people. The power seen in the life of Jesus is a reflection of unfallen man, the perfect image of God. In Jesus we see power to calm the storm, to heal diseases, and to walk on water. The disciples were not in danger of drowning in the storm because Jesus was with them. We never hear of Jesus being subject to sickness or accident. This is a reflection of his identity as the son of man, an image of perfect and restored humanity.

The defense I here put forth has been called the classical *free-will defense*.[8] A full understanding of it requires that we understand the concept of *corporate solidarity*. This concept means that the whole of mankind is bound up together—that we are part of one another. We are rooted in Adam; in fact, the whole of earthly creation is intertwined with the human race. Therefore when Adam fell, the consequences of his fall affected the whole race, since we are part of him. Although our individuality is important to note, we are not to overlook the dimension of reality in which we are part of each other. So Scripture says concerning Adam's fall that "death passed upon all men," even that, in a sense, we sinned in Adam. Our weakness of nature, our propensity to selfishness, and our inability to avoid accidents and disasters is all part of our Adamic inheritance. Even our free choice is severely limited by our inability to consistently choose righteousness. The judgment over the fallen race is such that we find opposition, disaster, and tragedy between man and animal, man and nature, and man and man.

Furthermore, we suffer evil that is not a result of our own personal sin because we participate in the curse over the race of Adam. If I have a son die in an accident, it does not mean that I am worse than my neighbor whose son lives. It simply means that the nature of accidental natural disaster has fallen on my family as a result of Adam's sin. There is a surd character to evil, a chance, irrational quality in which it indiscriminately falls upon people. This is part of the judgment on the race and part of Satan's work. This is the desert of the race because, as traditional Augustinian theology taught, all human beings are totally depraved. This doctrine of total depravity is often misunderstood. Total depravity does not mean that man is of no worth, but simply that no part of man's nature is not affected by the fall. His mind, his emotions, and his physical body are all warped. In addition, the law of sowing and reaping precludes God from intervening in any way inconsistent with his justice. Hence, when human beings forsake God's law and do evil to one another, whether limited or of the grossest character, this must be allowed as part of the sowing and reaping of the race, even if on an individual basis some suffer more than others.

However, God has put restraints on this evil through the laws of society given by His common grace. He restrains evil so the race is not totally destroyed. To the extent that societies maintain a degree of law, evil is thwarted and restrained. When lawlessness and tyranny are chosen by societies, then the evil that can be experienced is huge. War, famine, torture, and unspeakable suffering result from societies rejecting restraining laws. All social laws that are good are reflections of the law of God revealed in the Bible. These basic reasons explain most dimensions of evil. Evil is the result of judgment; it is the work of Satan; it is the recompense of "sowing and reaping"—for in rejecting God's law we reap suffering. It is the result of man's choice of evil.

With this dark picture, why would God in his mercy simply not end it all? Why does He let generation after generation continue in this sad situation? The answer to this question is in the concept of *redemption.*

Redemption means that God's intervention within the boundaries of his justice and love will produce greatly worthwhile fruits from the mess of the fallen world. God will save out of this world those human beings who turn to Him and will preserve that which is of worth within society for the Age to Come. The fallen world is a proper context for producing a redeemed community of such value that the costliness of evil and destruction are seen to be worth it. The quality of redeemed community, saved out of the fall, will be so rich, meaningful, and full of depth and understanding that it is sensible to put up with evil. Indeed the evil fallen world is a tool that is used to produce a quality of redeemed humanity.

This concept is well presented in the last volume of the *Narnia* stories by C. S. Lewis. Lewis shows that in the world which followed the end of Narnia, all that was of true worth in Narnia was preserved in the world which followed. God can continue to preserve the world despite the evil because it can be used to produce a higher redemptive good: a redeemed, experienced, tested, and loving human community that has turned back to Him. This redeemed community, produced through the crucible of the world, is so highly esteemed by God that the evil suffered is not worth being compared to the glory that will be revealed in them (Romans 8:18). In Eternity, this will be more clearly seen.

It should be noted that we have presented an out-of-balance picture of the world and its suffering. There is great beauty and goodness also. We need to note that if believers in God are called upon to solve the problem of evil, unbelievers should be called upon to solve the problem of good. If this is a blind-chance universe, with no loving and good God behind it, from whence come goodness, truth, and beauty? Not only is there evil, but there is the love of nursing mothers, the joy of newlyweds, the wonder of heroism, the beauty of thousands of sunsets, the miracle of a newborn baby, and the deep joy of loyal friendship. Mountain views still inspire, even if storms in the valleys depress. The one who rejects a good God has a great problem in explaining this. Within his world view he has a huge problem of good.

Yet when all this is said, is the classical defense of Augustine fully adequate? Some serious objections have been raised which need to be faced. The Augustinian view stated that God created Adam and Eve perfect. If they were perfect, would not a free but perfect being always choose good? After all, the picture of the final redeemed community is one of human beings who always freely choose that which is good. Others have argued that it is possible to conceive of God creating a free being who always chooses what is right. There is no apparent logical flaw, for good people do freely choose what is right. This issue was most forcefully raised in Antony Flew's *New Essays in Philosophical Theology*. These questions have raised a lively debate in theological and philosophical circles. Several responses have been given.

Hyper-Calvinism rejects the free-will defense outright, claiming that free will is an empty concept; everything is caused by God in the ultimate sense. Human beings are secondary causes that carry out His will. By denying free will and thus the classical free-will defense, the hyper-Calvinist seeks to return us to his "definitional solution" to the problem of evil. Whatever God does is by definition good. We have already rejected this solution for the reasons stated earlier in the chapter.

THE NATURE OF FREE WILL

Other solutions seek to bolster the free-will defense by clarifying the meaning of freedom. The concept of free will is the source of extensive philosophical debate beyond the scope of our present endeavor. Yet the debate leaves us with certainty that there is much to the concept. No philosophical argument has adduced sufficient evidence and logic to destroy the basic intuitive sense of free will as fundamental to human life. Moral philosophers have argued for centuries that free will is a necessary corollary of holding human beings accountable for their actions. If a person is not free to choose otherwise, at least within limits, can he be held accountable, punishable, or praiseworthy? The great eighteenth-century philosopher Immanuel Kant (*Critique of Pure Reason*, *Critique of Practical Knowledge*) held this to be an axiom of ethics itself. If all is caused by God or by material causation, the meaning of moral responsibility is destroyed.

I hold that free will is a basic, intuitively grasped aspect of human moral experience. It is not therefore explainable by other explanatory concepts, but is an ultimate concept that explains many other aspects of human experience. Free will is tied up with creativity. It is behavior that is unpredictable since it is a creative act that manifests freedom. Creative acts are rational, but not fully accountable on the basis of causation. An invention, a work of art, or a scientific discovery partakes of creative insight and execution which go beyond the data of past experience.[10] The nature of creativity and free will is best perceived through descriptions of human existence. The literature of recent continental European philosophy has been helpful in revealing the components of freedom and creativity in human life.[11] Freedom is perhaps best perceived in reflecting on those inner experiences of temptation and struggle. There is the awesome sense of the ability to choose either way; the person either resists and does the right thing, or yields to base temptations of greed, lust, or deception and does the wrong thing. Moral responsibility assumes freedom and a moral law which can be obeyed or broken, and a conscience which brings forth the claims of the law and produces guilt when the law is violated. This is part of the structure of human existence.

Usually our choices are simple or easy. We naturally choose to wait in line, rather than to break in; to feed our children; to pay our bills; and to be truthful in paying taxes. This is habitual moral behavior; we have been trained into it. However, we best know our freedom in the choice of right over self-protection or self-furtherance. In severe temptation we are more aware. Free will is thus part of the meaning of the fall as a basic category of explanation for the world of human experience.

FINE TUNING THE FREE-WILL DEFENSE

However, having said all this in defense of free will, what of the argument of those who say God could create free beings who always choose what is right? This is the meaning of perfection. There are several responses to this argument. Evangelical analytic philosopher Alvin Plantinga has forcefully argued that God cannot create a free being that always chooses right. It is rather of the essence of moral freedom to be able to have a real choice of doing wrong—a choice that can be actualized.[12] Once a choice of right is made, other right choices may be said to freely and naturally follow, but somewhere it had to be really possible to choose either. To create a truly free moral being who would always choose right is not to give real choice at all.

Similar argumentation is found in the monumental book by John Hick *Evil and the God of Love*. Hick also brilliantly argues that it is wrong to ascribe moral perfection to Adam and Eve as representative of original humanity. Moral perfection for created, free-will–type beings is gained through choosing right in the midst of a temptation in which either good or evil could be chosen. Hick thus breaks with Augustine's view of Adam and Eve as created perfect and returns to the view of Irenaeus, an early–second-century church father who argued that Adam and Eve were created innocent, not perfect.[13] As children, they were naive, could be foolish, and could misuse their freedom. Hick believes Irenaeus' concept, that Adam and Eve were created in innocence and were given the opportunity to develop moral perfection, is a step above Augustine's view. I agree. This is similar to the portrayal found in the writings of apologist C. S. Lewis and keenly put forth in his novel *Perelandra*, in which a new couple is tempted like Adam and Eve but does not fall.

Hick and Plantinga answer the question well of why God did not create a free being who always chooses good, and of why a perfect creature would choose evil. Yet two other questions are often asked. When Adam and Eve sinned, why did not God just start over again, and again, until He created a couple who freely chose right? Secondly, why couldn't God allow the free choice and simply thwart the evil consequences of these choices? C. S. Lewis' classic *The Problem of Pain*[14] provides the best answer to the second question. A world in which the evil consequences of our actions are thwarted would be a world without any moral seriousness. It would be a world in which real moral development would not take place. Imagine a world in which an assailant strikes with a club. It harmlessly turns to foam rubber and bounces off. Imagine a world in which the robber faints before he can take the money. No one would be tempted to do evil because evil could not be carried out. Moral freedom would be destroyed. Additionally, the experience of remorse at the consequence of evil, of guilt and repentance which could lead to progress, would be thwarted.

The first question overlooks the fact that the God of the Bible is a God of covenant. When God created Adam and Eve, He committed Himself in covenant faithfulness to the human race that was within the loins of this first couple. Unless they passed certain boundaries of moral depravity, which almost occurred before the flood, He would be committed to their preservation and to working for their redemption.

Secondly, God allowed the human race to continue after the fall because He saw the value of the quality of the redeemed humanity that could be rescued from the ultimate destruction resulting from sin. Many are the spiritual writers who have shown that redeemed humanity will be of higher value and character than a humanity that had never fallen. The position, wisdom, and character of the heavenly community will far surpass the humanity of original paradise.

Because God was aware of the potential of redeemed man, He continued to preserve the life of the fallen race.

A few more comments are in order concerning evil before we summarize an adequate solution to the problem of evil. First of all, most evil, although un- necessary, is allowed because of its usefulness in producing higher orders of goodness with regard to those who respond rightly. This was the argument of F. R. Tennant. Men, having seen the awful results of sin and selfishness, may be confronted with their need to repent. This may motivate them to turn from evil. Many lessons are taught by suffering the consequences of evil behavior. Furthermore, character in the righteous is developed by their resisting evil, re- lieving suffering, and taking up the battle of fighting evil in personal moral, social, political, and international affairs. The response to tragedy can develop compassion and also remind us that this is a world under judgment.

UNNECESSARY EVIL

There is evil that is indeed unnecessary. We can without qualification call it an unnecessary evil tragedy. It is not necessary that human beings choose to reject God and to suffer the destruction of Hell. It is not necessary that torture and human degradation be perpetuated. Yet even these ultimate evils are necessary to preserve the value or good of there being free beings created in the image of God who have real moral choice. Even Hell is a demonstration of the moral ser- iousness of our choices and the awesome power of choice we are given. The law of sowing and reaping requires that God does not unduly intervene in preventing the evil that results from our choices. A morally serious universe is one in which we as a race experience the results of our choices, even if *in this life* individual compensation is not fully balanced. However, as Kant taught, life after death provides recompense that will balance the scales of individual disparity. As the Scripture says, everyone will receive reward and punishment according to their just deserts for the deeds done in the body (I Corinthians 5).

GOD'S INVOLVEMENT IN SUFFERING

It is important as well that we do not see God as a distant observer. The under- standing of redemption is a crucial dimension in comprehending evil. God cre- ated man in His own image with an ability to rule the earth, with intelligence, and with moral and aesthetic ability. God created the potential for evil by cre- ating man with a free will and by allowing real temptation in the garden. God did not ever cause actual moral evil, but for his purposes, He allowed it. He thus immediately took action to promise redemption from the results of the fall (Genesis 3:15). God desires the fellowship of a human community He can love and that freely loves Him. There is no ultimate fulfillment without such fellowship for man. As Augustine said, "Man is restless until he finds his rest in thee."[15] God is involved with the race He created. He suffers the pain himself, for He is fully present in the experience of the race. He restrains evil through the gift of conscience and law, and through the prayer intercession of his people. He sent his Son to die for sin so that we might be connected to righteousness in Him and grow toward perfection.

THROUGH MAN GOD WORKS TO REDEEM

Furthermore, through man God works to remove the effects of evil in this age. First of all, through Israel and the Church, God is at work to reverse the effects of the fall and to limit evil. The community of faith carries on the same work of Jesus in restoring broken relationships, in healing diseases both—by medicine and prayer—and in freeing those in bondage to poverty and oppression. This poverty may be due to the actions of others against a person or group or may be due to the actions of a person or his ancestors. Because man fell, and because the law of sowing and reaping must justly be maintained, God must not unduly intervene. However, He can and will powerfully intervene through men and women who are submitted to Him because they are part of the human race. When God created man, He covenantally delegated control and responsibility for this earth to man for good or ill. Hence God's intervention is largely through man's invitation, the invitation of the righteous who know and walk humbly with their God.

God's intervention through man is seen through Abraham, through Israel, through the second Adam, Jesus, and lastly through all who are connected to Him by faith. Those connected to Him, whether Jew or Gentile, can remove mountains of evil and can pray worldwide change into existence. They can even do miraculous works to turn people to God and to stem the tide of evil. God provided a way for us to be reconciled to God through the death and resurrection of Jesus, the divine Messiah who is connected to God's own life. God was involved in the suffering death of Jesus the Messiah when He bore our sins. Only God can so empathize that His suffering in identification with us is fully experienced as His own pain. However, since evil came by man, so the reversal of evil must come through the work of man. It is not man's work in his own power, but his work in submitting to the power of God through Jesus. As man brought about evil, man is responsible to thwart it. Jesus is part of humanity and hence could lead the way in this reversal. This reversal is the responsibility of the whole people of God.

I also want to note that although man is a morally free being, the Bible makes it clear that we must not overlook the limits of this freedom. Atheist existentialist philosopher John-Paul Sartre argued that man is so radically free that he could choose to be whatever he wanted to be from moment to moment, even making radical out-of-character choices. In Sartre, this is a nauseating freedom which every authentic human must face.[16]

However, in the Scriptures, man after the fall lost his ability to choose the highest good without God's help. Even in choosing good over evil, man is often selfishly motivated. He still makes choices after the fall, but these choices are within the limits of his fallen character. They are options within a range of lesser and greater evil. Only by God's grace can people make a radically free choice opposite his fallen nature. For example, in Wesleyan theology (stemming from John Wesley), God provides prevenient grace to raise man to the level whereby he has a genuine choice between God and self, salvation in Jesus, or autonomy from God. As we grow in character, our free choices become more and more according to goodness. In moderate Calvinism as well, it is only by the predestining grace of God that man is freely able to choose God. God is totally free and always chooses goodness. When we are perfected we will also always make a free choice for goodness according to our perfected moral character. We shall choose among good options, never evil. However, as a person yields to evil, without God's grace their choices will reflect their evil character and will be more and more evil. There may be a choice that is less evil in the midst of temptation, but the bent of the person is still evil. The rapist may not choose to murder his victim. He has not yet fallen so far, but self-preservation may also be a motive, not real goodness. Depravity may so take over the person that behavior can be continually and obsessively motivated by evil.

It is also worth noting that the good humanist may not be really good in the biblical sense. Oftentimes a person can act very good out of motivations of self-preservation, learned civility, etc. Their motive is not one of genuine love at all. Therefore let us note the limits of moral freedom, the necessity of the grace of God to choose real good, and the selfishness that motivates even much so-called good behavior (as a result of the desire to be well thought-of, or to avoid punishment).

God created us free, but in yielding to sin we find ourselves in chains, unable to choose good over evil in many instances. Our character does not allow us to resist temptation; we become habitually trapped if we have previously gone too far in yielding. Such is a depraved person or community. Sodom and Gomorrah were just the products of persons choosing more and more evil. However, God provides grace through the word of the Good News to enable a truly free choice that reverses the process. C. S. Lewis said that the choice of his acceptance of God was the most free choice he ever made. Not only is there evil, but a solution in the redemption of Yeshua, Jesus the Messiah.

SUMMARY OF THE SOLUTION TO THE
PROBLEM OF EVIL

The problem of evil is solved and seen as an evidence for the biblical faith by the following:

1. A proper definition of *omnipotence* is crucial. God is all-powerful as the creator and sustainer of the universe; however, God can not do anything contradictory or against his own character.

2. God's goodness implies that God has a reason consistent with his love and justice in allowing evil to continue. This reason is that God has a good end in view that is worth the evil and pain in creation.

3. Goodness implies that God wills our ultimate fulfillment: a life of richness and love in a redeemed community consistent with our freedom.

4. God's goodness does not mean that He is a doting grandfather. He is just and punishes sin. Furthermore, God's love wills the perfection of his beloved. Trials, sufferings, and other modes of discipline are justly used to produce this end.

5. The *fall* is the basic category for understanding the presence of evil in the world. The fall is understood as the result of man's free moral choice against God's commandment. It results from his rebellion.

6. The fall explains both man's inhumanity to man and natural evil. The latter is the result of man's loss of capacity to avoid calamity and shows that this is a world under judgment. Therefore, this world with its disasters is a proper context or environment for the existence of a fallen race. I believe that unfallen man would have had power over nature, as demonstrated by Jesus in calming the storm. His intuitive and spiritual capacities would have been far different

than in the world of our present experience. This power or authority over nature and ability to avoid natural disaster was lost in the fall. Natural evil is thus God's corporate and individual judgment as well as the result of man's own behavior. Hence, in Romans 8 we read that the whole creation groans and travails waiting for redemption.

7. Suffering can sometimes be judgment for individual acts of evil under the law of sowing and reaping.

8. *Redemption* is the category which explains why God allows the world to continue with its accompanying evil. God can save out of this world both a saved humanity and all that is of true and lasting worth in this world. This can be preserved for the World to Come. Thus, God acts coherently in putting up with the evil of the world.

9. In this context, evil, although unnecessary, can serve many purposes. The experience of evil can lead man to see that he is under judgment and lead him to repentance. Those who fight against evil grow in character as they learn to respond with compassion and fortitude. As Joseph said to his bothers, "You meant it for evil but God has used it for good."

10. Evil also gives seriousness to our moral choices, even to their eternal consequences.

11. God is involved in limiting evil through giving humanity a sense of His law which is most fully revealed in Scripture.

12. God is also involved in fighting evil through the plan of redemption, for He is involved in the pain of the human race; He sent his Son to bear the pain of sin, evil, and judgment; and He has involved Himself through His people who have given themselves to the task of fighting evil. This is through prayer and through being empowered by God for works of faith.

13. Since man brought evil into the world, and since God covenantally gave dominion of the earth to man, it must be through man that evil on earth is thwarted. Therefore God fights evil through the *man*, the Messiah Jesus (perfect man), and those people who are connected to Him by faith.

14. Man corporately suffers for evil as a human race, not only as individuals. Thus there are disparities with regard to suffering and justice in this life. Life after death is the solution to the disparities of this life, for there will be a judgment with rewards and punishment in the world to come.

15. Hell is the final choice of evil by human beings. It is presently seen in the dimensions of depraved behavior and alienation among the human family. Hell and the ultimate choice against redemption are the only evil not redeemed.

16. Pain and suffering within animal creation is also explained by corporate solidarity; for the whole of nature is corporately tied to the human race, the rulers of nature. Romans 8 says that the whole of the creation groans and travails, waiting for redemption.

17. However, animal pain is not just like our pain since animals do not possess differentiated self-consciousness. This mitigates some of the problem. Lewis even holds that animals may be resurrected if they are a significant part of redeemed human community.[17]

18. Evil will be once and for all destroyed when the final redemption is complete in the New Heavens and a New Earth. In the ages to come, a redeemed humanity in fellowship with God will see it has been worth it all. All of great value, beauty, and truth will be a preserved as a reality in the ages to come. Nothing of real lasting value is ultimately and finally destroyed, excepting the destruction in Hell for those who ultimately choose evil and reject God.

IS THE QUANTITY OF EVIL A PROBLEM?

Some have objected to the existence of God because of the quantitative amount of evil. It is said that there is so much evil that we can not believe in God, but we could believe if there was much less evil. This argument does not invalidate our presentation. It is based on a fully arbitrary psychological grounding. How can we set limits as to what is and what is not an acceptable quantity of evil? What is not too much evil for one is too much evil for another. Lewis in fact argues that there is some limit to the amount of pain a human being can suffer.[18] It will cause him to pass out and ultimately to die. Actually, the amount of evil in the world is limited only by what sentient beings are able to suffer, by what inhumanities evil men are willing to commit, by what level of resistance good and spiritual people offer, and by the promise of God to preserve the world of humanity until the return of the Messiah.

As should be seen from our simplified summary, the biblical faith so well explains the problem of evil in human life—through its concepts of fall and redemption—that the nature of evil in human life gives credibility to the biblical world view. No other world view so well accounts for good and evil. This is what convinced formerly atheistic philosopher C. E. M. Joad.[19] Furthermore, all secular, atheistic, or impersonal world views have to explain the problem of good. From whence comes goodness, beauty, truth, love, heroism, etc.? Truly the biblical world view is superior to all others.

THE DEVIL AND THE PROBLEM OF EVIL

A common solution offered to the problem of evil is the concept that the Devil is the source of evil and responsible for evil, not God. Although this solution aids in understanding the gracious love of God and the nature of the evil we fight, it does not change the points of the solution as expounded. This is because the Devil is a *creature* and does not possess independence from the power of God. No created being continues in existence without the permissive will of God. Furthermore, the Devil was a free being who chose evil.

Certainly, the Devil is behind much of the evil in the world, through negative inspiration or thoughts broadcast to human agents. Yet, according to Scripture, human beings never can destroy their responsibility by saying, "The Devil made me do it." The Devil's power over the earth (including all evil spirits) as the "god of this world-system" is a power given him by man's individual and corporate choice. The existence of Satan and his minions, however evil, also serves within the framework of God's goodness.

First of all, God is just. Therefore man's bondage to evil caused by Satan is due to the *legal grounds* he has given to Satan. Therefore, this bondage is a just punishment for man's sin. Satanic power is part of that fallen environment that is proper to a fallen race.

Secondly, since God is just, he will not always use his power to directly thwart the power of the Devil without man's invitation through prayer, and man being a willing instrument of thwarting the power of the Devil in loosing people from bondage. Romans 5 says that since death resulting from sin came from an act of man, so redemption must come from man. Only people yielding to the power of God can undo the work of the Devil. Jesus the Messiah is that man who as the last Adam—totally yielded to God to destroy the Devil's work. His life of healing others physically and spiritually was a manifestation of destroying the Devil's work. We, as the body of the Messiah under our corporate head (Jesus), are given the legal right in Him to carry on his work of redemption. Evil can legally be reversed by men who yield to God in the Messiah and use their spiritual power for redemption.

Without at all changing the basic nature of our thesis on the problem of evil, we can say that it is indeed correct and helpful to understand evil in these terms. The world is a scene of spiritual warfare and strife which is physically manifested. This is a genuine war with casualties. Some are allied with God and his Messiah and some with the Devil. Many are used by both; by God when spiritually in tune with Him, and by the Devil when given over to bitterness, unforgiveness, and unbelief. We choose whom we will follow or who will inspire us. This warfare rages as those who submit to the power of God rescue others from the power of evil and its curse in sickness, poverty and death. Final redemption will only be manifest at the return of the head (Messiah) for his purified and submitted body (the Church, "Ecclesia," Qahilah, or Congregation).

This has very important spiritual implications. The followers of the Messiah are responsible to use their spiritual power—in prayer, fasting, spiritual warfare, and spiritual works (God-led action in the world)—to thwart the Devil's works. Let us apply this practically to that most horrible of recent events, the holocaust, in which six million Jews perished at the hands of the Nazis. Why? Secular historians will often use such reasons as: the humiliation of the Germans after World War I, the economic depression of Europe, the people's readiness for a charismatic savior figure, the tradition of anti-Semitism in Europe, Hitler's psychological megalomania, crowd manipulation and psychosis, and racial-evolutionary theories that were current.

There is more to be seen than in these naturalistic explanations. The concept of Satan's desire to thwart God's plan of redemption by destroying the Jews, who were given the promise of perpetual preservation by God, is helpful as well. During this period, the people of God in Europe, Jew and Gentile, had fallen to an astonishingly low spiritual state. Faith in God and biblical morality were at a low ebb. Knowledge of the spiritual means to oppose Hitler's evil was almost nonexistent.

Assassination attempts were made on Hitler, but he seemed to be almost miraculously delivered—I believe by malevolent power. Did Bonhoeffer realize the nature of Satanic power in this man and seek to overcome it by spiritual warfare before he joined in a plot to assassinate Hitler? Probably not.

Furthermore, the German church was cold and dead. Its clergy had been educated in German universities of unbelief in which the denial of spiritual realities and of the truth of the Bible was a century-old tradition.

It is no accident that deliverance, when it did come, came from Britain and the United States, whose spiritual tenor was stronger. Even the escape of the British forces from Dunkirk, which saved Britain, resulted in part, I believe, from a prayer meeting at a Bible college (cf. Rees Howells, *Intercessor*). The leaders of the prayer meeting received total assurance in the Spirit that the British were saved before there was any actual news of escape.

In this world, therefore, the only limits to evil are, firstly, the spiritual strength of the people of God who know and deal with the spiritual realities behind the world of the senses; and secondly, the covenantal promises of God to maintain the world of humanity in existence until the establishment of the New Heavens and New Earth. Once again we see that evil of all kinds is traced to the fact that men individually and corporately have allowed it. This world can only be truly comprehended by biblical categories of understanding. History written from this perspective would be far more true to the world of reality.

CLAIMS THAT THE BIBLICAL WORLD VIEW IS INCOHERENT

THE ARGUMENT THAT IT DOES NOT MAKE SENSE

People not only object to our world view as inconsistent, but also argue that it is incoherent. Although these two concepts are used interchangeably, it should be noted again that they are distinct. To be inconsistent is to be directly or indirectly contradictory, either in basic premises or in premises that can be clearly derived from those basic premises. To be incoherent is in some way to fail to make sense. We have explained that a true world view *ties together* all of the most significant aspects of human experience. When we speak of human experience being tied together, we are speaking of those dimensions of human experience that can be expressed in language which can be intersubjectively understood. Let us look at some of these objections.

WHY DID GOD CREATE?

The critic here states that there is clear incoherence, since a self-sufficient God who is eternal, who lived without a creation through the ages of eternity past, would have no reason to create. If He did not need a creation throughout these ages, why would He change? If He was satisfied for ages without the fellowship of the human race, why would the human race become necessary for Him?

This is a very old objection, and a discussion of this objection can be found in *Confessions* by Augustine, written in the fifth century. Augustine appealed to the timelessness of God's being to solve the problem. For God, with whom there is no time, who experiences everything in the fullness of present timelessness, the question of "Why create?" loses its meaning. The creation in all its dimensions is the eternal subject of God's present experience. For God, there was never a time without the creation. Time is only an aspect of our human experience in this world.

This very Greek concept of time and eternity appears at a glance to solve the problem. However, there are greater problems of incoherence in this solution. Can we really *tie together* the concept of human experience in time with a timeless divine experience? How are they related? For example, all human language is a language of time-conditioned relationships. We speak of loving, deciding, acting, etc., which all carry the basic sense of experiencing a before and an after. The situation changes; present conditions are different from the past. Can we even talk about experiencing without some dimensions of past, present and future? Yes, certainly there are experiences in which we say, "Time stood still." We mean by this that our experience was so concentrated that the flux of many experiences was not part of our focus. Yet, when we look at the clock, time elapsed. In fact, in the time-standing-still experiences, a great deal of time elapses before we realize what happened because we are absorbed in the present experience. This experience has a before and after.

In Einsteinian thought, time slows down at greater speeds in space. However, time does not stop; all dimensions of before and after do not halt. Certainly, God must experience before and after in a vastly different way than us. Yet if there is no before and after experience to God's life, it is hard to know how our human language can say anything about God at all. This is the conclusion of the East; ultimately nothing can be said about the Eternal Timeless Absolute.

Besides leading to its own incoherence, this solution is in all probability unbiblical. The Bible describes an everlasting God: a God who is *in his own way* time-conditioned; a God who changes his mind in response to man's repentance or sin; a God who loves, judges, forgives and creates. This time-conditioned language is not merely empty symbol. Oscar Cullman has to my satisfaction shown that the biblical concept of God is of a time-related being. God is affected by what happens in his creation; He experiences a before and after, not a timeless Being. The timelessness concept came into Christian and Jewish thought from Greek culture.[20]

How, therefore, do we solve the original problem?[21] The real issue is with the word "create." First we should note that the answer as to why God created man is biblically given—God desired the fellowship of a creature made in His image. Yet to the question of why God created anything at all, instead of not creating, is an invalid question. The reason God created is because it is his nature to be creative. The reason He created what He did when He did is because He chose to. No further reasons can be given, for "to create" and to "choose" are terms that are part of the meaning of creativity. They are ultimate concepts of explanation. One's ultimate concepts of explanation are the reasons for all else, but can not themselves be explained by other concepts or those other concepts would be ultimate. It is no more valid to ask the creationist why God created in this ultimate sense than to ask the materialist why there is a material world. The materialist would rightly answer that it just always was; it is an ultimate category of explanation in his world view. That God creates is an ultimate category in our world view. We then apply these ultimate categories of explanation to see if they better account for the realities of human experience than the ultimate concepts of other world views.

The solution to this problem is simply to state what we mean by the category or concept of "creativity." Creativity is a divine and human quality we all experience. It brings genuine newness into existence which did not exist before. God's creativity brings all creatures into existence. We cannot create life from no previously existing material base. Human creativity is thus both different and parallel to God's. Within God is the potential of all that is created. Human creativity is also not fully predictable, yet it is essential in the production of beauty and the solving of problems by *creative insight* and invention. It makes no more sense to ask why God created when He did than to ask why Beethoven created symphonies when he already had 104 of Haydn's symphonies to listen to. Nor could we ultimately explain beyond the concept of creativity why Beethoven chose at one time to create a sonata of a certain character and at another time a symphony.[22] If continually pressed, Beethoven could give many secondary reasons, but ultimately he would answer that he just had a creative desire to do so, and these were creative insights. The gift of human creativity is a reflection of the Creator. Both partake of the dimensions of decision, choice, and freedom. Creativity itself can not be fully accounted for in *causal* language.

Creativity is an intuitively perceived dimension of human and divine experience and cannot ultimately be explained by something else, but is itself an explanation for all else. God simply decided at a point in his experience to create the universe as a free act of His will.

This objection wrongly concludes that there is incoherence when there are no concepts to explain ultimate concepts. This is a false objection.

WHY IS THE UNIVERSE SO LARGE?

At first glance this objection seems almost foolish. Yet upon further examination, we can see why many people have concluded that faith in a loving personal God is impossible in the vastness of the universe. Recently scientist Carl Sagan stated,

> We find ourselves, trembling just a little, on the threshold of a vast and awesome universe, rich in mystery and in promise, that utterly dwarfs—in time, in space, and in potential—the tidy anthropocentric world of our ancestors. [23]

In other words, the world view presented in the Bible is a view in which man is important; he is created in the image of God and is an object of God's personal concern. Furthermore, God created this world and all that is in it. Sagan calls this an anthropocentric (man-centered) world view which we can no longer accept. Added to this objection is the sense that there must be other intelligent creatures in the universe, which Arthur C. Clarke of 2001 fame interpreted as follows: "The doctrine of man made in the image of God is ticking like a time bomb at Christianity's base, set to explode if other intelligent creatures are discovered." [24]

This is not a new objection. During my own years of personal skepticism, this objection seemed convincing. Picture, if you will, a large table as the universe. On this table is a speck of dust. Infinitely smaller yet is our own earth, for the speck of dust is the sun. On this sub-speck called earth are five billion minute specks or organisms called man. Can we really believe that the Creator is concerned with each of these creatures? We are so dwarfed in the vastness of it all that we can not begin to think we are of worth to a Creator. Perhaps it is easier to believe that there is no Creator.

Yet, strangely, some of the greatest scientists who were experts in space and time accepted the reality of a Creator God or at least a mind-design explanation for the universe. This included Albert Einstein, his great interpreter Sir Arthur Eddington, Sir James Jeans, and Wernher von Braun, the great architect of America's space and rocketry program. Perhaps this objection is not as forceful as it first appears.

Some also object that the Bible presents the earth as the center of the universe. We are told that the Earth is not even the center of our own solar system. However, this objection is totally false in the light of contemporary science and the relativity theory of Einstein (cf. pp. 75-77).

Several famous writers have dealt with these objections, and our answer will draw from three of them, along with our own comments. They are C. S. Lewis in "A Chapter of Red Herrings" in his book *Miracles*; William Temple in his Gifford Lectures entitled *Nature, Man, and God*; and Blaise Pascal in his *Pensées*.

First of all, we should note that the size of the universe as extraordinarily large is no new discovery, but was known by believers in antiquity and is reflected in classical literature. Ptolemy in his geocentric (earth-centered) astronomy, which held sway since biblical times, defined the comparative relationship of the earth to the rest of the universe as a point of no dimensions. Pascal noted the relative nature of size comparisons. Man in his physical size is halfway between the size of a galaxy and a micro-organism.

Actually, this objection is simply one example of that illogical reasoning that falsely derives valuational meaning from mathematical relationships. Mathematical relationships are not a source for interpreting personal meaning. It is only our projection of *poetic* meanings upon the astronomical figures of math that yields these false conclusions. Lewis, with his ever-keen imagination, notes that a small snug creation could be used as an objection to the Bible's teaching, for it would show God to not be nearly as great as purported in the Bible. We can note that the universe is only vast from two perspectives. One is the extension of a measurement that is small (miles, light years, etc.), and extending that measurement so that an astronomical figure results. This yields only a number that is hard to comprehend for its hugeness, but yields *no inherent* meaning by which we can refute the view that man is created in the image of God. The second perspective that yields a sense of vastness is imagining, *under our present physical limitations*, how long it would take to travel to a far-away galaxy. Yet we could easily imagine a universe in which we are not subject to physical-spatial limits. Simply by willing it, we could be anywhere in that universe we desire. Certainly all of this mathematical measuring tells us nothing concerning our significance.

William Temple provides a classic answer.[25] He notes that the most significant thing is not the vastness of scientific numbers, but that there is a creature with a mind to comprehend the universe. Our cognition is the most significant thing. In one sense, the whole universe is only something within our own conscious experience as humankind. This is also the case in regard to the ages of time. We *abstract* our present experience and extend it back in time and feel dwarfed. Yet to God, or to a creature who lived twice as long and did all his actions at half our speed, the vastness of the ages would be cut in half. The Bible teaches that in God's experience one thousand years is as a day. Perhaps the vast distances of the universe to God are as no more than our planet to us or even much less.

I am not arguing that the universe has no existence apart from my mind's perceptions of it. However, I do believe, as Eddington concluded, that the vastness of the universe is only a concept for how we presently subjectively and mentally experience our present limits. All of this vastness is only within our minds because God has made us all to have a common conscious experience. In a sense, the vastness of the universe is within human minds, a product of God's way of revealing his majesty to our minds. God's mind makes it to be so for all our minds in common. However, He certainly experiences it in a different way, since He is its creator.

Once we begin to reflect in this way, we can see why Lewis calls this objection a red herring, not a real, serious objection, but a figment—an invalid mental trick of the mind. It is derived from man's ability to be mathematically creative in extending and applying numbers to the physical world. This ability gives us figures for the vastness of the universe as well as the marvelous universe of the computer chip. Yet this is of little relevance to world view decisions. To make such considerations relevant is an arbitrary decision because dimensions of space, time, vastness, etc., are *all relative* to our own decision concerning the meaning of the tools of measurement. This should be even more clear after studying Einsteinian science, in which greater speeds cause mass to increase and time to slow down until we reach the speed of light. To go in the same direction long enough is to end in the same place, since space is curved.

This all says to me that vastness simply reflects the *present* physical-law limits to which God has confined our race. In the next life, the universe may be our playground and we might even play catch with the planets. For in the world to come the followers of Jesus are said to reign with Him.

These objections presume to understand how God (if He is presumed to exist, for argument's sake) experiences the universe, which the critic then finds untenable to his imagination. The invalidity of this is clear when we realize that we do not know what God's experience of space and time is like. Perhaps God experienced long geological ages as passing very quickly, but experienced the life of one human who did many good works as passing more slowly. He could savor this life. The subjectivity of lived time is amazing. To a child, next year seems an age away. To a senior citizen, life is amazingly brief. It is foolish to think that our scientific time-space measures have an absolute objective meaning that even reflects God's experience rather than simply being tools to order man's experience of the universe for scientific purposes. As to the objection from the possible future discovery of extraterrestrial life, I must admit puzzlement. If God is great enough to love six billion people on earth, then He can love other billions on other planets. C. S. Lewis found the thought of other civilizations on other planets to be quite compatible with his faith and wrote novels reflecting this perspective. Arthur Clarke's objection is simply subjective assertion with no philosophical validity.

📖

CHAPTER 6: STUDY QUESTIONS

1. How does the free-will defense deal with the problem of evil in natural events (earthquakes, hurricanes, etc.)?

2. What is the significance of the Devil as an explanation of evil?

3. Why does the atheist have a problem of good?

4. Was Adam created perfect or innocent? Explain. What is the difference?

5. Why is the size and age of the universe of little consequence to theism?

OBJECTIONS THAT THE BIBLICAL WORLD VIEW IS EMPIRICALLY FALSE

OBJECTIONS IN THIS CHAPTER BASICALLY CLAIM that the biblical world view fails to fulfill the criterion of comprehensiveness which I have shown to be a key test of truth. A true world view must be able to *comprehensively* tie together the basic whole of human experience and observation. If it does not, it is not a rationally defensible viewpoint.

THE OBJECTION FROM NATURAL LAW

The biblical world view presents a viewpoint in which a supernatural personal God intervenes in the natural world of His creation. This intervention is known as a miracle. Truly, the Bible presents the miraculous—from the dividing of the sea in the Exodus, to the healing miracles of Jesus, to the resurrection of Jesus the Messiah from the dead.

The objection to miracles takes on a twofold aspect. The first is that miracles are contrary to the natural laws discovered in human observation. The second is that when we closely examine the world of human life, we find that miracles just do not happen. First let us examine the proposition that human observation proves this to be a world of natural law. This objection was classically presented by philosopher-skeptic David Hume in the eighteenth century.[1] It is well reflected in contemporary skepticism as well. Rudolph Bultmann in *Jesus Christ and History* argues that it is impossible for modern man, who turns on and off electric lights, to believe in miracles. Modern man, in other words, is one who knows that all events in our world are governed by the laws of natural causation; a miracle is impossible. In both Hume and Bultmann, the universe is understood to be an interconnected cause-and-effect nexus. A miracle would be a violation of this nexus; cause and effect are the rules of the world. Furthermore, some have argued that God's intervention would be an indication that He did not make things right in the first place (this is the argument of deism).

This objection assumes that the nature of scientific laws is a *closed system* of cause and effect. An excellent philosophical response to it is C. S. Lewis' book *Miracles*. A full presentation of the historical debate is found in Colin Brown's *Miracles and the Critical Mind*. The basic problem with this objection is the totally *assumptive* nature of the argument. It assumes that which needs to be proved, that this is a *naturalistically* determined universe, at least as far as known history. By totally assuming one world view, it claims that the other is false. This is circular reasoning indeed.

The basic answer to this objection is to show that the nature of a miracle is compatible with scientific law within the framework of the biblical world and life view. Furthermore, it simply is not true that observation shows this to be a world of natural cause and effect alone. Modern science and physics do not look at natural law as a system like an integrated machine. Natural laws are rather statistical regularities with probabilities but not certainties. Physicist W. Heisenburg taught that in the more theoretical dimensions of atomic physics, there is an unpredictability in subatomic particle motion (called the Heisenburg uncertainty principle).

From a biblical perspective, what we call natural law is simply a manifestation of God's faithfulness. There is a regularity and order to creation that we can depend on. The Scriptures praise God for the manifestation of his faithfulness in continuing the order of the seasons, day and night, the cycle of the moon, and the order of nature. Such order is the product of God's word or command—part of His covenant love. Yet, God is not bound by the order He has created beyond the principle of His personal character of faithfulness. He is free to intervene in the universe of his creation. He is not boxed out of His own world. That moral agency can intervene in the natural world is seen whenever a human being chooses to act. Man creates an airplane and overcomes the law of gravity by the law of aerodynamics. When I hold up a pencil, I keep it from falling according to the law of gravity by applying the law of my energy to raise it and keep it from falling. In the same way, God, by his supernatural principle or law, can suspend or transcend natural laws when He intervenes in the world of His creation. Supernature is behind nature and in control of nature. Nature reflects God's general providential faithfulness; miracle reflects God's special intervention in love and judgment. Both nature and miracle fit together compatibly in a universe created by a personal God who relates personally to those created in His image.

There are misconceptions about miracles. Some hold that miracles are just unusual events that are marvelous to us but fully explicable in terms of natural law. They then say that they believe in miracles as a manifestation of God, but hold that they are fully compatible with and part of the natural cause-effect nexus. This, unfortunately, is not what the average person means when he speaks of a miracle, nor is it a reflection of what the Bible means.

The biblical sense of the word "miracle" is an event of such a nature that it has to be seen as a special intervention of the supernatural into the natural. Yes, some miracles are explained by skeptics in other than supernatural terms, even though the believer may be sure, due to his experience, that natural explanation is inadequate. Believers often speak of miracles in situations they believe would have developed differently if God had not intervened. Hence some may disagree concerning whether a particular happening is really a miracle or not. For example, a person dying of cancer calls for prayer. After a concerted all-night prayer meeting of his friends, he is healed. The cancer disappears. For him it is a miraculous intervention of God in answer to prayer. For a skeptic it is a spontaneous remission in which the body's immune antibody system was somehow kicked into gear. He doesn't yet know the trigger but is confident it can be found. Since he doesn't have an explanation, but does have some examples from the lives of unbelievers in remission, he remains skeptical. The believer still maintains that it was supernatural due to the timing and its association with prayer. This is *his* experience of it.

However, there are other recorded miracles for which there is clearly no explanation from the natural-causation angle, even though God used natural elements as part of the miracle. This includes the many biblical miracles—from Elijah causing the axe head to float in the water, to Yeshua supernaturally multiplying bread and fish to feed the five thousand to his raising Lazarus from the dead after four days, to the resurrection of Jesus from the dead. Miracles fit coherently within the framework of God's purpose in the biblical world view. They more clearly reveal God; they comfort, restore, and motivate. Yet, they are in no way contrary to the revelation of God through the natural regular processes of His ordination. God is free to work through both means. There is absolutely nothing in the nature of scientific, law as properly understood, to preclude the possibility of miracles. Certainly the whole of reality is not limited to our sense realm or not impinged upon by any other realm.

One of the objections to miracles is the claim by many skeptics that they have never experienced one or found one that could be adequately verified. As a college skeptic, I recall my search to find a bona fide miracle. I would hear of one and pursue it. Upon checking it out it would often be found to be a blown-up story. It evaporated upon investigation, at least as far as its evidential value for supernatural investigation. However, I later discovered amazing bona fide miracles, some so wonderful that some readers might doubt my objectivity in reporting them. No matter, I did carefully check them out. For skeptics there is a fine little book by a physician, Dr. Richard Casdorph, entitled *The Miracles* that documents some amazing healings with X-rays and medical analysis. In a future chapter we shall be presenting evidence for miracles.

At this point I only want to note these two things. First of all, that I can testify to the reality of the experience of the miraculous both by first-hand experience and by reputable testimony. Secondly, that the experience of miracles is dependent upon the circles in which we move. As I began to move in circles that believed in miracles, I discovered more bona fide miracles which were not amenable to natural explanation. This pursuit took some patience. Some skeptics assume that miracles are impossible because they have never experienced one or have never seen credible evidence to change their opinion. They are unaware of the problem of the limits of the communications structure of human society. Miracles are found among communities of deep faith. Most skeptics are amazingly isolated from the goings-on in these communities. Their circle of experience is very narrow; this violates the criteria of comprehensiveness as a truth test.

In general, when miracles do happen, the report of them is squelched by the general skepticism of the media or communications vehicles that could report them. They are dismissed as myths. Bona fide miracles do not yet get reported on the national evening news. The reports are discounted without any serious research. This is the certainty of unbelief. Furthermore, unbelief is bolstered by the fact that many seemingly good miracle reports would have to be followed up to find a few that would really hold up. Our circle of communication is extremely limited. It is as if there is a wall between the evidence and the potential reporters.

However, if one can break out of the limited circle of unbelief and be willing to accept the truth that miracles point to, there is in today's world, as well as in the recordings of good historic testimony, fully adequate evidence for miracles. The cynical will find a barrier between himself and the discovery of miracles, but the honest, persistent, and sincere seeker will find them.

It is amazing that David Hume, who popularized the objection from natural law, argued in other writings that the concept of causation was an unprovable assumption drawn from the frequent association of events. Although this eighteenth-century philosopher argued in contradictory ways for different purposes, he is still the fountainhead for much modern skepticism. As I stated in the section on the nature of truth, it is possible for a naturalist to dismiss all evidence against his view by the gross assertion that he just does not yet have a natural explanation, but that one will eventually be found. Yet, when one talks of resurrections and instant creative miracles, we certainly see evidence which does not cohere with his stance.

Actually, although he can deny the evidence that would lead to a reevaluation of his world-view stance, he cannot do so without revealing that his own view is as much of a faith stance, or even more of a faith stance, than the stance of the believer.

In summary, natural law only proves that there is significant regularity in nature. It says nothing about other kinds of events which do not *fit* our usual experiences of cause and effect. The biblical world view provides a context for integrating both scientific information or law as well as miraculous occurrence. There is nothing in either experience or valid philosophical reasoning to invalidate these conclusions. The biblical world view is again shown in its superiority by being able to integrate all kinds of experience as part of the total evidence to be evaluated by world view thinking.

OBJECTIONS FROM PSYCHOLOGY

Psychology has been the source of several objections to the biblical world and life view. These objections are not at all inherent to the study of the human mind or human behavior.

THAT RELIGIOUS PEOPLE ARE POORLY ADJUSTED

The first objection states that religious people are more poorly adjusted than nonreligious people. The argument would be that a psychologically healthy human being is more likely to choose the correct world view. This objection suffers from several major defects. First, the author knows of no published study that objectively correlates psychological health and religious belief. George Gallup, Jr., recently conducted a poll which is not published as of this writing. In an interview in the June edition of the *National Christian*, he states that committed Christians are the most fulfilled members of American society. Secondly, even if there was truth to the allegation, it would only show that poorly adjusted people seek help from religion, which may help them to be better adjusted. The author's personal experience with many maladjusted people has been that religious faith has provided a means of significant growth in adjustment. This objection is no more valid than to claim that psychology is invalid because people who go to psychologists are less well adjusted than those who do not. It is a well-known fact that psychologists and psychiatrists have a higher percentage in their ranks who are mentally ill and who commit suicide.

Thirdly, this objection is without truth value since it is a species of *ad hominem* argument—that is, dismissing the truth of what a person says solely on the basis of other personal accusations against the person(s) who put forth a view. However, a view is true on the basis of its correspondence to reality. Every viewpoint has good and bad and healthy and unhealthy representatives. Ad hominem argument is a classical fallacy of logic.

Skeptics never tire of pointing to unstable people who have weird religious fantasies so as to invalidate religion. This is very foolish. There are many examples of healthy religious people, from a rocket scientist like Wernher von Braun, to Abraham Heschel, to Billy Graham. Religious schizophrenics express their psychosis in religious delusions, nonreligious ones in secular delusions. Secular atheism is represented by Bertrand Russell and by Joseph Stalin. The former is usually praised as a humanist; the latter is despised.

RELIGION AS A NEUROTIC PSYCHOLOGICAL NEED

This classical objection to religion is based on *psychologism*, which holds that all human behavior can be explained by psychological concepts. Sigmund Freud sought thus to account for religion in his book *The Future of an Illusion*.[2] Previously Ludwig Feuerbach (a significant influence on Karl Marx) gave a similar argument. Basically, these men argued that religion could be explained as the product of a childish wish for a protective parent figure. It is an illusion that arises from our insecurity. Religion is thus seen as a sickly inability to grow up and face the hard realities of life with courage. It is an infantile illusion that fosters dependency—an illusion that provides a father figure to reassure us in trouble and to give us life after death. Several responses to this are in order.

First of all, if we are truly created in the image of God and are his children, to deny our dependence on Him is foolish rebellion. If it is our nature to find fulfillment in a relationship with our heavenly Father, then it is not spineless to acknowledge it. The objection claims that religion is a crutch to get us through life. Perhaps. However, wouldn't we think a man with a broken leg was foolish if he refused to use a crutch?

Secondly, this view proves too much. Any view can be dismissed as the product of wish fulfillments, subconscious needs, desires, and neuroses. The naturalistic world and life view could be seen as a wish fulfillment for those who fear God's judgment and who desire to live lives contrary to God's law. This is not far off the mark. Psychiatrist David Baken has written a revealing book called *Freud and the Jewish Mystical Tradition*.[3] In this book Baken extensively documents Freud's fear of God, of judgment, and of guilt and condemnation. Surely some of Freud's own personality theory is derived from a projection of his own fears. Freud, according to Baken, saw himself as a Messiah figure saving people from the harsh realities of the law and judgment of God. The psychiatrist provided comfort by accepting the patient; "It's O.K. if you broke some taboos."

Freud was incredibly superstitious and influenced by the libertarian wing of the Jewish mystical tradition. Freud's own analysis of Michelangelo's statue of Moses is so revealing. Although Moses, holding the tablets of the law, looks fearful, the tablets will not crash down upon us. Moses is a frozen figure, we need not fear. Freud's unbelief is as much a wish projection as it is belief. The biblical faith provides a solution to sin and condemnation through the atoning sacrifice of the Messiah. Freud tried to save us by lessening the severity of the law. How easy it is for those who desire to break the law of God, the hedonists of our own day, to deny in wish fulfillment that there is a God.

The argument that religion is a projection of our wishes cuts both ways. If it disproves the biblical world view, it can be used to disprove any world view. How much better then to comparatively examine world views in the light of evidence according to the basic criteria of truth: consistency, coherence, and comprehensiveness.

PSYCHOLOGY AS AN ADEQUATE EXPLANATION OF MAN

Psychologism leaves us with total skepticism about truth and meaning. It claims that the highest explanation of human life is in terms of needs, drives, propensities, upbringing, and conditioned behavior. Therefore all world views stand on a level of subjective choice. This is radical relativism. Yet psychologism itself is purporting to be the highest concept for understanding human life. By its own argument it is condemned. Psychologism as a viewpoint can then be explained as simply the product of the drives, needs,and upbringing (mental conditioning) of its proponents. There is no truth; this is a self-defeating claim, for either this statement is claiming to be true, which would be contradictory, or it is meaningless. If psychologism is true, which it cannot be, then even psychological theories themselves are myths that cannot be true or false.

Actually, psychology must be explained or comprehended as part of a comprehensive world view which provides us with an interpretive scheme for understanding the social sciences. A world view gives perspective for understanding the limits and truth value of various fields of study. Underneath psychologism is an incipient scientific naturalism. Scientific naturalism is a significant world view, though we believe a false world view. Yet the person who espouses psychologism frees himself from arguing for a bona fide world view in comparison with other world views. He takes a short cut to authenticity by making statements about the implications of psychology which on the surface appear to be wise but are foolish.

Psychologism is one form of the *reductionist fallacy*, which seeks to reduce the meaning of existence to one of its descriptive aspects. Yet psychological terms are only partial descriptions of human life.

OBJECTIONS FROM SOCIOLOGY

The field of sociology has added a dimension of importance for our understanding of human life and religion. This is the important aspect of the social component of life, group dynamics, and the study of community. There *are* sociological sources and reasons for some religious groupings and behavior. An example is the origin of some denominations documented in H. Richard Niebuhr's *The Social Sources of Denominationalism*.

The world view known as *sociologism*, however, seeks to account for all of the dimensions of human experience, including religious beliefs, in ultimately sociological terms. Social influences and needs are dominating concepts. This sociological explanation leads to *relativism* concerning religious truths and values. It teaches that world views are not true or false but are the images and symbols expressing the needs, desires, aspirations, and preferences of a social group.[4]

Max Weber's and Ernst Troeltsch's studies gave great impetus to sociologism.[5]

Sociologism seeks to explain all with sociological concepts. It thus explains away religious truth in terms of social forces, conditioning, influences, and patterns. Therefore sociologism is subject to the same objections which were raised against psychologism.

First, and most simply, if all world-view statements are neither true or false but a product of social conditioning, then this statement itself is neither true or false, but is a product of social conditioning or represents a baseless commitment. We need not take it seriously. A person who argues for sociologism wants us to take his statements as *true* reflections of the nature of reality. However, it cannot be so. Actually, the proponent of sociologism is not without a world view. He simply does not want to argue for his world view. Underlying sociologism is a naturalistic, secular-humanist world view. It is relativistic concerning ethical values which were traditionally rooted in religion. It is a world view in which the universe can be accounted for in terms of natural forces.

As we shall later demonstrate, naturalism does not adequately account for the total phenomena of human existence. The social sciences produce information that is ultimately integrated and interpreted in terms of our ultimate world view, whether naturalism, biblical theism, or pantheism. The insights of sociology do not provide us with those ultimate concepts of explanation and cannot be used to dismiss those concepts. Ultimate concepts are tested by applying them to human experience and testing them by the criteria of truth. Sociology may give insight that is part of a world view, but cannot itself either provide a world view or dismiss one unless by a hidden agenda of fostering undisclosed premises. The world view of scientific naturalism is one which gives us ultimate concepts to be tested, but sociologism alone does not.[6]

POLITICS

The objection that religion impedes social and political progress is most commonly recognized in Marx's claim that "religion is the opiate of the masses." Yet this claim is not unique to Marxism, but is common to all who hold that religion is a diversion from facing and dealing with the practical problems of the real world. Marx taught that religion is a means used by the privileged to keep the oppressed in subjection. Christianity teaches submission to authority, for example, while at the same time offering the oppressed justice and a better life in the

next world. Hence this view claims that religion lulls the masses into complacency just as if they had been drugged with opium. Opium produces the illusion
of wellbeing; religion causes the masses to acquiesce in injustice done to them
under the illusion of a better life to come. Marx's analysis is a serious attempt
from the stance of unbelief to discredit religion. However, everyone who snick-
ers at religion as a foolish waste of time is a partaker of Marx's basic attitude.

To give adequate answer to this objection it is necessary to distinguish between the teaching of a religion itself and the interpretation of that religion as an
agent for perpetuating the unjust status quo. For example, it can be easily shown
that Hindu religion in many forms can act as an opiate to induce complacency in
the face of injustice. This is most clear in the doctrine of the caste. One is born
in high or low castes depending upon deeds from a previous life. Poverty—
being born into a low caste—is the just result of the law of recompense (*karma*)
operating in reincarnation. Thus Gandhi found great struggle in arousing the
masses to reject their caste status. Gandhi's pacifistic revolution was greatly influenced by the passive-resistance orientation of the life of Jesus.

However, even good ideology is perverted and is used as a means to oppress
the people. Certainly, privileged oppressors have been quite willing to propa-
gate forms of religion to enable them to maintain status. The Bible has been
twisted to support many types of injustice. This includes apartheid in South
Africa and American slavery, in which blacks were seen as being under the curse
of Canaan and therefore their enslavement was justified—it was their due. Yet
Canaan was the father of the Canaanites of Palestine. The Canaanites served
Israel in ancient times. This prophecy, found in Genesis 9:25, was historically
fulfilled and has no relationship to African blacks.

Scripture has also been twisted to encourage people to acquiesce in crimes
against Jewry during World War II and is used today to support other forms of
oppression. Is this inherent in religion or only a manifestation of the depth of
human sin and perversion? It is interesting to note that Marx's followers set up a
privileged communist class and oligarchy that lives in superior wealth and
oppresses the masses. Yet all of this is done while interpreting Marx to support
it. One of the great manifestations of perversion was in the Polish communist
repression of the worker's union movement called Solidarity. Communism was
thus called upon to suppress a worker's revolution, but the workers triumphed
and threw out the communists. Eastern Europe and the Soviet Republics dramatically threw off the chains of communism.

It is in the nature of human beings to use any twisting of religion, or whatever else gives credibility to their designs, to gain their ends. We *should* expect a better religion to have a better effect. Yet this will not fully protect us against human perversions. The real impetus from the biblical world view, however, has been toward social change and improvement. This is especially so where an open Bible has guided the conscience of leaders in the West. Biblical revolutionary concepts are plentiful. Every man is created in the image of God and is of great worth. Scripture amazingly commands "to love our neighbor as ourselves." Jesus specifically applies this in a situation to show its applicability to a despised race. In the story of the good Samaritan, Jesus describes a Samaritan who fulfills the law of love better than a heartless Jew. Deeds of love and kindness are the essence of loving one's neighbor, who may be from any races and culture.

The Exodus tells the story of God's intervention for the deliverance from slavery and the leading of the people of Israel to a promised land of freedom. God identifies with the outcast slaves and empowers them to conquer the unrighteous residents of Canaan. This is hardly the stuff of an opium-type religion.

As the New Testament spread in the Roman world, infanticide was ended along with abortion. Laws required greater justice. The Bible taught that the king was not absolute but under the law of God and gave many examples of God punishing unjust kings. It even warned against the dangers of oppression in a monarchial order in the days of the prophet Samuel, when Israel, while being a loose confederacy, asked for a king.

It is no accident that democracy first flourished in those lands most influenced by the Protestant Reformation, the open-Bible movement. Democracy was born in the land of the Puritans who looked to Scripture as the legal basis of society and the reason for the dignity of all. The early Puritans were not all democrats by any means, but the implications of their principle of conscience before the Word led to the statement of the Declaration of Independence, that "All men are *created* equal." William Wilburforce was inspired by the Bible to fight for laws which led to the elimination of child labor and slavery in the British empire. An open Bible informed his conscience, and, through Wilburforce, the conscience of Parliament and the nation was formed.

Those who most strongly fought slavery in America were religiously committed. This included the evangelist Charles Finney, whose Oberlin College became a bastion of slave liberation, and Jonathan Blanchard, whose Wheaton College participated in the underground escape network. The civil-rights movement of Martin Luther King derived its inspiration from the biblical Exodus.

Time can not begin to tell of those who established hospitals, gave themselves for the social betterment of all, fought for legislation, were jailed for the sake of conscience, and at great sacrifice gained victory in these battles. Where the Bible reigns most supreme, people find their greatest freedom and dignity. The lands most opposed to Scripture are most oppressive.

Marx's argument is only valid by a very selective reading of the evidence. A more *comprehensive* reading shows that the Bible has been the greatest influence of all in producing human liberation. The fathers of the American revolution were inspired by it, and Lincoln quoted it as his source of inspiration and guidance.

Of course, certain Greek interpretations of the Bible have undercut the fullness of its power. Concepts such as saving the soul and not being concerned for the body are foreign to the biblical spirit. Jesus went about healing *body and mind*. He said in Luke 4, "The Spirit of God is upon me. . . to proclaim liberty to the captives." His quote from Isaiah 61 referred to the year of Jubilee, in which wealth was redistributed every fifty years by returning all lands to ancestral ownership. One could acquire wealth, but within limits. The concept of economic justice was a biblical concept 3,000 years ago. James well remarked that those who say to the hungry and thirsty, "God bless you" but give not what is needful profit nothing.

The biblical faith has nothing to fear from Marx's objection, or any akin to it. Marx's idea that history progresses in linear direction toward a utopian conclusion is derived from the Bible. If one recognizes in Marxism the perversion of the biblical concept of history and the millennial age, one can easily see the biblical influence on Marx. A linear concept of history followed by a better age is a Western concept in lands influenced by the Bible. It was unknown in the East.

SUMMARY OF THESE OBJECTIONS

A fair appraisal of these objections to the biblical world and life view shows them to be seriously deficient. Their inadequacy, along with the ease of response that is derived from the biblical framework of understanding, is itself significant evidence for the truth of the biblical world view. We will be dealing with some objections in presenting the positive evidence for our world view. At this point, however, the material discussed appears to provide significant, if not overwhelming, pointers to the truth of the biblical view.

CHAPTER 7: STUDY QUESTIONS

1. What are the basic objections to the biblical faith taken from psychology?

2. What is the objection(s) to the biblical faith from political considerations (especially Marxism)?

3. What is the interpretation of religion from sociology which leads to relativism?

4. Why do some think that natural law precludes miracles?

PART FOUR

POSITIVE EVIDENCE

SUPPORTING THE

BIBLICAL WORLD VIEW

THE EVIDENCE FROM
CREATION

A S PREVIOUSLY STATED, *CREATION, FALL, AND REDEMPTION* are those most basic root concepts of the biblical world view. These concepts do the best job of tying together the whole of the experience, evidence, and data provided by the world of our experience. Since we have already covered the fall, it is now our task to cover the evidence from creation and the history of redemption.

Creation is a category (root concept) of understanding through which we perceive the world. Creation means that the world of our experience is the product of an intelligent conscious being (a personal God or gods). There are several classical arguments for the concept of creation—namely the ontological, cosmological, teleological, and moral arguments for the existence of God.

The *ontological argument* argues from the *idea* of the creator to the *necessary existence* of God as following from the *nature* of the idea. Anselm's classical case is still widely studied in philosophy and theology. This twelfth-century philosopher argued that God was a being such that a greater could not be conceived. If, however, God did not exist, we could think of a being that was greater, namely one with all the attributes of God with the addition of existence. Therefore, the greatest being must exist. The seventeenth-century French philosopher René Descartes provided a different form of this argument. He argued that the idea of God was a clear and distinct idea of a most perfect being. However, a most perfect being must have the attribute of existence or it wouldn't be most perfect. Therefore the idea of God necessitates the acceptance of the truth of His existence.

Amazingly, this argument has been forcefully restated by renowned Cornell University analytic philosopher Norman Malcolm (to the incredulity of his peers.). The argument does not have the power of conviction for most people.

This is its central fallacy: Is existence an attribute of a perfect idea? Does any idea *entail* existence? This question has engendered debate for centuries. However, it is so unique a question that it is at least clear that this argument is not a key to convince most people. It does for some point to the unique difference between God and all others.

The *cosmological argument* seeks to prove the existence of God by the concept of causation. It is argued that every present reality is caused by something before it. I am the product of many causes: my parents, their parents, etc. This law of causation is true of every object of creation. A tree comes from previous trees. The earth itself is the product of causes that preceded it. However, the argument says that it is unthinkable to accept an infinite series of causes into the past. There must be a first, un-caused cause behind all of the other causes in the universe. This un-caused cause is God. Some argue that an infinite regress of causes is self-contradictory, for if there is not a first cause there is no explanation of the causal series.

This argument is more widely held than the ontological argument. It has been a pillar of Catholic thinking from Thomas Aquinas to the present (e.g., the writings of Etienne Gilson). It is held by Bible-believing philosophers such as Stuart Hackett (*The Resurrection of Theism*) and Norman Geisler (*Christian Apologetics*). Yet the argument is very controversial. Is an infinite regress of causes really self-contradictory? Many Eastern and other philosophers allow for an infinite regress of causes. Do we only think it is contradictory if the concept of a beginning of creation is a part of our mindset? It is my view that this argument simply does not have sufficient convicting power to be widely useful. It raises as many questions as it answers.

The teleological argument is an argument drawn from the marks of design in the world to the conclusion of a great designer. It was put forth by the British writer Paley in the eighteenth century in his famous analogy of the watch and the watchmaker. If we found a watch, we wouldn't assume it to be a product of chance, but that it was the work of an intelligent watchmaker. So it is with the design we perceive in the world: nature's intertwined workings, and the amazing structure of human beings. This argument was given a serious blow by the philosophy of natural evolution. However, it is still forcefully argued by many noted thinkers from British philosopher A. E. Taylor to Norman Geisler and Stuart Hackett.

The usual objection to the design argument is that it reads design into the world and then naturally assumes a designer. What if what is called design is merely our reading or projection into what are really chance material arrangements? We will respond to this objection in our new restatement of the argument. Suffice it to say here that chance evolution is an old argument known from the ancient Greeks. What is convincing to many about today's evolution is the seeming scientific mechanism of evolution through mutation and adaptation. This seemingly explains how natural evolution could take place. Many, however, still find the teleological argument convincing.

The last classical argument is the moral argument which argues from the existence of human moral laws to an ultimate lawgiver, or argues from human conscience as an evidence of God as a creator-judge. C. S. Lewis has brilliantly restated this argument in *Mere Christianity*. A new form of this argument of great merit is found in E. J. Carnell's *Christian Commitment*. We will draw from these sources. The moral dimensions of human life are explained by those who reject the moral argument as simply a reflection of the social patterns of our particular time and locale.

It is relatively easy to call into question arguments used to prove something. My approach to the area of the evidence from creation is to present the concept of creation in a comparative context with its alternatives. Is there a better means of explaining the world? In the light of this comparative approach, do creationist concepts best tie together the world of our experience? These concepts include such terms as design, moral law giver, creator and sustainer of the world, etc. Creationism holds that personal categories are the best terms of explanation. Let us therefore look at alternatives to the concept of creation.

CLASSICAL MATERIALISM

Classical materialism seeks to account for the whole range of existence in terms of combinations of material. All personal experiences—love, hate, morality, consciousness itself, and the outer physical world as a whole—are to be explained in material terms. Love is simply a chemical reaction in the brain or a particular configuration of molecules. Classical materialism seeks to reduce all to its material basis.

Physicalism is a more sophisticated, twentieth-century version of materialism. Modern science has called into question the concept of basic material, or particles, which are the building blocks of all reality. Matter has been defined in terms of energy since Einstein $(E=MC^2)$. Energy is the ability to do work. Classical materialism sought to find the basic building blocks of the universe, first in atoms (a term from the ancient Greeks), then in the parts of atoms.

However, in a world of relativity science, a world of subatomic particles, anti-matter, black holes, and curved universes, this goal is certainly impossible. Therefore, the new physicalists seek to explain all reality in physical terms, terms which find their locus of meaning in the sensory realm of human experience, without resorting to a search for ultimate building blocks of matter. Scientific terms, tested by experiment or measured by instruments of observation and empirical methods (what is observed, or heard in repeated experience), are the ultimate terms of explanation. Thus love may be explained both as a chemical reaction in the brain and as a brain state that is part of distinctive physical behavior. Speech is simply one kind of physical behavior. The brain state of being in love is expressed by its empirical behavior (hugging, staying with the other, kissing, doing for the other, and engaging in speech acts connected to love) and nothing more. The mind itself is explained in terms of brain states and physical responses to the environment and nothing more. These kinds of explanations are called reductionisms since they seek to reduce all life to its physical and/or material dimensions.

This world view leaves us with two huge problems. One problem is the explanation of the origins of this present world. The other is the impossibility of living life without the use of *personalistic terms* which imply a consciousness and a spiritual dimension to life which transcends the physical. For example, when behavioral psychologist B. F. Skinner expresses his love for his wife, what does he say? Does he say, this body is in a brain state which inclines this body to press the lip part to your lip part (remember, terms such as "I" and "my" give the illusion of a conscious, nonphysical center according to physicalists). If Skinner followed through consistently with his philosophy in all levels of life, he might soon find himself in marriage counseling. If reductionist physicalism were true, human beings should be able to speak about all areas of life with physicalist terminology without the loss of anything significant. However, only complete dehumanization would allow for this. With his wife, the physicalist uses personal language, "I love you." This is because personal language, as a part of ordinary language, reveals something about the nature of reality that we cannot do without.

Realities beyond the physical are so certainly known and experienced in everyday life that we can not part from the language that expresses their reality. This explains the aborted attempt of the positivists of a few decades ago to create a language that would be totally physical and precise as a replacement of our ordinary language. It was an impossibility. The absolute necessity of personal language, poetry, and religious speech to human life is well brought out by F. Matson in *The Broken Image*. Matson well documents the extraordinary effort to destroy the unique sense of human worth in the history of these reductionist efforts.

A devastating blow is given to reductionist philosophies in the writing of German philosopher Martin Heidegger in *Being and Time*. Heidegger forcefully argues that all scientific language (which is the basis of the language of physicalism) is an abstraction from the life-world (the world of normal human experience and language). These abstractions have a use in organizing and controlling the world of our experience. However, they are dependent for their very use upon the acceptance of the reality and truthfulness of ordinary life-world speech. Not to accept this is to saw off the limb upon which the abstractions of scientific thought sit.

Let us give an example of what Heidegger means. Love is sometimes spoken of as a chemical brain state. We can conceivably imagine a set of sophisticated scientific sensors which could be hooked up to the brain. These sensors could give us a reading of chemical changes in the brain. Now all we have to do is hook up the subject and bring a picture of the woman he loves before him and tell him to think loving thoughts about her. When he tells us that he is feeling love, we can mark the chemical readout. After going through the procedure with several subjects and finding similar results, we could conclude the nature of the chemical brain state during the experience of love. Conceivably, the same procedure could be followed to identify guilt, hate, fear, worry, and more. The formula could be complex and might include more than the brain (even the whole body), but the principle would be the same.

What is the rub? It is this; how does the scientist find his chemical state? It is by asking the subject when he is feeling love. Indeed he tells the subject to think thoughts of his beloved. Without the subjects understanding of the meaning of love, hate, fear, and guilt as transcending the mere physical chemical reactions, could the chemical reactions ever be identified? No indeed, we admit that man is a complex physiological being, but is the physical a cause of the personal-psychological, or a part of it? The brain state accompanies and is part of the state of love, but it is not the whole of love. Love is an intuitively real conscious experience known in the community of human beings. It is understood in personal terms and experienced in our conscious life before we identify a chemical brain state connected with it. It is part of what Heidegger calls the life-world. It is simply not the chemical state in itself; it is what we know and experience it to be in basic human experience. Even our physical terms are dependent upon life-world experience as the real and most basic level of reality.

The second objection comes from the physicalist-materialist explanation of the present world order. In simple terms we could say that it consists of using the concepts of time, chance, and matter to explain the origin of the universe and the world we know. Because other atheistic world views depend upon evolutionary naturalism to explain the world, a critique of this viewpoint will be presented after the next section.

EMERGENT NATURALISM

In my experience, emergent naturalism is the most widely held popular view among people who do not believe in the God of the Bible. The emergent naturalist believes that the original components of all existence are matter and energy. However, when matter and energy are organized into new patterns, these new patterns produce wholes which are more than the sum of the parts. Just as hydrogen and oxygen produce water, with new properties unanticipated by past elements, so matter and energy in certain patterns produce biological properties that can only be adequately described by biological laws. Biological patterns of the right complexity and interrelation give rise to animal instinctual properties and, in the human sphere, a mind which must be spoken of in terms of mental and psychological properties or laws. Emergentism argues against the reductionism of materialism and physicalism.[19]

It is well stated that the biological levels of reality cannot be adequately described by the concepts of physics and chemistry. New laws and concepts are necessary to describe biological life. In the same way, the mind must be described by mental and psychological concepts; a reductionist description in terms of biology or physics and chemistry can not fully account for the realities of mental life. The emergentist would agree with much of the content of the argument against materialism and physicalism in the last section. In our view the emergentist is correct in his argument against materialism.

However, emergentism has its own problems, for it thoroughly violates the principle of coherence. It offers an explanation for our mind's existence which is no explanation at all.. It is simply and crudely stated that at certain levels of patterning (material arrangement), the mind makes its appearance. When this patterning disappears in the disintegration of the body, the mind ceases to exist. Emergentist levels of reality are dependent upon the organization of the material levels. The analogy with hydrogen and oxygen producing water does not hold water. On the basis of a description of the molecular structure of water, including the interrelation of the bonding taking place between the atoms, a coherent material explanation can be given as to why the properties of oxygen and hydrogen will yield the properties of water. The properties of neutrons, protons, and electrons coherently give reason as to how oxygen and hydrogen give rise to water.

However, there simply is no coherent explanation as to how the organization of matter gives rise to the mind. The physicalist and materialist can rightly fault the emergentist for incoherence. On the other hand, the emergentist rightly points out the impossibility of material or physicalist terms adequately describing human existence. We ask, from whence comes the intricate organization of material which produces the emergent level of mind and psychological law? Secondly, how does the mind arise from matter, which is described by laws and principles of a different order than the psychological? Matter simply does not adequately anticipate psychological laws. Emergentism asks us to believe that something comes from nothing, that the mind comes from matter in which mind does not exist. Organized matter is said to give rise to something that is not inherent in it. There is no answer to the question as to why an arrangement of matter is simply nothing more than an arrangement of matter. Emergentism is merely the product of the sociological influence of the nineteenth-century spirit of evolution. There are no rational grounds for its acceptance, for emergentism accepts the ultimate incoherence, the ultimate philosophical irrationality—that something comes from nothing.

Perceiving the detrimental incoherence of this view, some naturalists have posited a mental dimension to all material existence. It is said that every molecule has a dimension of mind. This view certainly is superior, for it holds that the mind or consciousness as a reality is a self-existent part of the "everlasting is." However, the belief in mind's inhering in all things is partly a strange return to animism, a most primitive viewpoint, which is now put forth in more modern terms. Animism spoke in terms of spirits in all things. Yet this certainly does not provide an explanation of the emergence of the human being with all his qualities. Nor does it explain the organization of existence. How developed are these myriad minds? We see no evidence of mind in inorganic life, and little evidence if any in lower forms of plant and animal life. There is no evidence of mind in the sense of thinking (reasoning, problem solving, and communicating). It is speculation without evidence.

At this point it is well to note the problem of all merely scientific explanations of the universe and human life. All such explanations describe a taste-less, colorless, odorless, feelingless, and mindless world. The scientific world is a world of electrons, protons, neutrons, subatomic particles, anti-matter, energy, stimulus and response, and other scientific abstractions. Is the tasteless, color-less, odorless world of science the real world or only an aspect of the real world mathematically and otherwise abstracted from the real world and useful for human endeavors? Is the color red in itself real, or is it merely a measurement of one particular wavelength of light? Or is the wavelength one of the accom-paniments of "redness" which is known directly and perceptually as red? Fur-thermore, color can not be explained in terms of any one color or combination of waves. Rather, the experience of various colors is something that we trust as a shared common human experience. The experience of consciousness itself in-cludes all types of experiences, including material experiences. However, con-sciousness cannot be explained by one type of conscious experience, such as the experience of material things.

All philosophies discussed so far assume evolutionary naturalism as an expla-nation for the present world order. Before leaving this discussion it is important to discuss briefly the theory of naturalistic evolution. We are not here speaking in regard to those who believe that God created in a slow progressive manner by causing one species to evolve into another (theistic evolution). We are speaking rather of evolutionary theories that claim that material explanations of origins are fully adequate without resort to any divine, supernatural, or spiritual forces. (There are other geological, biological and biblical reasons for questioning the-istic evolution).

EVOLUTIONARY NATURALISM

In simple terms, naturalistic evolution is the view that time plus chance plus matter produced our world. Beyond the problem of reductionism already dis-cussed, evolutionary naturalism is full of incoherence. First is its philosophical incoherence. This is especially apparent in the concept of chance. Although chance is used in sentences to appear to give an explanation, does chance explain anything? Chance has only two meanings. One is its use in common speech, meaning that there is no explanation for an event. It just happened. We often say of tragedy that it is chance or surd in character, that in this world there is no particular spiritual or divine cause or explanation behind the event. Certainly the evolutionist does not believe in a spiritual explanation, but he does believe in a material explanation. Yet chance says there is none. Chance only appears to explain because it is inserted in a sentence with the syntax of an explanatory proposition. That chance explains at all is an illusion. Hence the evolutionist finds himself saying that part of the explanation of the world order is the absence of explanation. Chance means that if we can't find a reason, there is no explanation.

Chance is also used as a term in mathematical probability theory. We speak of the laws of chance. By this we mean that in random material events we can predict how much of one combination will come up over against another. If I flip a coin without seeking to impose a particular thumb force to it, there is a fifty-fifty chance of having it come up heads. The more times we throw the coin, the more the total throws will equal about fifty percent heads and fifty percent tails. The results are similar if I throw a hundred coins at the same time. However, the probabilities of throwing ten heads in a row are very small, the percent being equal to one-half multiplied by one-half ten times. The laws of chance enable us to predict probable outcomes of random material events when we do not know or *cannot measure* the forces that would enable more precise prediction.

Actually, no event is truly random, but it is random to us in our inability to measure the forces. Broadly speaking, it is random, but is not random in an ultimate sense. The coin comes out heads because of the combination of forces from my thumb's pushing force, gravity, the weight of the coin, and the position of the coin during the beginning of the toss. If I could measure all of the forces involved, I could predict precisely. It is the lack of adequate knowledge that causes me to use the laws of probability or chance to predict.

In scientific use, the laws of chance or probability help us predict probable events where we cannot adequately know and calculate the innumerable causes and forces that yield a specific result. Chance, in this sense as well, provides no explanation for the order of our world. In fact, further studies on the laws of chance connected to the nature of chemical-biological functions strongly disprove any possibility of the complex material patterns of life just happening. Matter tends to undifferentiated disorder, not to order.[9] Probability theory shows that random combinations remain within limited boundaries and never would produce the material arrangements of life. The nature of the material reality itself never suggests any probability factor for the complex interrelationships that produce human life.

The evolutionist is fond of saying that *given enough time* and a large enough universe of cosmic events, although it is extraordinarily improbable, the order of matter which will produce human life will occur. In other words, all conceivable material arrangements will occur given enough time. Let us press this argument. I believe that it is an exact analogy (that can be pressed to the limit) to say that if a monkey, who is taught to punch typewriter keys, was given enough time he randomly would eventually write *Hamlet*. These are false and misleading applications of the concepts of probability theory and chance. Furthermore, there is nothing in the order of chance that explains the trend toward higher more differentiated life as we find in the evolutionist's scheme. Certainly the survival of the fittest or the domination of the most adapted does not explain it. Many of the simplest forms of life have the greatest survival potential. There is nothing to drive the evolutionary engine upward.

Let us take another analogy. Let us say there was a world in which cloud formations over every country spelled out, in the languages of the various countries, "Jesus is the Messiah, follow him." Most would certainly conclude that this was the work of intelligence. However, we do sometimes see letters and pictures in the sky. According to naturalistic theory we should expect that, given enough time, there will be a world someday in which this message will be spelled out in the clouds by chance. Somehow we know that this is not a true application of probability theory. This example should cause us to question the validity of any argument that uses chance as an explanation. Yet naturalistic evolution rests on "chance" as its key concept.

Sometimes evolutionists point to other concepts of explanation. Mutations and the survival of the fittest are the two most prominent concepts. The latter concept has been refined by newer phraseology: "the predominance of the most adapted forms." However, the whole system of survival or adaption *rests on chance* to explain how the conditions are produced that will lead to a system producing higher life. Furthermore, mutation itself is a chance mechanism that tends to disintegration, not order. While it is true that there are genetic variations in life forms, such that some of these variants will be environmentally favored, there is no clear evidence from history, philosophy, or science that suggests that change and adaptation as such produces change from lower to more highly differentiated forms. An insecticide wipes out insects with the exception of those few that are genetically resistant. These few multiply and replenish the population. This kind of genetic variation does not lead mosquitoes to become other kinds of insects or to become non-insect animals.

Beyond this, one must note the total inability of mutation and survival (adaptation) to provide any explanatory power in accounting for higher life forms, especially human life. It is well known that many lower life forms have far greater survivability and adaptability than the human species. Insects and amoebas are all more resilient as species. Why is there, according to the evolutionary picture of history, an *upward* development toward greater complexity and mental intelligence? There is no adequate explanation. Some have been led back to the concepts of emergentism with the addition that there is latent mind or unconscious mind in things that is pushing toward this higher form of life. This has already been dealt with earlier. Others have said that human life is not higher at all—only different.

This book is not a scientific treatise. Our notes do list books that deal with naturalistic evolution in greater depth and from a scientific perspective. Nevertheless, it is well to note those aspects of science that are devastating to the theory of evolution.

The first is the second law of thermodynamics. It shows that the whole of the universe is moving from order to disorder, from usable energy to unusable. A. E. Wilder-Smith has shown as well that there is a law of disintegration in all biological systems. Such systems tend toward an equilibrium of disorder and not toward order unless there is intelligent intervention. Michael Denton argues in a similar way from a different perspective on probability.[10]

The second is the *extraordinary* nature of the geological record in regards to the history of life forms. This record does not just show gaps between major life form groups. Rather, among all major groupings it shows *systematic* gaps, which fit a creationist picture more coherently than an evolutionist picture. Whole orders of life simply make their appearance in a geological stratum without any previous warning or hint. This has prompted some evolutionists to posit an alternative to gradualism wherein some unknown mechanism could produce rapid and radical change that is unpreservable in the geological record.

Thirdly, the concept of mutation cannot explain complex organs. A. E. Taylor in *Does God Exist?* brilliantly notes the nature of the eye and its supposed evolutionary predecessor, the light sensor.[12] Between the light sensor and the eye are thousands of changes. The evolutionary concept would lead us to believe in a slow development from the sensor to the eye over hundreds of thousands (millions?) of years, with ever-increasing abilities and survival value to organisms, until the eye is ultimately developed. Yet, Taylor points out, the light sensor performs its function well and so does the eye. Any state between the two would have less survival value than the light sensor and would be detrimental to the organism. To go from the light sensor to a stage of equal survival value would require thousands of integrated mutations all at once, or the exceptional survival of organisms in the in-between stages during a long period of time in which survival potential is hugely compromised. This is not only so for the eye but for many other organs—from wings to developed mammalian sexual organs.

Problems such as these have prompted amazing responses by some who are naturalistic. G. A Kerkut, an atheist, exposed many of these problems in his writings and decried the unwillingness of the majority of evolutionists to face these issues squarely. He then calls for further research to find the true mechanisms behind naturalistic evolution.[13] Others have posited unaccounted-for jumps in evolution over historically brief periods in contrast to accepted evolutionary time scales. This, it is said, would account for gaps in the geological record. It is believed that these gaps have occurred during times of great environmental upheaval, thus producing tremendous pressure for change. Yet this still assumes change with no adequately defined mechanism. It gives no explanation of upward movement to higher more differentiated forms. These are really stabs in the dark to save a intellectually deficient theory.

So severe are the problems that some have even returned to the theory of Larmarck, the nineteenth-century naturalist. Larmarck posited an inner desire in the organism that supposedly explained the direction of evolution toward higher intelligence. Organisms developed the eye because there was a desire to see. This blind desire is very much like the unconscious consciousness of Henry Bergson that supposedly drives the evolutionary process upward. As we argued before with regard to emergentism, what *is* unconscious consciousness; what *is* a nonconscious desire to see? These are incoherent concepts. However, we note that these concepts are suspiciously closer to intelligent direction. Paraphrasing C. S. Lewis, these people get the benefits of an explanation somewhat like intelligent design, without having to face any personal responsibility before the creator.[14]

It is only one step further to the concept of *theistic evolution*, the idea that God was the intelligence directing evolution and is the ultimate explanation of it. We have no *philosophical* objection to theistic evolution. We do strenuously object to the view held by some that God created the circumstances for an evolution which would produce the world as we know it, with little or no divine intervention. This view (we could dub it deistic evolution) has philosophical problems, such as the concept of "chance" and most of the rest of the problems of naturalistic evolution. However, even theistic evolution, which sees God as thoroughly involved with the whole process and thus eliminating chance as a factor, has these several non-philosophical problems. First the geological and biblical records combine to show that macro-evolution was not the process of God in creation. Secondly, philosophically, I have never read a heistic evolutionist who has made clear the relationship between such evolutionary concepts as mutation and survival, which seem to derive from an ultimate chance-materialistic viewpoint. A coherent theistic theory of evolution would, it seems to me, have to drop these mechanisms for explanation totally and replace them with the view that new forms evolved by God's creative and preserving involvement.

I believe that naturalistic evolution is one of the most extraordinary deceptions ever believed by human beings.[15]

PANTHEISM

Pantheism is the last view which should be noted. There are two types of pantheism. One was rightly called "paneverythingism" by Francis Schaeffer.[16] In this view, the world is God. Beyond this nothing can be said about God. However, a God that is the world, of which nothing can be said, certainly can give no adequate explanation of the world of our experience.

The other view, called *panentheism* (all is in God), holds that God is the soul or consciousness of the world, as our soul is within and pervades our bodies. God as the soul directs the universe. He is the intelligent direction behind all. Panentheism was argued centuries ago (sixth century) by the Hindu philosopher Ramanuja and is finding new popularity in the East and West. Theism differs from panentheism in holding that the material world we see is not the everlasting body of God, but was brought into being by God, the great and mighty Spirit-Creator. I believe that the choice of theism over panentheism is justified mostly because of biblical revelation. However, since the world appears as inanimate and is not a body organically like ours, the analogy of panentheism does have some weakness. Both panentheism and theism explain the order of the universe by the concept of personal intelligence. Pantheism on the other hand, because it holds that God is ultimately beyond understanding and unknowable, or is not the subject of rational propositions, cannot really be the explanation of anything. Pantheism only appears to have explanatory value to the extent that it is expressed in more panentheistic terms. Both pantheisms are found in Hinduism.

In the light of this discussion, we now turn to the reasons for believing that conscious intelligence is the foundation of the world order, an explanation given from Moses to Einstein, from St. Paul to rocket scientist Wernher von Braun, from Thomas Aquinas to such noted scientist-philosophers as Arthur Eddington, Sir James Jeans, and Arthur Compton. All saw, as Einstein did, that the universe and its order reflected the work of a great mathematical genius.

PERSONAL EXPLANATION - THE CASE FOR THEISM

The exceedingly difficult problems with the alternatives to theism are evidences for theism and should cause all true seekers to seriously examine theism more carefully.

Theism argues that the source of this world order is personal, that the concept of creation or a Creator–Personal God best ties together the most significant dimensions of our world. We are not lacking for proponents of theism who argue on this basis. They include Frederick Ferre, William Temple, B. Mondin, and many more.[17] We hold, as shown in the writings of Nicholai Hartman, that the various levels of phenomenological reality are inherent in the world order. These levels cannot be reduced to something else.[18] Conscious experience cannot be described by materialistic terms. Love, hate, guilt, and anger are not reducible to chemical reactions and hormonal combinations. Beyond this, however, we note that the world reflects a universe of change. Human beings, animals, and plants are not themselves everlasting. They constantly come into being and pass away. When human beings come into being, they display those personal qualities of thought and emotion that we intuitively and immediately experience. Since we do not hold to the possibility of something coming from nothing, and because the world of our experience is transient (all that has been has passed away, and all that presently is will pass away), those characteristics we call personal must inhere in the permanent or everlasting ground of the world order.

Most philosophies hold that there must be something that is everlasting behind the world of our experience. This is the ground of our experience or the ground of being. There are essentially only two choices: one choice is that the ground of being is material (matter, energy, forces, etc.) and the other choice is that the ground or our being is spiritual (consciousness, mind, intelligence, love, etc.). If we say that the ground of existence is material, we are closed either to the notion of reductionism or to the idea of the incoherence of something coming from nothing. If we hold that the unchanging or everlasting ground of existence is spiritual, there is no problem. Indeed, all experience is an aspect or part of consciousness. The physical is an *aspect* of the spiritual in the ultimate sense. For example, the *experience of matter* is the experience of levels of hardness, sharpness, visible shape, etc., that is a conscious experience of a mind. Mental experiences like thoughts and emotions are also aspects of my conscious experience. We need to reflect a bit to see it, but when we do so it becomes apparent that the material world is nothing but a shared medium between or among individual conscious centers.

We perceive the same material experience together. Subjective experience is my experience alone. Objective experience is simply an experience in common in community or intersubjectivity. Material experiences are more easily experienced as the same by various individuals than are more nonmaterial experiences. We together have an experience of a green chair that can only be occupied by one of us. We distinguish between our body and the body of another person because my body produces pain and pleasure for me in a way that other bodies do not. It is uniquely with me and expresses me. Yet more nonphysical experiences can be objective. Prophets can separately hear the same message from God and write it down and show it to be received separately. Actually, objectivity is recognized through persons sharing the same experience or having a common intersubjective experience.

Since consciousness is the most basic reality of all experience, it is utter foolishness to think that consciousness itself can be explained in terms of one dimension of conscious experience—namely the experience of matter and energy. By the same rationale, it makes the most sense to hold that the ground of being is of the nature of consciousness. Thus mind gives rise to mind; the ability to love gives rise to the ability to love.

In the same vein, C. S. Lewis argued that it is foolishness to hold that an irrational universe gave rise to rational beings.[19] E. M. Blaiklock as well argues that conscious personal being must be the originator of conscious personal being.[20] Let us therefore conclude that conscious personal being is the ground of the world of our experience.

Can more be known about this ground of being without revelation? According to Scripture, the existence of God can be intuitively known from the observation of the creation order (Romans 1:18,19). Scripture does not explain this statement—whether this is a conclusion from our perception of marks of design in the creation, or from an argument like ours, or is just intuitively known. Certainly the argument from design again becomes powerful once the incoherence of naturalistic evolution is shown. Yet Romans 1 says that men have suppressed this knowledge and have produced foolish reasonings as a means of maintaining this suppression. Indeed, how much this fits the theory of naturalistic evolution, a theory that suppresses truth.

Scripture indicates that the reason this knowledge is suppressed is that we also intuitively know that God is our moral judge. Because we know ourselves to be morally deficient, and because we want to live our life in our own way without submitting to the Creator, we suppress this knowledge. Yet, we really do know we are a race under judgment. Our moral consciousness of right and wrong makes no sense unless there is an absolute standard of right and wrong inherent in the nature of God as moral lawgiver. When we say that something is wrong, we mean to claim that there is an objective standard that can be shared among human beings by which the action can be judged. A moral standard is a standard of someone for someone. This is the essential nature of the argument of C. S. Lewis in *Mere Christianity*. It is a brilliant argument worth reading; it is an argument of real force in the light of the knowledge that conscious personal being is the ground of existence. Conscious personal being must also be the ground of the moral dimension of life.[21]

It is often argued that the different moral standards held among various cultures show this argument to be suspect. In response to this objection, several points should be made. First, moral standards in advanced civilizations are not as divergent as often argued. The appendix of C. S. Lewis' *Abolition of Man* lays out those moral and social standards that have been held in common by a wide variety of cultures.[22]

Secondly, the Bible itself argues that the level of fallenness in a culture can lead to an inability to properly know moral truth. It is possible to be perverted to the point of calling good evil and evil good.

Thirdly, Scripture, in Romans 2, does not argue that we know that God is moral lawgiver because we all have the same moral standard as the content of our conscience. Rather it is that our moral motions are indications of God as our judge. For example, when we feel guilt because we *have broken our own moral code*, we sense we are guilty before someone and fear judgment. We either suppress this knowledge or come to know forgiveness. Scripture also argues that no matter how limited or twisted our own moral standards may be, we do not live up to these standards. Yet we judge and condemn others for wrongs of which we ourselves are guilty. Therefore, according to the argument of Scripture, all human beings should know themselves to be guilty before God. The human problem is the suppression of this knowledge, the suppression of guilt. E. J. Carnell called this argument *the argument from our judicial sentiment*.[23]

In the light of all of this, we can say the category of intelligent purpose is clearly the one that best ties together the world of our experience. This includes the whole dimension of human community, the male-female relationship, the whole interrelation of man with flora and fauna, and the integration of the ecosystem.[24] We can clearly understand why the great German philosopher Immanuel Kant argued that God, freedom, and immortality were the conclusions of practical reason in reflecting on the creation and in maintaining any seriousness in morality.[25] He argued that since justice is not perfectly applied in this life, there must be a life after death with rewards and punishments according to our moral deserts.

So far we have not fully looked at the biblical concepts of *creation, fall, and redemption* as the best categories to tie together and make sense of the whole of human life. We have only noted in this chapter those aspects of the world of our experience which would best square with the idea of creation. However, there is much that is not clear without the Bible's revelation. The concepts of the biblical revelation are excellent in making sense of our world, yet the full meaning of these concepts are not discoverable without revelation.

For example, is the personal intelligent ground of being to be conceived as a singular consciousness as in Rabbinic Jewish monotheism? Or is this ground a plurality of beings that is in significant enough accord that we can speak of the universe as a cosmos rather than a chaos? There must be some principle of unity behind the order of the world.[26] Is the ground of our existence a singular consciousness or a community consciousness that is the ground of human community? Francis Schaeffer argues that the triune concept of God makes the most sense because of the existence of relational love. Love is interpersonal and must have an interpersonal ground.[27] These are interesting indicators of truth, but without revelation can we really come to firm conclusions about the personal intelligent ground of existence? We can affirm that this ground is the source of moral law; but, beyond this, is the physical world created or is it the everlasting body of God which is rearranged or made into new forms and interrelationships?

Besides these there are other important religious questions. Are human beings immortal? Does the soul survive the death of the body? Is life after death conditional upon our moral character or religious belief? These and many other questions remain unanswered without revelation. Yet it is reasonable to believe, because of the extraordinary nature of human life, the amazing marks of design in nature, and the moral and purposeful dimensions of human life, that the intelligent personal ground of existence is manifest in those communities that live out the teachings of Scripture and believe in life after death.

The reader at this point has probably noticed similarities and differences between my writings and the traditional arguments for God's existence. The following comments should help clarify the relationship.

First of all, since reductionism and the naturalistic theory of evolution are shown to be incoherent, there is real force to the teleological argument—that is the argument from design. New discoveries in genetics and the analogy to computer programming give greater strength to the argument. It certainly seems that the genetic codes are divine programs for life forms.

Secondly, the moral argument gains new force on the basis of our argument for a personal intelligent ground of existence. Lastly, our argument is a replacement for classical cosmological arguments. The old argument depended upon the concept of a first cause beyond time and on the concept that an infinite regress of cause and effect is contradictory. These claims are so disputed that, in my opinion, the old cosmological argument is no longer useful. My argument, a new cosmological argument, simply notes that there must be a ground of existence behind that which comes into being and passes away. We then ask what this everlasting ground of existence must be like—material or spiritual, intelligent or nonintelligent. Something must always continue in existence. Therefore we ask, what is inherent in this everlasting something? It must be analogous to the nonreducible aspects we perceive in experience or something would come from nothing. I believe that this argument is superior to the traditional cosmological argument.[28]

The concepts of *creation, fall, and redemption* will find further credibility through an examination of historical evidences. These categories fully make sense of human experience.

📖

CHAPTER 8: STUDY QUESTIONS

1. What is the cosmological argument?

2. Why are the foundational concepts of evolution problematic (chance, mutation, survival, and adaptation)?

3. Why is it likely that the ground of existence is conscious personal being?

4. Compare and contrast the old cosmological argument with the new one given in this chapter.

EVIDENCES FROM FULFILLED PROPHECY

HISTORICAL NON-MESSIANIC PROPHECIES COVERING NATIONS, CITIES, AND KINGS

A N EXAMINATION OF HISTORICAL EVIDENCE is part of fulfilling the criteria of comprehensiveness. By such an examination we seek to show that the biblical world view can best tie together the relevant historical material, including historical non-Messianic prophecies covering nations, cities, and kings. The primary relevant material for this study is biblical or Near Eastern history. When we study such history we find that all our evidence is intertwined; from the moral character of Scriptural teaching and its prophetic teaching, to the fulfillment of predicted events. This includes the high quality of the biblical miracle accounts in the gospels and the evidence of the historic trustworthiness of the gospel writers. All of this forms a whole that is powerful. Yet, for purposes of exposition, it is necessary to divide out areas of revelation history for examination. This is important to remember.

THE ROLE OF THE BIBLICAL PROPHET

As we look at prophecy, it is important to understand the role of the biblical prophet.[1] The biblical prophet was not a soothsayer or someone who sought ecstatic states to see into the future. A study of comparative culture shows the office of the biblical prophet to be completely unique among the institutions of the world. The primary purpose of the biblical prophet was to *forth tell* the Word of God, rather than to foretell. He was a spokesman for God and His

covenant with his people. As part of this function, he proclaimed God's righteousness and his judgments. Oftentimes this righteous judgement included specific blessings and judgments to come upon historical personages, cities, nations,
and empires. This proclamation also looked forward to the time of ultimate
human redemption, and it included the understanding that history is moving
toward this redemption. The predictive element of prophecy should be seen in
the context of this understanding of history and of proclaiming the word of
Israel's covenant God.

The covenantal material given to Israel during the days of Moses provided for
the office of the prophet. Furthermore, the book of Deuteronomy provided the
standards for the testing of a prophets in ancient Israel. It was not only that predictive elements would be fulfilled (Deuteronomy 18). (Indeed some dimensions of prediction were for the far distant future and untestable.) It was that
the prophetic teaching was morally and theologically in accord with the original
covenantal material (Deuteronomy 13). The biblical revelation uniquely presents
us with an infinite personal God whose moral and social commandments are a
reflection of His eternal character. This high moral quality is so unique that it is
in itself an evidence of the truth of the biblical revelation. The Scriptures present us with an amazing unified revelation of a God who loves and seeks fellowship with his human creatures. It presents a God of compassion who is concerned for social justice and high moral standards, and who is involved in the historical process by directing it to a redemptive future.

THE PREDICTIVE ELEMENT

Having given this proper context, I still must note that the fulfillment of the
preictive elements of prophecy in history past is an important dimension of the
veracity of the Scriptures. However, some prophecies still await fulfillment and
were earmarked for the distant future. Other prophecies were conditional.
Jonah predicted the destruction of Nineveh, but when Nineveh repented she
was spared from destruction. Human response to prophecy can thus suspend
the fulfillment. Jonah sought to not warn Nineveh because he perceived that
her repentance would avert judgment. Because Nineveh was an enemy of Israel,
he desired her judgment.[1]

This somewhat complicates our task. Some prophecies are stated as clearly
conditional with regard to human response. Some are clearly without conditions
—God states that He has made his decision, and human response will not make
a difference. There are some prophecies, however, that do not make clear

which kind they are. Therefore, we will choose those prophecies which are clearly given in nonconditional terms, or have already been fulfilled in history.

The prophetic material of Scripture is without parallel in its moral-ethical quality. The prophets share the moral concern of God. They heard His voice; sometimes an intuited inner sense was the means, sometimes a vision, sometimes an audible voice was heard commanding the prophet what to write.

Predictive prophecy neither destroys human freedom, nor does it provide us with a predestinarian fixity for the future. It is simply that God shares His mind and tells His prophets what He will do. As Scripture asks, "Surely the Lord God does nothing, unless He reveals it to his servants the prophets" (Amos 3:7).

For predictions to have real evidential value, they must be specific enough so that they are not easily applied to a whole variety of possible fulfillments and meanings. In other words, prophecies for apologetic purposes must not be vague.

AFFIXING PROBABILITY QUOTIENTS

Some writers on predictive prophecy, especially with regard to prophecies about the Messiah, have tried to affix probability quotients to prophecies. This was to show the unlikelihood of chance fulfillment. They will say that the chances were one in a thousand that one city would be destroyed and another remain.[3] However, I see no valid means of fixing such probability quotients. The fulfillment of specific predictions which are incapable of being fulfilled by human conscious intent gives clear evidence of supernatural involvement in both the prediction and the fulfillment. Many such fulfilled prophecies demonstrate evidence for the supernatural beyond any possible calculation of probabilities. To set probability quotients, one would have to be able to tabulate the likelihood of cities continuing or being destroyed as if these events were capable of equal quotients for various periods of time. These quotients would then be set in the same way that we set probability quotients for random events. History, however, is the stage of human and divine purpose, and no chance probability factors can be set. The attempt to do so, although well meaning, adopts a category from mathematical science and seeks to apply it to the realm of historic events. I believe this is a mistaken application.

WHAT PREDICTIVE PROPHECY PROVES

We must not think that predictive prophecy proves too much. If it is prevalent and accurate in one literary tradition (e.g., the Bible), it certainly shows a non-normal source of knowledge. Combined with moral and doctrinal teaching of a coherent nature, it may indicate an interrelationship between the truth of the teaching and the prediction. It gives evidence that both aspects are from a supernatural and trustworthy source. It is no absolute proof, but is for the genuine seeker an indication of the truth of the material, especially in the context of the quality of the whole biblical revelation.

Lastly, before looking at specific predictions, I want to comment on my procedure with regard to dating. This is not a book on Bible introduction. Therefore we can not give a full discussion of the dating of specific biblical books.[4] Liberal critics have tended to "late date" biblical books and to claim that the writer wrote his material after an event as if he were predicting it. This would give his writing greater credibility, as if it were from a bygone age and hence inspired. This certainly is not in accord with the high moral tone of the writings, although some excuse this practice as an aspect of ancient culture.

William Foxwell Albright, the greatest archaeologist of the twentieth century, has written that "prophecy after the event" simply was not a part of Hebrew culture, though it was known among the first-century Greeks.[5] We believe that the conservative traditional dates for the books of the Bible are correct according to linguistic and historical evidence. However, to prevent uncertainty, we will only pick those prophecies whose supernatural character in prediction and fulfillment is not affected by the theories of late dating. Even more prophecies can be found for apologetics if the arguments for conservative dating are accepted.[6] Our procedure will enable us to avoid the complexity of critical theories of dating.

Those who claim errors in Old Testament predictions have not adequately taken into account both the conditional nature of prophecy and the evidence that some prophecies await a distant-future fulfillment. They were not intended to be fulfilled within a shorter time period. Some words had a partial fulfillment in the immediate context but awaited, or still await, a more distant fulfillment. We believe that an honest evaluation of biblical prediction shows an astonishing trustworthiness.

Predictive prophecy is miraculous. Miracles are biblical apologetic evidences. Some have dismissed the miraculous because of an assumption of its impossibility. Others argue that miracles can not be corroborated by historical evidence. If one has bought the limited thesis that all history is to be understood by weighing evidence which must conform to the analogy of our experience of *natural cause and effect*, then the miraculous is indeed a problem. This positivistic view of history holds that the right explanation for events is always a natural explanation. History research and writing is then seen as finding that *natural* meaning or *naturalistic* explanation. Liberal theologian Rudolph Bultmann was one of the most noted proponents of this viewpoint.[7] Yet it would certainly appear that this viewpoint is built on mere anti-supernatural prejudice.

Although we might require more than the usual level of testimony to give credibility to supernatural occurrences, the evidence for such events is the corroborated testimony from people of moral character, just as it is for other historic events. We may not be able to know how a miracle is done, but we can recognize an event whose occurrence transcends the normal laws and processes of the natural realm. A withered arm restored, a deaf ear that is healed, a dead person who has become alive again, the restoration of an emaciated, cancer-ridden body, and the fulfillment of a prediction that is not in accord with normal expectations—are all events that can be experienced and testified to. When the miraculous takes place as part of attesting a religious tradition, and when these events take place in the name of God, they give credibility to that tradition. This is especially so in the case of the biblical tradition, including the history of Israel and the Church. In this tradition, such occurrences are numerous. Accounts of the miraculous are given with testimony professing their evidence for the presence and character of God. They reflect a high moral quality beyond the miracle stories of other religious traditions.

We now turn our attention to specific prophetic predictions.[8]

SPECIFIC PREDICTIVE PROPHECIES

HOSEA 1:4,5,7

This is a passage written during the prosperity of the northern kingdom of Israel in the early eighth century B.C. At this time the prophet predicted the destruction of the ten-tribe northern kingdom as a significant national entity. Yet at the same time, the southern tribes making up the land of Judah were given the prophecy that they would survive this destruction. This is amazing, considering that the northern tribes making up Israel were more powerful by far, at the time, than the southern kingdom. We read, "Yet I will show love to the house of Judah and will save them, not by bow, sword, or battle, or by horses and horsemen, but by the Lord God."

The end of the eighth century B.C. saw the destruction of the northern kingdom but the amazing deliverance of Judah during the period of Assyrian expansion. This is recorded in Isaiah, II Kings, and II Chronicles. Even though Assyria was at the very gates of Jerusalem, besieging the city, Assyria amazingly withdrew, probably due to a plague among her troops (II Kings 20:35). The Stele of Sennacherrib records his military victories and his invasion of Judah, but absent is any claim that Judah and Jerusalem were finally conquered. This archaeological find confirms the fulfillment of prophecy as well as the biblical account of the fulfillment.[9] There is no doubt among scholars with regard to the fact that Israel fell, but Judah did not.

HOSEA 3:4,5

This text provides an amazing prophecy of Israel during the ages. It states,

> For the Israelites will live many days without king or prince, without sacrifice or sacred stones, without ephod or idol. Afterward the Israelites will return and seek the Lord their God and David their king. They will come trembling to the Lord and to his blessings in the last days.

At the time this text was delivered, all of the features listed were part of the national life of both the northern and southern kingdoms. The ephod was part of the high priest's attire, in which were kept Urim and Thumim. These objects (stones?) were used as an indicator of either "yes" or "no" in discerning the will of God. Israel was also plagued by idolatry. A future for Israel was described that was totally without precedent. Israel would be without any of these elements for a significant period (yomim rabbim: "many days"). After this period they would return and seek the Lord and David their King (a euphemism for the Messiah to come). This amazingly describes Jewish history to the present day.

JOEL 3:6–8: ON TYRE AND SIDON

The prophet Joel was also one of Israel's early–eighth-century B.C. prophets. This passage proclaims judgment upon these cities for selling Jewish people as slaves. It is predicted that the people of these cities will become slaves of Judea and sold to Sabians, faraway traders. This whole region came under Jewish rule during the period of the Maccabees (165 B.C.). Herodotus, the Greek historian, also records that Alexander sold 13,000 Tyrians as slaves. However, prophecies concerning Tyre and Sidon become even more specific in the book of Ezekiel.

EZEKIEL 26:3-23

This passage was probably composed from 592–570 B.C.E. So specific is the fulfillment of this prophecy that critics want to date this passage as an interpolation added during the days of Alexander. There is no other reason for this late-dating, but further details of the prophecy remain valid even if late-dated.

At the time this prophecy was delivered (during the days of Nebuchadnezzar of the Babylonian period), Tyre was a powerful city. Tyre had both a mainland settlement and a significant island settlement offshore. The prophecy states:

1. Nebuchadnezzar will conquer the mainland portions of Tyre (vv. 7–14).
2. Not only Babylon, but many nations (peoples) would come against Tyre (v. 3).
3. They will scrape away the rubble of Tyre and make her a bare rock (vv. 4, 5).
4. Stones, timber and rubble will be thrown into the sea.
5. Out in the sea, she will become a place to spread fishnets.
6. She will never be rebuilt.

History records detailed fulfillment of the prophecy. Nebuchadnezzar did indeed conquer the mainland. However, the complete destruction awaited the coming of Alexander the Great with his naval force. Alexander scraped the mainland and threw the debris into the sea. With land and naval forces, the city was finally destroyed. He left the mainland bare rock.[10] Although the mainland is an excellent city site, it has never been rebuilt. Present-day Tyre is a small fishing village and is not geographically in the same place as the old city. Other settlements in the area were finally destroyed during the Crusader-Muslim period of wars. Today, fishing nets are spread from the causeway. Tyre is desolate.

This prophecy is even more astonishing when considered in parallel to the passage concerning Tyre's sister city Sidon. Ezekiel 28:22-23 predicts that Sidon would experience punishment, a plague, and blood flowing in her streets with a sword against her on every side. Yet there is no prediction of Sidon's utter destruction. Sidon still exists today on the same site. However, her bloody history perfectly fits this prophecy. Whatever God speaks comes to pass.

AMOS 1:3-8 (PARALLELED IN ZEPHANIAH 2:4-7)

Amos was an early–eighth-century-B.C. prophet. Several predictions concerning several cities are included in these passages. They include the fire devouring the palace of Ben Hadad which occurred under Tiglath-Pileser of Assyria. Syrians would be exiled to the east in Kir (732 B.C.). Gaza would be burned, captured, and plundered for its ruthless slave trade. This occurred under the same Assyrian conquest. Ashdod would find its inhabitants cut off. The records of Sargon II record his attack and plunder of Ashkelon. The prophet says the ruler (he who holds the scepter) would be cut off. Sidqia revolted against Assyria in 701 and was deported. Amos 1:8 then says the remnant of the Philistines will perish. "After 165 B.C. the former Philistine cities regarded themselves as Greek; the other elements in their population seem to have largely disappeared."[11] Jonathan Maccabee captured Ashdod and Ashkelon (I Maccabees 10:84–86) and in 146 B.C. burned and plundered Gaza (I Maccabees 11:60–62). Zephaniah 2:4–7 predicted the eventual Jewish settlement of the area, which took place. Ancient Gaza was destroyed and is a bald city. The new Gaza is not located near the old site.

AMOS 2:1–3

This passage predicts the destruction of Moab, a rich and powerful nation. Fire will be sent upon her. Jeremiah 48:47 adds an unusual twist, for God is quoted as saying He will restore the fortunes of Moab in the days to come. A fuller, more detailed prediction is given in Ezekiel 25:8–11, with a parallel prediction concerning Ammon. Moab and Ammon were relatives or national cousins to Israel—descended from Lot (Abraham's nephew). Ezekiel predicts destruction and captivity for both from a people from the East. The reason for the punishment is their action and attitude toward Israel. In 23:4 it is said that the people of the east would "pitch their tents among you . . ." and that Rabbah would be a pasture for camels and Ammon a resting place for sheep.

All of these prophecies came true historically. These lands were overpowered and deported under Nebuchadnezzar. Yet Moab did not experience a restoration after Babylon's fall. This is in accord with Jeremiah's prediction. The people of the East did make it a place of settlement and Arab palaces. The land now is part of present-day Jordan.

JEREMIAH 49:7-11

This passage predicts the destruction of Edom during the same period. Esau was the brother of Jacob and the first son of Israel. Hence this is another cousin-nation. The biblical prediction concerning Edom requires a survey of several other passages. Here we read of her being diminished by Babylonian aggression (Jeremiah 22) and returned to her land after Babylon's fall. Isaiah 21:11, Jeremiah 33, and Ezekiel 47 all indicate that the Edomites would be driven out—they were, by Nabatian Arabs. They were incorporated under Judah during the rule of John Hyrcanus. The latter event was predicted by Obadiah's book on Edom's judgment. 1 Maccabees and Josephus' *Antiquities* record that the Edomites held out against Israel, but were occupied during the Hasmonian period of Israel's history.

AMOS 3:12-15

This passage again predicts the complete doom of Samaria (the northern ten tribes of Israel), but not of Judah.

NAHUM

This book deals with God's judgment upon Nineveh. This great prediction was given during the height of Nineveh's power as capitol of Assyria. Nahum 1:8 predicts Nineveh's destruction by a flood. Chapter 2:1-6 describes how Nineveh's attacker (Cyaxares the Mede) will advance wearing scarlet. This was a Persian practice.[12] Of special note is verse 1:8, for during the battle, the channels which ran into the city overflowed as the waters rose to a new level. The waters washed away the wall, after which the attackers poured into the city, conquered it, and set it on fire. This was a natural event favoring the attackers (cf. 2:6). Diodorous II.26 also records that carelessness and drunkenness prevailed in Nineveh during the battle, which encouraged the attackers. This was predicted in verse 1:10. Nineveh is to be utterly destroyed, according to the prophecy, and would not only be uninhabited (vv. 1:8, 3:11), "it would be hid." Nineveh became a mound; it had to be excavated for the ruins to be found.

MICAH 4:10

This prophecy was given before the time of Babylonian power. It was given during the Assyrian period and predicted, amazingly, "O daughter of Zion . . . you shall go even to Babylon, there you shall be delivered." Micah saw far off to Babylon's great power a century later. He saw the seventy-year captivity of Judah—its exile under Babylon. He also saw the return of Israel to the land.

ZECHARIAH 1:12-21

In this passage we find that the exile of the Jewish people will be temporary. Jerusalem would continue until Messianic times. The cities of Judah would overflow with prosperity. This, of course, has been the pattern of history.

EZEKIEL 29:13,14; 30:8–15

The history of Egypt and some of its chief cities, especially Thebes and Memphis, was outlined in this chapter. It should be noted that Egypt had been a world power for millennia and continues to be a nation even at the time of this writing. Egypt's domination by the power of Babylon was brief. Judah had looked to Egypt for deliverance; this was a false hope. The passage teaches that Egypt would survive. She would be made desolate and would experience a scattering of her people. She would not again be a world power, but would be a lowly kingdom. (This is most interesting in the light of the prediction of the total destruction of Babylon and Babylonia later to be discussed.) Thebes and Memphis are also to be destroyed along with their idols. There is no record of such destruction during the Babylonian period, but there is a significant record of Persian triumph under Cambyses in 525 B.C., recorded in Herodotus. Yet it was not until 89 B.C., in the Roman period, that Thebes saw the destruction spoken of in this chapter. Once again, biblical prediction has been fulfilled.

ISAIAH 13:19–22, 14:23; JEREMIAH 51:2

This amazing series of prophecies concerning Babylon greatly contrasts with the prophecies concerning Egypt.

The capital city of Babylon is to be totally destroyed and never again inhabited (13:19,20). Indeed no one would pitch their tent there. This is a word that has been true through the centuries due to Bedouin superstition about the area. There would be no sheep folds and no reuse of the stones for rebuilding (Jeremiah 51:26). This is contrary to the usual reuse of materials and mounds in ancient cities. This prophecy is all the more amazing since it was delivered at the height of Babylonian power. It was also several centuries until the complete fulfillment.

During the Persian period Babylon was conquered. It still survived as a center, but it would never regain sovereignty. A steady decline ensued as reported in Herodotus. Contention caused plundering and destruction during the Seleuciud period before Rome's control. Much business and commerce moved from Babylon to Selucia. By 60 B.C. the city had become desolate, a veritable desert. In the early first century only a small group of astronomers and mathematicians continued to live in the city. In 363 A.D. the emperor Julian broke down its remaining walls to prevent its use in rebellion. Once again we have an amazing prediction, the decree of God.

Although it is true that there is disagreement in identifying the details of fulfillment in some predictions, yet the overall evidence of clear fulfillments and identifications shows the extraordinary nature of biblical predictions.

Of nations we note:

1. Egypt will remain but be a weak nation.
2. The Jewish people would remain and be regathered after worldwide scattering.
3. The Philistines would cease.
4. Samaria would cease.
5. Edom would totally cease.
6. Moab and Ammon would return from exile but would eventually be absorbed and lose their distinctive identity.
7. Assyria would cease as a nation.

Of cities we note:

1. Tyre would be destroyed.
2. Sidon would remain, although with a bloody history.
3. Memphis would be destroyed.
4. Thebes would be conquered, its idols would remain.
5. Nineveh would be utterly destroyed.
6. Babylon would be destroyed.
7. Jerusalem would remain.
8. Damascus would remain.

SIMILAR NEW TESTAMENT PREDICTIONS

The New Testament also contains qualitatively similar predictions. Luke 21 notes that Jerusalem would be trodden down by the nations but not eliminated as a city. However, Chorazin, Bethsaida, and Capernaum would be destroyed. History has confirmed the fulfillments (Matthew 11:20–24).

In my view, prophecy is accurate in its predictive dimensions because God carries through on his pronouncements. He speaks into reality judgment and redemption.

PREDICTIONS OF THE SAGA OF THE JEWISH PEOPLE

The most amazing dimension of biblical prediction, however, has been the saga of the Jewish people. The biblical accuracy with regard to the outline of Israelite history is one of the key signs that awaken us to the amazing nature of Scripture. The early books of Moses give a picture of Jewish history. Deuteronomy 28 and Leviticus 26 are noteworthy. They predict the worldwide scattering of the Jewish people and the persecutions and the trials they would suffer. This picture is expanded by the prophetic books. However, the Jewish people would never cease to remain a distinct people and a covenant people of God. Scripture states,

> Yet in spite of this, when they are in the land of their ene-
> mies, I will not reject them or abhor them so as to destroy
> them completely, breaking my covenant with them. I am the
> Lord their God. For their sake, I will remember the covenant
> with their ancestors whom I brought out of Egypt in the sight
> of the nations to be their God. I am the Lord. (Leviticus
> 26:44)

This covenant includes the land of Israel as an everlasting possession. Yet it also notes the fact that Israel would not always dwell in this land. Faithfulness to God's revelation was required. The scattering of Israel as well as a great re-gathering of the Jewish people was predicted by most of the major prophets. According to Isaiah 11 there would be a second return, beyond the return from Babylonian exile in the sixth to fifth centuries B.C. This return, according to Jeremiah 16 and Jeremiah 23, would be from the four corners of the earth. It would eclipse the first exodus in power and renown, and would especially fea-ture the land of the North giving up its Jewish people. Is the Soviet Union in view here? The reclamation of desert land—desolate, but now productive—was a major part of these predictions (Isaiah 35, Ezekiel 36:33–35).

Jesus even noted that Jerusalem's domination by foreign nations would be temporary. In Luke 21 we note that Jerusalem would be trodden down by the nations *until* the times of the Gentiles would be fulfilled. The biblical sense of all these passages is that the covenant land of Israel only prospers when Jewish people inhabit it and control it. When Jewish people are in the suffering of exile, the land suffers and becomes desolate—a desert. This has certainly par-alleled Israel's history and the history of the land with extraordinary accuracy.

CONCLUSION

What can we therefore conclude concerning nations, cities, and peoples? It is clear that the prophets spoke from a source of knowledge that was not normal or that did not belong to the natural order of things. It is worth noting that bib-lical predictions did not arise from an interest to know future events, as in oc-cultism. Biblical prediction is instead a secondary element that accompanies the prophetic message concerning God's judgments, his mercy, and his redemption. They fit within this context of preaching; they are not contrived. This is extraordinarily unusual in the history of religions. Prediction is almost an aside, an accompaniment of the message of justice, judgment, and hope. The accuracy of the prophetic material, coupled with the moral insight contained therein, provides persuasive evidence concerning the truthfulness of the claim of the prophets that they were speaking from God or under His inspiration. This in turn gives persuasive force to the truth of the whole of their message—theologically and morally. Of course, trusting these books is like trusting a person. We, out of our own moral perception, need to be able to recognize the ring of authenticity or the marks of trustworthiness in these books. Just as people of poor moral perception do not recognize a trustworthy person, so not all will be persuaded by the force of this argument. Once again we are thrown back to the crucial necessity of the work of the Holy Spirit to open the heart of a person to be able to rightly weigh this evidence. As stated in our section on value pervasity, all argument can be challenged and our premises denied. Some may say that their prophetic accuracy is coincidental, or that the prophets had an Eastern type of clairvoyance so that their accuracy is unrelated to the truth of their message. Our arguments are only persuasive to the open heart that is willing to find persuasive evidence on historical grounds to make a religious decision based on this evidence that would entail a change in life direction. It is good to challenge a people to express what marks of trustworthiness and evidence they required as sufficient for believing the biblical revelation.

CHAPTER 9: STUDY QUESTIONS

1. What are the standards showing that predictive prophecy is from a supernatural agency?

2. Does the Bible "prophesy after the event?" Explain.

3. What is the biblical picture of the destiny of Tyre and Sidon?

4. What is the evidence from historical non-Messianic prophecies?

EVIDENCES FROM MESSIANIC PROPHECY, I

TYPES, FORESHADOWING, AND EARLY PREDICTIONS

THE EVIDENCE FROM MESSIANIC PROPHECY IS CENTRAL TO APOLOGETICS. The images, hopes, predictions, and foreshadowing concerning the Messiah are best seen as fulfilled in Yeshua of Nazareth. Jesus is the promised Messiah. His unique life, death, and resurrection fulfill the predictions of the Tenach and give fullness to the meaning of Israel's religion and life.

The argument that Yeshua is the Messiah from predictive prophecy is a classical argument rooted in the New Testament Scriptures themselves. In our view, however, the biblical argument for prophecy and fulfillment in the life of Jesus is both more subtle and more powerful than many present-day formulations.

Recent formulations put forth several Old Testament prophecies and point out how Jesus fulfilled these Old Testament predictions. Sometimes a probability quotient is affixed to a prediction to indicate how unlikely it would be for it to be fulfilled (e.g., one chance in three hundred). Parallel to probability theory, quotients from many predictions are multiplied together to show how astronomically impossible it would be for these prophecies to be fulfilled in one man unless it was by supernatural working (e.g., one in three billion). This then proves that the Bible is true and that Yeshua is the Messiah.[1]

There are several problems in this approach. They are as follows.

1. Some passages chosen are not clear predictions. We can not always *prove* that they were predicting exact events in the life of Jesus. To set a probability figure looks impressive until we realize the need for a clear exegetical meaning and solid reasons as to why the prediction's fulfillment is improbable to the degree claimed. From whence come these quotients.

2. Secondly, it is crucial that prophecy, if used in a scientific-probability context, be incapable of self-fulfillment. However, Yeshua consciously sought to fulfill some prophecies, such as when He had his disciples obtain a donkey upon which to ride into Jerusalem to fulfill Zechariah 9:9.

3. Many New Testament passages that quote the Old as being fulfilled are not quoting *predictions* from the Old Testament at all, but are quotes from passages which illustrate the meaning of Yeshua's life as epitomizing and climaxing the meaning of Israel's history. For example, Matthew 2:15 quotes Hosea 11:1, "Out of Egypt have I called my son." This passage is not speaking of the Messiah at all, but is speaking of Israel as the Son of God being called out of Egypt. Israel is here described as rebellious in spite of being called out of Egypt. As in other passages, Matthew is not claiming that Jesus' coming out of Egypt fulfills a direct prediction of Hosea 11:1. It is that Yeshua, being Israel's representative of the Messiah, recapitulates the life of Israel at significant junctures in his life, thereby *filling full* the meaning of Israel's history. The New Testament word "fulfill" is not limited to the concept of a prediction coming to pass but has the broader meaning of "fill full;" the simple change of syllable order more expresses the truth of the biblical concept.

4. The model of prediction used is generally a wrongheaded use of a mathematical method applied to biblical and historical material. It yields ground to the idea that evidence must conform to a scientific-mathematical mode to be valid. This is simply not true. Historians must reconstruct the past by testimony, primary documents, and by analogies to their experience. Sound judgments are required. There is no scientific (in the sense of the pure science) way to do this.

5. The argument must also give reason to believe that the purported fulfillment event really occurred and was not just purported to occur because the prophecy was known. For example, that the Messiah would be born in Bethlehem was a commonly known prediction. Was Jesus really born in Bethlehem or did the biblical writer say He was because he knew the prophecy? The prediction-fulfillment arguments rest on the case for the trustworthiness of the New Testament documents. The case for this is very good, but this case is part of the

total evidence for fulfilled prophecy and cannot be disassociated from it. Therefore this chapter is partly dependent for its value on Chapter Fourteen, where
the case for the trustworthiness of the New Testament is argued.

We sum up by saying that one must not divorce prediction and fulfillment
from the *fullness of life* which fully convinced his Jewish disciples that He was
the promised Messiah. This was even more amazing in that the disciples were
blind to the idea of the Messiah who would suffer, die, and rise again. Their
Messianic hope, based on their biblical interpretation, differed from the interpretation of Jesus—yet they were convinced. By hindsight the Scriptures were
now clear to them.

Robert Culver makes the point that prophecy needs to be clear enough to
identify fulfillments, but not so clear as to set an easy probability quotient. It
must not be so vague that it is capable of many conflicting fulfillments, but clear
enough that the disclosure of the fulfillment gives real evidence.[2] The use of
Messianic prophecy to prove that Jesus is the Messiah has a long history in the
debate between the Church and the traditional Synagogue. Jews have claimed
that Christians (based upon New Testament usage) use passages out of context
—passages which are not even Messianic prophecies. It is claimed that these
passages are twisted to try to prove that Jesus is the Messiah even though these
passages prove nothing of the sort. Christians have argued that the Rabbinical
community is blind to the obvious evidence. At the same time, Christians have
missed truths to be discovered in Judaism and Jewish interpretation. Most
passages which have been claimed as pointing to Jesus as the promised Messiah
have a long history in Jewish interpretation as being Messianic. The concept of
the Messiah is so central to Judaism that Judaism loses its heart without it.
Therefore, as part of our presentation, we shall seek to give reference to supportive ancient Jewish interpretations.

MESSIANIC CONCEPTS
AT THE TIME OF JESUS

Jewish interpretation was not unified in regard to the concept of the Messiah
in the first century. All agreed on the coming of the king-Messiah, David's descendant who would reign on David's throne. Yet beyond this, agreement breaks
down. Qumran (usually considered an Essene community), which gave us the
Dead Sea Scrolls, was part of a major ascetic sect of Judaism. They looked for

the coming of a prophetic Messiah (Deuteronomy 18:18), a Davidic kingly Messiah, and a priestly Messiah like Aaron.[3] The Pharisees looked for two Messiahs, one a prophet-king and another who would be a priest. The prophet-king would be like unto Moses and would combine both rulership over the nation and the prophetic mantle. This is reflected in John 6, especially verse 15.[4] Most expected that the Davidic Messiah would bring a glorious period for Israel as the center of a worldwide kingdom of peace. Did Jesus' disciples also expect this to happen in their day? This explains Zebedee's wife requesting that her sons would sit to his left and to his right in the Kingdom (Matthew 20). One of the early legends of Judas' betrayal is that it was done to force Jesus' hand to establish the Kingdom. Into this milieu, Jesus brought his own interpretation.

FULFILLING ISRAEL'S HISTORY

As explained previously, the concept of fulfillment in the New Testament is best understood as bringing the meaning of Israel's revelatory history to its fullness. This includes bringing to fullness the meaning of *Israel's feasts*, or holy days, the meaning of *the temple sacrificial system*, the meaning of *Israel's history* (He recapitulates the life of Israel in his person), and the meaning of Israel's prophetic tradition concerning the person and work of the Messiah.

The Gospels present Jesus (Yeshua) as bringing Israel's history to its fullness. Under this concept we see that parallels in Israel's history and the Messiah's history show forth the meaning of the Messiah. Yeshua is Israel's representative; He is the light of Israel, the personal revelation of what Israel is meant to be. Recent studies have shown how Jewish methods of biblical interpretation have been used by New Testament writers to make this point. Rabbinical methods are evident in Paul, and Qumran-type methods are evident in Matthew and John.[5] The Qumranic method is known as "peshar." It is recognized by the formula, "This is that."

Matthew 2:15 is one example of highlighting the fulfillment of Jewish history by Jesus. Joseph took the holy family to Egypt to avoid the wrath of Herod. He later returned to Israel after Herod died. The danger was past. Matthew 2:15 then quotes this as a fulfillment of Hosea 11:1, "Out of Egypt have I called my Son."[6] A contextual reading of Hosea 11:1 shows that this passage does not explicitly speak of the Messiah. The Son called out of Egypt is Israel, who is described as unfaithful despite God's marvelous deliverance. Matthew is not foolishly claiming to find a prediction where there is none. He is rather showing how Jesus fills up the meaning of Israel's history. As her representative He goes down into Egypt and comes out of Egypt. It is a God-intended parallel. As Israel's representative He is fully faithful and righteous in a way that contrasts with Israel. Matthew's method is to convince us of the truth of the Gospel by showing the depth of the meaning of Yeshua.

This theme continues in Matthew 2:18, which refers to Jeremiah 31:15. In this passage Rachel is weeping for her children, who suffered the literal destruction of war and captivity under the Babylonians. Rachel was the mother of Joseph and Benjamin. The descendants of Joseph are the children who suffer. Matthew sees parallels in the destruction and captivity suffered under Herod.

Matthew 2:23 reflects upon the coming of Jesus to settle in Nazareth and says "that it might be fulfilled . . . He shall be called a Nazarene." Where in the Scriptures do we find a prediction that the Messiah would live in Nazareth? Yet Scripture does call the Messiah the "branch," or Netzer (Isaiah 11:1,2). Also, we note that He was totally dedicated to God at birth, parallel to Samson. This is a quality of commitment that can only be compared to a lifelong Nazarite commitment. A Nazarite vow was a special vow for dedicated service to God (Numbers 6). The name of his town reminds Matthew of these truths concerning the Messiah, a spiritual Nazarite, and the branch. It is not an accident that the Messiah is called "the Nazarene," for it reminds us of these truths—it is a play on words.

These examples reflect the ancient Jewish idea of corporate solidarity. This concept puts forth the truth that our lives are bound up with one another. The father is part of his children and their later descendants. The Messiah is part of His ancestors and one with Israel and her key leaders. This forms a reality that is part of one whole. Hence "Hebrews" sees the sacrifice of Isaac by Abraham in Genesis 22 as foreshadowing the later sacrifice of his greater descendant, the Messiah Yeshua (Jesus).

Matthew's account of the baptism of Jesus and his being tested in the desert for forty days (Matthew 4) parallels Israel's passing through the sea and being tested in the wilderness for forty years. Yeshua is fully victorious in His tests, whereas Israel lost a generation to rebellion and sin.

Paul picks up this aspect of solidarity and applies it to all believers. He notes that Israel was baptized in cloud and in water (I Corinthians 10:1ff.). These parallels point out that Yeshua is our righteousness, not only by dying for our sins, but by perfectly living out what Israel failed to do. He thus makes up for Israel's failures. In dealing with these passages, Walter Kaiser notes that certain key phrases in the Old Testament have Messianic implications according to the concept of corporate solidarity: examples are *seed, son, messiah*, etc.[7]

As Israel came to the mountain to receive the Law, so Yeshua, as the prophet like Moses, goes up to the mountain to reveal the true issue of the meaning of the Law (Matthew 5-7). These chapters reflect covenantal forms with a closing statement of blessing and cursing for those who respectively heed and those who do not heed the Word of God.[8]

Finally, Matthew 27:9-10 reveals foreshadowing parallels in the betrayal of Yeshua by Judas for thirty pieces of silver. Matthew probably has two passages in mind (as is common in Jewish exegesis) but he only refers to the major prophet Jeremiah even though the significant part of the parallel is from Zechariah 11:12-13 (cf. Jeremiah 32:6-9. 18:1,2). Zechariah is a highly symbolic book often fraught with Messianic meaning. In this passage the good shepherd Zechariah is rejected by Israel's leadership and is paid off with thirty pieces of silver, the price of a slave (Exodus 21:32). This, God tells him, is the price they put on their relationship with God. It is of little value. It is fitting, therefore, that when a price is set to betray God's perfect representative, the true shepherd of the sheep, it is thirty pieces of silver.

For Matthew, the degree to which Yeshua's life parallels the life of Israel and recalls key events recorded in the writings of the prophets is an evidence that He is the Messiah. This is not an argument from prediction-fulfillment. It is rather an argument from coherence based upon seeing the depth of the meaning of His life. Yeshua fulfills (fills up) the meaning of Israel's history.

JESUS FULFILLS THE RELIGIOUS SYSTEM OF ISRAEL

Raymond Brown in his monumental commentary on the Gospel of John[9] devotes an extraordinary amount of his writing to showing how, in John's theology, Jesus fulfills (fills up) the meaning of Israel's principle feasts. Although this is most prominent in John, it is also found throughout the New Testament writings. The book of Hebrews centers on the relationship of Jesus to Yom Kippur (the Day of Atonement) and Sabbath. The writings of Paul reflect his connection to Passover.

First of all, let us look at *Passover*. The New Testament continually presents Passover as a foreshadowing of Jesus. All of the Gospels present Jesus celebrating the Passover with his disciples. Passover was a covenantal meal in which the worshipping family renewed the covenant through making a blood sacrifice and by sharing in a fellowship meal. The memory of the Exodus, and the events leading up to it, were and are prominent in the celebration. Blood sacrifice was in ancient days the means of symbolizing the receiving of life from God and the giving of our lives to God, since the "life of the flesh is in the blood" (Leviticus 17:10). The sacrificial animal served as a substitute in blood covenanting for both the deity and the human party. Knowing that He was to die for our sins, Jesus presented Himself as the Passover lamb substitute through whom we could yield our lives to God and receive His life in return. Hence the elements of the Passover meal take on new explicit meanings; the broken unleavened bread speaks of His broken body; the red wine speaks of His covenantal life-blood (Matthew 26:26–29).

Central to all this is the biblical understanding that the animal sacrifices were only pointing-symbols to the sacrifice of Jesus. This is because to really receive God's life and for humanity to give its life to God requires that the blood covenant sacrificial substitute be genuinely a part of the covenanting partners. Jesus is both connected to God and is genuinely part of humanity so that He can be the "one mediator between God and man" (II Timothy 2:15). With regard to Passover, He became the lamb as well the spiritual food of the believer. He is called the Passover lamb slain from the foundation of the world (Revelation 13:8).

Passover concepts are not only behind His sacrifice as the Passover lamb for our sin, but many other New Testament concepts: that He is the bread from heaven; that He is the means of a new exodus from sin (John 6:33, I Corinthians 10:1–6), this exodus being foreshadowed in the old exodus in which Israel was baptized in type in the Red Sea; had spiritual food and drink (as foreshadowing the Messiah's communion supper); and was led by the Rock of their salvation who is Yeshua (I Corinthians 10:1–6). Scripture also speaks of purging out the leaven of sin (leavened bread being a type of corruption, since it will turn moldy). The feeding of the five thousand is looked at in Passover terms, for in this act the bread from heaven (the Messiah Jesus) gives supernatural bread and fish as God provided bread and quail in the wilderness. Hence, Jesus brings the meaning of Passover to its fullness. In Matthew, Yeshua himself recapitulates the Exodus by going down into Egypt as an infant, being baptized by John (parallel to Israel and the Red Sea), and in being tested in the wilderness forty days, parallel to Israel in the wilderness for forty years.

The Feast of Sukkot (Tabernacles) is also used as a means of showing the fullness of Yeshua. The context of this feast is the background for John 7–9. The lighting of lights in the Temple courts was no doubt the occasion for Yeshua saying, "I am the Light of the World, He that follows me shall not walk in darkness, but shall have the light of life." The Temple lighting ceremony, according to the Talmud (Tractate Sukkot), was one of the most extraordinary ceremonies in beauty. This feast also featured a massive pouring of waters of libation. This is the context of:

> In the last day, the great day of the feast, Jesus stood and
> cried, saying, "If any man thirst, let him come to me and drink,
> He that believeth in me, as the Scripture hath said, out of His
> belly shall flow rivers of living water." (John 7:37,38)

Shavuot (Pentecost) finds its fulfillment in the giving of the Holy Spirit. This was the feast of the early-summer harvest festival. It was also celebrated as the anniversary of the giving of the Law at Sinai. Acts 2 records this as the day in which the believers first received the outpouring of the Spirit promised by Jesus (John 16:7). It is the fulfillment as the early harvest of souls for the Kingdom. It is also a fulfillment because the Spirit was given as the power within by which the Law can be kept (Jeremiah 31:31ff.). Though He was no longer physically present on earth, Jesus brought another feast to fullness of meaning by sending the Spirit.

Most notable of all is the presentation in the book of Hebrews that Jesus is the fulfillment of *Yom Kippur (the Day of Atonement)*. In the amazing central chapters of this book, He is presented as our high priest who alone could go into the most holy presence of God (symbolized on earth by the inner sanctum of the Tabernacle and the Temple). Only the high priest could go into the Most Holy Place in the days of the ancient Temple, and only once a year on Yom Kippur (Leviticus 16). Jesus, however, enters with the blood of atonement from his own self-sacrifice. He is both the high priest and the sacrificial animal, the true meaning of Yom Kippur. He is *both* the Passover lamb and the Yom Kippur sacrifice. The meaning of this Kippur (atonement) includes the inauguration of the New Covenant.

Because the inner sanctum of the Temple most clearly portrayed the separation between God and man and was most clearly depicted in the Yom Kippur ceremony, Matthew records,

> The veil of the Temple was rent in twain, from the top to the
> bottom; and the earth did quake and the rocks rent.

All of this shows that in the Messiah, we may enter into the presence of God. He is the fullness of the meaning of Yom Kippur.

The fulfillment of Israel's religious system includes more than the feasts. The Scripture also present the whole *ritual sacrificial system* as finding fulfillment in the Messiah. This is also a central theme of the Book of Hebrews. The whole concept of the mediating priesthood comes to its fruition in the priestly ministry of Jesus "who ever lives to make intercession for us" (Hebrews 10:12–19, Hebrews 7:25). The book of Hebrews has as its central argument that the temple sacrifice system must be understood as a symbolic representation. It is clear, according to the writer, that the blood of bulls and goats cannot really take away sin (Hebrews 10:4). This is because the sacrifice is only a representation of our life being poured out to God in repentance and total commitment, and of God giving His life to us (Romans 12:1,2). Offering a bull or a goat through a priest is a step removed from the reality of our sharing life with God in its deepest spiritual sense. Ancient blood-covenant ceremonies originally involved both parties sharing their blood in the ceremony. Animals sometimes represented the two covenant partners. However, the sharing of the actual blood of the participants more clearly represented the life-pledge and covenant. The question looms, Can an animal really be offered to God in my stead? Can it really mediate the life of God? No, according to Hebrews; it is only an important pointer. Jesus can, however, be a real substitute because He is part of the human race, which Scripture looks at as one great corporate reality. As a human race, we are all part of one another, either tied together in Adam or in the Messiah. This is a spiritual reality. In Him the human race can give itself up to God totally. He can die for us.

Jesus is also part of God; therefore, in His life being poured out (his blood shed) the life of God is offered to us. Because He is part of God and part of humanity, He can be "the one mediator between God and man" (I Timothy 2:15). All the temple meanings find their fullness in Him: priesthood points to His priesthood; sacrifices point to His sacrifice; ceremonial washing points to His cleansing us from all sin and uncleanness; the most holy place in the temple to His work in God's own presence; incense to His prayers and the prayers of His people.

Lastly, Scripture represents His teaching as bringing Israel's revelation to its fullness. In Matthew 5–7, He shows us that the laws and commandments point to the deeper issues of the heart—to attitudes and intents. "Thou shalt not kill" is dependent on "thou shalt not hate thy brother in thy heart," as the Torah taught. To not commit adultery is fulfilled by faithfulness and not looking at a woman lustfully. As Israel's great teacher, He brings the teaching of Torah to its fullness. The student would do well to study Yeshua's teaching to note His profundity and power. The biblical argument is that there is an amazing coherence to all the aspects of Israel's heritage as finding fullness of meaning in Him, that it reveals Yeshua (Jesus) as the Messiah. This coherence is broad, deep, and so pervasive as to be amazing. Yet the dimensions of fulfillment herein summarized are recounted by many different biblical writers with an artlessness that is truly extraordinary. Truly, He is the one who makes sense of Israel's history and religious system.

The next dimension of fulfillment, however, is most noteworthy for its objective quality. It is the fulfillment of promise and prediction concerning the Messiah.

YESHUA FULFILLS PROMISES AND PREDICTIONS

It must be pointed out that we do not believe that Jesus exhaustively fulfilled all the promises and prophecies concerning the Messiah. This is because Scripture points to *two* comings of the Messiah. Much of Messianic prophecy speaks of the Second Coming. The Scriptures predicted that the Messiah would come as a suffering servant as well as a reigning king. All interpretation must deal with these two aspects of the Messiah's work. Classical Judaism in the Talmudic period (200–500 A.D.) theorized the coming of two Messiahs, one a suffering servant, and the other a reigning king; one called Messiah ben Joseph and the other Messiah ben David. (The Talmud records the rabbinic discussions on the law from this period.) However, this is speculation without historical foundations.[10] I believe that when the Messianic material of the Old Testament is studied, the most coherent fulfillment is to be found in Jesus who comes twice. He is the climax of history.

THE OLD-TESTAMENT MESSIANIC "SEED PROMISE"

We do not propose an exhaustive treatment of all Scripture that may be used in the case for Jesus as fulfilling promise and prediction. Our goal is to trace the development of the Messianic hope in the Old Testament with reference to New Testament fulfillment and to point out the emergent implications. There are certainly passages that are vague until they are seen in the context of New Testament fulfillment. However, the light of the New Testament provides clarity of perspective. Some dimensions of typology not seen as clearly Messianic do manifest implications and a God-ordained predictive value when seen in the light of the whole.[11]

Genesis 3:15 is the beginning of the Messianic hope. This passage initiates what I call the *seed-promise dimension of Messianic prophecy*. The promise comes through the seed, or the descendant(s) of a man or woman. After the fall, when Adam and Eve had partaken of the forbidden fruit in disobedience to God, this first promise was given:

> I will put enmity between you and the woman, between your seed and her seed, he shall bruise your head and you shall bruise his heel.

This verse about the fall has been variously interpreted. Most farfetched was the comparative religionist who saw the passage as a mythological account of why men beat snakes on the head and snakes bite at the heels of people. This interpretation has been largely abandoned. Even students of mythology, who do not accept Genesis as a more literal account, see the passage as a profound attempt to deal with the issue of the origin of evil and the human predicament. Hence, the serpent is the embodiment of evil and the temptation to evil.

Traditional Christian and Jewish interpretation saw the serpent as a manifestation of Satan, that great malevolent spirit who works destruction and evil in the world. Satan spoke to Eve to deceive her into disobedience. Ancient Jewish interpretation identified the seed of the woman who would bruise the head of the serpent as the Messiah to come. The Targum (ancient Jewish Aramaic paraphrases of the Scripture) identify the fulfillment as in the days of the Messiah. Targum Onkelos specifically identifies the seed as one specific son.[12] Most significant is the interpretation of Rabbi David Kimchi:

> As thou wentest forth for the salvation of thy people by the hands of the Meshiach, the Son of David, who shall wound Satan who is the head, the King and Prince of the house of the wicked, and shall raise up (overturn) all his strength, power, policy, and dominion.[13]

Similar interpretation is found in Pesikita Rabbatai 3:6.

Looking specifically at Genesis 3:15 produces some fascinating insights. As traditionally pointed out, the seed of the woman to come is to bruise the head of the serpent, this being a fatal blow. However, the seed of the woman is bruised in the heel, a nonfatal injury. Also, we note that the passage specifically emphasizes the seed of the woman, not the seed of Adam. This is a significant confirmation of the virgin birth of the Messiah (cf. Luke 2; Matthew 2 in interpreting Isaiah 7:14). The virgin birth teaches that the Messiah is born without a human father. In Near Eastern thought the seed of the male was most prominent for several reasons. Patriarchal society understood that one's status was determined by relationship to the father, not the mother. All other seed promises were given to men for their descendants (e.g., Genesis 12:1–3, II Samuel 7). The male was looked at as planting seed into the fertile ground of the womb in which it could grow. The emphasis of the seed of the woman was therefore remarkably unusual. Yet this emphasis makes perfect sense if Jesus is the Messiah. He is truly the physical seed of the woman only. The male chromosome was not received from a human father. It was directly supplied by God. In addition, his crucifixion reveals the bruising of the Messiah by Satan. Yet his triumph through the cross and resurrection has given the death blow to the head of Satan.

The seed promise is a central theme of the book of Genesis. When Cain murdered Abel, a new child was born to Adam and Eve whose name was Seth. Noah was descended from Seth and eventually became, after the flood, the sole father of a future humanity. In Genesis 9:26 Noah states, "Blessed be the Lord God of Shem." Shem evidenced righteous respect toward his father. These passages show a line of blessing through whom the promise of redemption would come, a line that finds a key person in Abraham. In the patriarchal narratives of Genesis, we see the importance of the seed promise as God brings into being the beginnings of the nation that plays a key redemptive role.

Genesis 12:1–3 is the first of a series of seed promise passages addressed to Abraham. These promises are extended and elaborated in Genesis 15 and 17. These passages compose what has been known as the Abrahamic Covenant. Abraham, who is in the line of promise, is told to leave his father's house and to go to a land of God's choice. The promise is given,

> I will . . . make your name a blessing. I will bless those who
> bless you, and him who curses you I will curse, and by you all
> the families of the earth shall bless themselves (in you all the
> families of the earth shall be blessed).

Those familiar with ancient cultures will recognize this as a covenant of strong friendship. In such a covenant both parties to the covenant became bound up with one another so that friends of one are friends of the other, and enemies of one are enemies of the other. This was a blood covenant as indicated by Abraham's blood-based circumcision and God's passing between the sacrificial pieces in Genesis 15. The special promise of this covenant was to make Abraham into a great nation and to give him and his descendants the land of Canaan as their possession forever.

Genesis 15 and 17 further specified this promise. This promise must come through Abraham's wife Sarah, not her maid Hagar. Circumcision is to be the sign of this covenantal relationship between God and Abraham and his seed. This context is significant in understanding Abraham's only child through Sarah, through whom the seed promise was continued. Isaac is to be the child of promise, not Ishmael.

Genesis 22 gives an amazing account of God commanding Abraham to sacrifice Isaac on an altar as a burnt offering. The covenant of strong friendship meant that Abraham could withhold nothing from God. Yet God had stated that the promise was to come through Isaac. This seemed an alarming contradiction, but Abraham obeyed the voice of God which he had come to recognize. Isaac was still a boy and submitted to the will of Abraham. Let us note some salient points about Isaac, who receives the same promise given to Abraham.

1. He is the child of seed promise through whom redemption is to come.
2. He is the only child of Abraham and Sarah.
3. He is offered by his father as a sacrifice.
4. He voluntarily yields himself as a sacrifice.
5. After the act of obedience, Isaac is received back by his father and his life continues.

The parallel to Jesus is amazing. Some have called this a parallel by typological correspondence. Isaac is the grandfather of the twelve tribes of Israel who corporately are recipients of the seed promise. No individual after Jacob receives such a redemptive seed promise until David. Judaism saw this act of obedience as one which contained sufficient merit as to be a basis upon which sin would be forgiven. This is recorded both in the daily and High Holiday prayer services. Abraham is required to believe in the promise of blessing even though the substance of that promise, Isaac, is offered on the altar.

Ancient peoples saw in this concept the idea scholars call "corporate solidarity."[14] A people, its ancestors, and its future descendants were bound up together as one whole reality. Under this concept, significant ancestors parallel the lives of their significant descendants at key points in their lives. When we look at Yeshua we note that He is also the only son of his father—a child of miraculous birth—offered by his father as a sacrifice. Yeshua voluntarily submitted himself, and continued his life after the act of obedience (resurrection). He is the child of promise who does bring blessing to the nations of the world. We see such a strong coherent parallel that Genesis 22 is rightly taken as foreshadowing the Messiah Jesus.

Genesis continues the story concerning the inheritor of the seed promise. Of Isaac's sons, Esau and Jacob, we read, "The elder shall serve the younger" (Gen-

esis 25:23ff.). God's promise will not pass to the older brother, as was cultur-
ally the tradition of inheritance. Jacob is thus blessed by Isaac in words reminiscent of Genesis 12 (Genesis 27:29).

The Messianic hope, the inheritance of the promise, now passes to the group
of twelve children of Jacob, whose name is changed to Israel. For the rest of the
Old Covenant Scriptures we read of this nation and their mission to be a people
of purity, example, and blessing to the world. However, the promise again fo-
cuses on an individual in later Bible passages. This is not to exclude Israel as subject of the promise, but to note the importance of Israel's corporate representative, Israel's king, as the key to the seed promise.

Genesis 49:10 is the first hint of this. In this passage we read of a key representative to come to whom belongs the scepter or symbol of rule. We are told:

> The scepter will not depart from Judah, nor the ruler's staff
> from between his feet, until he comes to whom it belongs and
> the obedience of the nations is his.

Traditional Jewish interpretation has always identified this person as the Messiah
who would be of the tribe of Judah (Targum Onkelos, Targum Jonathan)[15]. In
Hebrew, He to whom it belongs sounds like "Shi-lo-ah," which some rabbis took
as a name of the Messiah, Shiloh (Sanhedrin 98:b). The passage at least is noting
that Judah would be the tribe through whom kingly rulership would come; the
dynasty would always be Judean. This passage probably implies, as ancient Jewish interpretation affirmed, that the Messiah would come from the tribe of
Judah and be Israel's final permanent ruler. The question is well raised as to
whether this ruler is connected to the seed of the woman, promised in Genesis
3:15, who would crush the head of the wicked one. Later prophecy will clarify
this.

Although the Scriptures from Exodus through Deuteronomy point to the
work of the Messiah through feast, tabernacle, priesthood, and sacrifice, as is
especially emphasized in the book of Hebrews, there is only one *direct* reference
to the Messiah in these books (in my view). It is a passage found in a prophecy
on Israel's character and future delivered by the seer Balaam,

> I see him, but not now;
> I behold Him, but not near.
> A star will come out of Jacob;
> a scepter will rise out of Israel.
> He will crush the foreheads of Moab,
> the skulls of all the sons of Sheth.

The star is a king-ruler of Israel. Is this the Messiah? In itself the passage is not clear; it could refer to David. However, ancient Jewish interpretation referred this to the Messiah and the final destruction of evil. This was the reason for Rabbi Akiba and others calling the Jewish Messianic claimant *Bar Kochba* ("son of the star") in the second war against Rome (130s A.D.).[16]

We should note the reference in Deuteronomy 18 to the prophet whom God would raise up. In context, this refers to the office of the prophet in Israel and has application to many prophets. However, the passage was seen well before the ministry of Jesus as a reference to the Messiah who would be a prophet-king.[17] This passage is not one that clearly fits our present purposes of seed-promise exposition.

Seed promises concerning the coming of the Messiah are not again found until the time of King David. In II Samuel 7, God speaks to David through the prophet Nathan. David is herein promised an *everlasting* dynasty. In and of itself, this passage does not speak of one Messiah-king to come, but of a line of kings. However, that the kingly line is everlasting is most significant:

> I will establish the throne of his kingdom forever, . . . your
> house . . . and kingdom shall be made sure forever before me;
> your throne shall be established forever.

It is only later, in the book of Isaiah (9:6,7; cf. Hebrews 9:5) that we find that this promise is to be fulfilled in *one final and ultimate king*. Now that Davidic descent is no longer traceable (cf. genealogies of Jesus in Matthew 1 and Luke 3), how could this promise be fulfilled? If Jesus is the Messiah descended from David, resurrected from the dead and eventually returning, the solution is clear. Also, since the seed promise traced to this point finds fulfillment in Israel, and Israel's life is bound up in her king-representative, the Messiah, it is clear that seed promises concerning the Messiah (David's dynasty of descent) are to be tied together with earlier seed promises. All these seed promises are connected in meaning and fulfillment in the Messiah. It is worth calling attention to the point that there was one time in biblical history when these prophecies were almost nullified (II Kings 11). This was when the wicked Queen Athaliah sought to destroy the whole kingly line and only one child, Joash, was saved by the high priest Jehoiadah. Through his brave action, Joash eventually became king.

THE ISAIAH PORTRAIT

The book of the prophet Isaiah gives a most wonderful portrait of the Messiah to come. The book of Isaiah is grand in its universal import. The development of the portrait of the Messiah begins in Isaiah 7. In this chapter, the prophet Isaiah speaks with King Ahaz, urging him not to fear the alliance of Ephraim (the northern Israel tribes) and Syria, but to place his trust in God. The king is bidden to ask a sign to encourage faith. He refuses with the false pretense that he does not want to test God. Despite his refusal, Isaiah gives a sign to the whole house of David:

> Therefore, the Lord Himself will give you a sign; the virgin will be with child and will give birth to a son and will call him Immanuel (*God with us*).

We then read that before the child reaches the age of personal accountability, the nations Ahaz dreads will be defeated. Despite this word, Ahaz makes an unholy alliance with Assyria (alliances in ancient times involved sharing one another's gods).

Traditional Christian interpretation looked upon this passage as a prediction of the virgin birth of Jesus (as interpreted in Matthew 1 and Luke 2). Several objections have been raised to this. First, it is said that the word *almah* in Hebrew simply means "young woman." Secondly, the sign is for Ahaz. It must be a contemporary child whose growth to the age of accountability will not have occurred before the northern alliance against Israel is crushed.

Some have held that the son of Isaiah 7:14 must be Mahershalalhashbaz, born to Isaiah and his wife in Isaiah 8. His name is interpreted as "quick to the plunder, swift to the spoil" and refers to Assyria's defeat of the northern alliance against Judah. Against this interpretation are two grave objections. The first is that the names Immanuel and Mahershalalhashbaz are of a totally different character and meaning. It would be strange indeed to give the same child two such different names. The second objection is well stated by Sigmund Mowinkel.[18] Mowinkel was not a great friend of traditional interpretation, yet his words on this chapter bare repeating.

> In the situation to which Isaiah VII refers, the continued existence of the Davidic dynasty is at stake. The enemy's plan was to depose Ahaz and make another king in Jerusalem. . . . the inevitable conclusion is that in the Immanuel prophecy . . . the reference is to the wife of King Ahaz, to the queen, . . . yet to find fulfillment, the king had to trust in God.

In other words, the Isaiah 7:14 prophecy is a prophecy of the continuation of the Davidic line, despite the threat to the dynasty from the northern alliance against Judah, and a confirmation of the promises given to the line of David. It concerns the birth of a king whose name demonstrates that "God is with us." This king will be a righteous king over against the wicked, vacillating King Ahaz. Hence Mahershalalhashbaz, Isaiah's son in chapter eight, cannot be the primary subject of the prophecy. Rather this prophecy concerns the anointed (Messiah) king to come; the child of Isaiah 7:14 is to be identified with the everlasting ruler-king whose birth is again spoken of in Isaiah 9:6,7 (Hebrews 9:5).

Mowinkel, however, also wrestles with how a prophecy of the distant future would be relevant to King Ahaz. His conclusion is that the hope of the prophecy is that Hezekiah, the son of King Ahaz, would be the king of Isaiah 9:6,7—a king with whose reign would be a worldwide reign of righteousness. Since he did not fulfill it, the prophecy remained for a future king to fulfill (cf. the opinion of one rabbi recorded in the Talmud and resoundingly rejected by the majority of other rabbis, that the Messiah had already come and was Hezekiah).[19]

This is not an adequate solution. According to the chronology of II Kings, Hezekiah would have already been a young boy at the time this prophecy was delivered. Secondly, a solution is ready at hand which solves all the problems.

First of all, this solution recognizes that Isaiah 7:14 is purposely cryptic in nature. Shouldn't we expect that the book of Isaiah itself would explain the mystery of chapter seven? This is indeed the case. Isaiah chapter eight and nine provide the explanation of Isaiah seven. My view is that two children are involved in Isaiah seven. One is the coming Messianic king, the other is a contemporary of Ahaz, a child who would not reach the age of accountability before the destruction of the northern alliance against Judah. The meaning of the latter part of the Isaiah 7 prophecy concerning the child's knowing how to refuse evil and choose good is explained in Isaiah eight. In Isaiah eight a child is born to Isaiah and is given a name which predicts the destruction of the northern alliance. In verse 4, we learn that all this occurs before the boy knows the difference between right and wrong. It is further emphasized in the words "Before the boy knows how to say my father and my mother" (Isaiah 8:4).

In Isaiah 9, the promise of the continuation of the Davidic dynasty fulfilled in the final Messianic king is given as the exposition of the first part of the Isaiah seven prophecy, specifically verse fourteen. Isaiah seven through nine therefore knows of only two children, Mahershalalhashbaz and the coming, final Messiah-king. This is born out by these salient facts:

1. The name of the child, *Immanuel* ("God with us"), is of the same quality or character as the names given to the child in Isaiah 9:6,7: "Wonderful, Counselor, Mighty God, Everlasting Father, Prince of Peace." These names do

not fit with Mahershalalhashbaz. Isaiah 7:14 fits naturally together with Isaiah 9:6,7 as parallel prophecies.

2. The issue in Isaiah 7 is the survival of the Davidic dynasty; the future Messianic king is the ultimate answer.

3. Isaiah 7:14 does predict a virgin birth, as also described in Matthew 1 and Luke 2. There are several reasons for this conclusion:

a. The word *almah*, although also meaning "maiden," in every biblical use meant "an unmarried maiden presumed to be a virgin." The so-called word for virgin, *betulah*, was used of a married woman with children in at least one case (Joel 1:8).

b. The Septuagint translation of the Hebrew Scriptures into Greek, done over a century before the New Testament period, translated *almah* as *parthenos*. There is basic agreement among experts that *parthenos* means "virgin."

c. This passage is also connected to the seed-promise passages of the Bible. The first of these passages unusually predicts that it is the seed of the woman, not the seed of the man, who would crush the head of the evil one.

d. Matthew and Luke did not write in a vacuum, but must have interpreted Isaiah 7:14 in a way that many Jewish people at the time would have considered likely.

Furthermore the actual testimony to the virgin birth in the New Testament gives credibility to this interpretation of Isaiah 7:14. This fits Mowinkel's idea that the passage implies a *supernatural* sign. We therefore are on solid ground in holding that Isaiah 7:14 is a continuation of the seed-promise theme of Scripture, is a prophecy of the future Messiah-king, and is a prediction of a supernatural virgin birth. We shall also see that Isaiah's development of the Messianic hope further establishes this view.

Isaiah 9:6,7 (Hebrews 9:5) is the first crystal-clear prophecy of the fact that one individual would fulfill the word given to David that he would be the father of an everlasting dynasty. Of this king to come we read:

> Of the increase of his government there will be no end. He will reign on David's throne and over his kingdom establishing and upholding it with justice and righteousness from that time on and forever. The zeal of the Lord Almighty will accomplish this.

One individual will have an everlasting reign. More remarkable are the names or titles given to the king:

> For to us a child is born, to us a son is given and the government will be upon his shoulders, and he will be called Wonderful Counselor, Mighty God, Everlasting Father, Prince of Peace.

These titles have been a source of great controversy. Although Hebrew children were given names that included the name of God, there is no child that was ever given, *directly*, such names as these. These names are clearly descriptions of God. This passage is a mystery which is not resolved until we turn to the New Testament Scriptures which reveal the Messiah as carrying a divine nature from God. The Messiah is conceived without a human father. Attempts to interpret the passage by adding interpretive words and phrases to the translation (such as in the New English Bible) are speculative. The New International Version translation is a more literal rendering of the Hebrew itself.

The Isaiah 9:6,7 passage predicts a Messiah who would bring the age of worldwide peace. This age of peace has not dawned upon earth. This is one of the key stumbling blocks to Jewish people in accepting Jesus as the Messiah. Followers of Jesus argue that He will yet fulfill the prophecy of universal rule and peace. As we will find, Isaiah says much more, giving weight to this viewpoint.

Isaiah 11:1–16 (especially vv. 1–3,10) calls the Messiah a shoot from the stump of Jesse (David's father) and, in verse 10, the root of Jesse. We read of the extraordinary anointing upon Him which gives Him ability to make supernaturally correct judgments (vv. 3,4). He will bring judgment to earth (v. 4), and will bring an age of peace and harmony to humanity and nature (vv. 6–9). Amazing new content predicts that the Messiah will be followed by peoples other than Israel, for He is a "banner for the peoples" and the nations (Gentiles) will "rally to Him." The passage goes on to predict a great second exodus of the Jewish people from all over the world. This, I believe, is still partially future. The new Messianic content here, consistent with the Genesis 12:3 promise that Abraham's seed would bring blessing to the world, is the promise of deliverance and salvation for Gentile peoples through the Messiah. This is a key to interpreting passages concerning the Messiah in Isaiah 40–66.

📖

CHAPTER 10: STUDY QUESTIONS

1. Explain how the New Testament concept of prophecy-fulfillment is broader than is generally understood.

2. How does Jesus fulfill the history of Israel and its religious system?

3. Explain what we mean by seed prophecies in the Hebrew Scriptures.

4. Why is it reasonable to hold that the prophecy of Isaiah 7:14 points to Jesus?

EVIDENCES FROM MESSIANIC
PROPHECY, II

THE SUFFERING SERVANT
AND HIS LIFE ON EARTH

THE SERVANT OF THE LORD PASSAGES of the second part of Isaiah's prophecy are keys to all Messianic prophecy. Bible scholars are unified in identifying four key literary units in these chapters of Isaiah as unique *servant songs*.
These passages are Isaiah 42:1–7; 49:1–7; 50:1–11 and 52:13–53:12. Ancient
Jewish interpretation as well as elements within these passages show that the
primary figure represented in these passages is the Messiah. The Targum, the
ancient Jewish paraphrases of the Scriptures (first century), explicitly add the
words "the Messiah" after "my servant" in both chapter 42 and 52:13–53:12.
Secondly the Talmud, in Sanhedrin 98b, identifies the suffering servant as the
Messiah. Is it possible that the Messiah's suffering and death precede the fulfillment of the age of peace the Messiah brings? These passages do indicate this.
However, even more important than these ancient Jewish identifications is the
internal evidence of the passages. Jewish interpretation since the time of Rashi
in the late Middle Ages has sought to identify the suffering servant as Israel. As
Israel is bound up with her Messiah-king, surely she is involved in suffering servanthood, but the primary referent in these chapters is none other than the Messiah-king of Isaiah 7:14 and Isaiah 9:6,7.

The first song in Isaiah 42:1–9 speaks of the servant as God's chosen one who
has God's Spirit upon Him and brings justice to the nations. Verse 4 notes that
He establishes justice over all the earth and that the islands will put their hope in

Him. Furthermore verse 6 declares Him to be a covenant to the peoples and a light to the Gentiles. The parallels to Isaiah 11 and its portrayal of the root of Jesse are unmistakable. It is the same person and the same promise. It is looking toward the universal rule of the Messiah described in Isaiah 9:6,7. In his personal dimension, the Messiah is described as quiet and confident (v. 2), and amazingly gentle to those in weakness: "A bruised reed He will not break / and a smoldering wick He will not snuff out." Each song adds to the portrait of the servant.

Isaiah 49 is the second and very significant song. It portrays the plan of God in the Messiah's birth. He is concealed in the quiver of God before His birth (v. 2). It then addresses the Messiah as "my servant Israel," but this is Israel's corporate representative, not Israel as a nation, for it says of Him, "He who formed me in the womb to be his servant, *to bring Jacob back to Him* and gather Israel to Himself." The name "Israel" connotes his representative connection to the nation. He is the spiritual head of Israel as Jacob, called Israel, was the physical father of the nation.

It looks as though the labor of the Messiah is in vain (v. 4). This reference fits Jesus at the end of his pre-resurrected life, forsaken by his disciples, and ending in the ignoble death on the cross. Yet "his reward is with my God." It is not hopeless—he will succeed. Again it is predicted that He will yet restore the tribes of Jacob, be a light to the Gentiles, and bring God's salvation to the ends of the earth (v. 6). This connects the servant with the Messiah's mission in Isaiah 9 and 11. The last part of the chapter adds a significant new piece of information, "He is despised and abhorred by the nation," yet "kings will see you and rise up, princes will see and bow down." Though at first rejected by Israel, He is honored by Kings and will restore Jacob to God. Does not this wonderfully fit the Messiah Jesus?

The third song, Isaiah 50:1–11, continues the description of the true servant of the Lord. The song begins with a description of Israel's sin. Verse four describes a man with a tongue instructed of God with a word sustaining the weary. Then follows the most explicit description to this point in Isaiah's material. So submitted is the Messiah to the will of God that He yields his back to those who beat Him, His cheeks to those who pulled out His beard; He does not hide his face from mocking and spitting (v. 6). The description perfectly fits the Messiah Jesus. Yet the servant's vindication is near; none can substantiate charges against Him (v. 8). Those who fear the Lord obey the word of his servant (v. 10).

The most detailed description of the servant's suffering and vindication is found in Isaiah 52:13–53, the climax and the fourth song. This chapter finally describes the extent of the Messiah's suffering, the reason for it, and His subsequent vindication. Rashi was noted for identifying the servant of this passage with Israel. However, more ancient Jewish interpretation identified the person as the Messiah. The Talmud in Sanhedrin 98:b identifies the person as the Messiah by answering the question, What is the Messiah's name? This answer is given by quoting Isaiah 53:4, wherein it is stated that the Messiah bore our sickness and carried our diseases. It then refers to Him as the "leper Messiah." The first- and second-century Aramaic Targum inserts "Messiah" into the passage, stating, "See, my servant the Messiah" (52:13).

Certainly the figure in this passage is the same as the one in the other servant songs. This parallels the material in Isaiah 9:6,7 and Isaiah 11. Despite the influence of Rashi's new interpretation in the twelfth century, Rabbinic references are not lacking which identify the servant with the Messiah, even to the point of noting that the Messiah suffers for our sins that we might not suffer for them ourselves.[1]

The servant is described as disfigured in verse 14—as not attractive to the people through external appearance (v. 2)—and as "despised and rejected of men, a man of sorrow and familiar with suffering." This rejection comes not only from men in general, but the Messiah is also rejected by Israel, for the prophet states, "we esteemed Him not." The servant of Isaiah 53 suffers for Israel, and thus cannot merely be Israel. Indeed, if one asserts Israel into the passage for the "He" of the Servant and reads Isaiah 53 accordingly, it is incoherent. The description then notes that He bore our sicknesses and sins (v. 4) though we considered Him stricken by God. However, "He was pierced for our transgressions, the punishment that brought us peace was upon him, and by his wounds we were healed." Verse 6 notes that our iniquity was laid on Him.

Verse 7 describes Him a lamb to be sacrificed and verse 8 notes that He is falsely judged in oppression. Such description fits the Gospel accounts of the trial and sentencing of Jesus. In verse 9 we read that He meets His death with the wicked, and with the rich in His death, "though He had done no violence, nor was any deceit in His mouth." These references remarkably parallel the fact that Jesus died between two criminals, but in His death was with the wealthy Joseph of Arimathea, who took Him down from the cross and buried Him in His tomb (Matthew 27:38, 27:57ff.; Mark 15:27,42; Luke 23:32–43, 23:50–56). Verse 10 clearly notes that His life was a guilt offering. Yet in this verse, there is an amazing transition: the one who died as an offering will be again alive:

> He will see his offspring and prolong His days, and the will of
> the Lord will prosper in His hand. After the suffering of His
> soul, He will see the light of life and be satisfied.

The suffering servant of Isaiah 52:13–53:12 perfectly fits Jesus of Nazareth and
no other figure in history. The servant of the servant songs from Isaiah 40–66 is
identified with the Messiah of Isaiah 9 and 11.

Other interpretations simply are not supported by the evidence. Israel cannot be the subject of these passages, for the servant brings Israel back to God,
and we (Israel) rejected Him. It cannot be a righteous remnant within Israel,
since the passages give no indication of this. Furthermore, the descriptions fit an
individual, not a corporate national entity described as an individual. He is buried with the wicked and with a rich man in His death. Yes, Israel as a nation also
plays a representative role among the nations, but the figure here is Israel's representative King. Yes there are parallels to His life and Israel's, but the figure
here is more than the nation. It cannot be that the passage describes the prophet unless we want to hold that the prophet was the source of kings being astonished and of being the light of God to the Gentiles.

All of the other interpretations provide a viewpoint that simply does not fit
all the features of the passage or they deny that any specific fulfillment can be
found. The denial of the view that the fulfillment of this passage is found in
Jesus seems to be a case of special pleading from those who wish to deny the
most obvious and clear interpretation and fulfillment.

Everyone who interprets Scripture should face the evidence that a Messiah is
presented who suffers even unto death, but who also rules victoriously over the
whole world. How can these two dimensions be squared?

Early Jewish interpretation came up with the novel idea of two Messiahs, one
who would suffer and die, called in the Talmud and Midrashim (early Jewish
commentaries) Messiah ben ("son of") Joseph. The other Messiah who would
rule is designated Messiah ben David. Yet there is no warrant for these interpretations. The Scriptural evidence indicates that both the suffering and reigning
are aspects of one person's work. Raphael Pattai notes that the two Messiah
concepts are constructs which are sometimes laid out in a way as to belie the
underlying sense of the early rabbis that the two figures were really one.[2] The
New Testament interpretation of one Messiah who comes twice is a coherent
means of tying together the data of Messianic prophecy.

OTHER PREDICTIVE TEXTS
POINTING TO JESUS

Other significant texts lend further evidence to the identification of the seed promises of the Messiah as being fulfilled in Jesus. The Psalms contain numerous significant references, of which a few shall be dealt with here. Many Psalms are ascribed to King David. At various times David writes in a way that does not fit his own life, but does fit the life of his greater son, the Messiah-king. As stated before, the ancient concept of corporate solidarity gave rise to the common concept of an ancestor's life paralleling the life of his later descendant. This is certainly true in that the Messiah is the greatest king over Israel, whereas David as king was second only to the Messiah.

Parallels and prophecy that go beyond the life of David are to be noted in Psalm 22, wherein the trials of David became the occasion for David's vision of a suffering that does not fit his own life, but does fit that of the Messiah Jesus. Jesus quoted Psalm 22:1 on the cross indicating that He saw His life in the psalm (Matthew 27:46). Numerous references in the Gospels show that the apostolic writers considered the psalm as a prophecy of the Messiah. Salient features of the psalm parallel Isaiah 53. In verses 6–8, the person of the psalm is scorned, despised, and mocked. Insults are hurled at Him and heads wag (Matthew 27:3–9, 41–44). Even the words of Matthew 8:44 are parallel to verse 8 of the psalm. As do other passages about the Messiah, verses 9–11 describe His trust in God from childhood and God's plan for Him from before birth. Verses 14 and 15 vividly parallel the experience of crucifixion (though written centuries before crucifixion):

> I am poured out like water, and all my bones are out of joint.
> My heart has turned to wax, it has melted away within me.
> My strength is dried up like a potsherd, and my tongue sticks
> to the roof of my mouth; you lay me in the dust of death.
> Dogs have surrounded me, a band of evil men have encircled
> me, they have pierced my hands and my feet; I can count all
> my bones.

Controversy surrounds the phrase "pierced my hands and feet." This would be such an extraordinary prediction that some have sought to blunt its force by maintaining that the Hebrew does not mean pierced, but "like a lion [at] my hands and feet" (the bracketed word supplied). Of this other possible reading it must be said:

1. Although possible through a variant vowel pointing (substituting vowels for the ones traditionally passed down), it is an awkward reading to say the least. (Ancient Hebrew was largely written without vowels.)

2. The Hebrew does lend itself to be pointed so that it means "pierced."

3. The Septuagint translation, well before the time of the New Testament, translated the phrase "pierced my hands and feet."

4. Zechariah uses the same word, which is translated by all: "they shall look upon me [him] whom they have pierced" (12:10).

Therefore the weight of the evidence is toward "pierced my hands and my feet."

Verse 18 of Psalm 22 recounts the dividing of his garments by casting lots (Mark 15:24, Matthew 27:35). Yet what is a seeming end in death ends in victory, for God vindicates His suffering afflicted one. Indeed, the suffering and victory are a basis for the earth to remember and to turn to God. The Messianic prediction of all nations bowing before God is found in Isaiah 11 and the early servant songs of Isaiah. The parallels to Messiah Jesus are pointedly obvious.

Psalm 16:11 is also quoted in the New Testament as pointing to the Messiah. Acts 2:25–28 quotes, "because you will not abandon me to the grave, nor will you let your Holy One see decay." The fact that David died and was entombed is used by Peter to show that David spoke not of himself, but as a prophet of his greater son, Messiah Jesus.

Psalm 2:7,8 states:

> I will proclaim the decree of the Lord: He said to me, "You are my Son; today I have become your Father. Ask of me, and I will give you the nations for your inheritance, the ends of the earth your possession."

Verse 12 states,

> Kiss the Son, lest He be angry and you be destroyed in your way, for his wrath can flare up in a moment. Blessed are all who take refuge in Him.

Hebrews 1:5ff. significantly uses this and other Messianic psalms to show the high position of the Messiah. This psalm is certainly Messianic and points in verse 8 to the eventual worldwide rule of the Messiah, as in Isaiah 9:6,7. Also significant is the language: "Today I have become your Father" or begotten you (more literally). The Messiah is uniquely designated the Son of God to be given special homage, in a higher sense than other kings of Israel or the nation of Israel (also designated a son).

Psalm 110:1 is of a similar quality. Quoted in the Gospels (Matthew 23:41–

46, Mark 12:35–37) by Jesus, it is used to show the strange mystery that David called his "son" his Lord. Unless this son was of a higher special nature or function, how could David call the Messiah his Lord? "The Lord says to my Lord, 'Sit at my right hand until I make your enemies a footstool for your feet.' " This is given in a Messianic context predicting the universal victory of Israel's ultimate Messiah-king.

These are not the only passages in the Psalms that foreshadow and fit New Testament concepts of the Messiah Jesus. Yet these are the clearest and most significant.

Other worthwhile references to study for Messianic content are Psalm 45:6,7 (Hebrews 1:8,9), Psalm 110:4 on the fact that the Messiah-king is a priest like Melchizedek (not descended from Aaron but superior to Aaron, as argued in Hebrews 6:6 and 7:1–22), and Psalm 40:6–8 concerning the Messiah's perfection of obedience to God's will.[3]

In comparing these and other New Testament references to the Old Testament, the student should be aware that the New Testament often quotes what at that time was the authoritative Jewish translation into Greek, the Septuagint. This was written about 150–200 years before the time of Jesus. There is a basic content of agreement between the Septuagint and the authoritative Jewish text from the Middle Ages, the Masoretic text. Most biblical scholars believe that the different text traditions need to be compared to approach what was the original text. The student should not be put off by traditional Jewish arguments against the accuracy of New Testament quotes of the Old as though it was twisting the text for its interpretation. Since the New Testament writers wrote in Greek for the sake of worldwide distribution, they would naturally quote what was already considered the authoritative Greek translation of the Old Testament in first century Jewry.

Deuteronomy 18:14–22 gave directions to Israel concerning true and false prophets. The passage calls upon Israel to test the prophetic Word (also Deuteronomy 13) and to follow the words of the true prophet. Yet Jewish interpretation at the time of Jesus also saw this passage as pointing to the ultimate true prophet like Moses who would be the Messiah-king:[4]

> I will raise up for them a prophet like you from among their brothers; I will put my words in his mouth, and he will tell them everything I command him. If anyone does not listen to my words that the prophet speaks in my name, I myself will call him to account.

These two verses were seen as not speaking of prophets in general (as verses 20–22) but in saying, "like Moses," it was taken to imply one who would, as Moses, combine civil and prophetic offices together. Moses was Israel's ultimate civil ruler and priest (before he anointed Aaron) and the head prophet as well. In these regards, Yeshua is like Moses.

Zechariah 9:9,10 is a prophecy concerning the universal rule of the Messiah, who is pictured as coming in a lowly way (gentle) and riding upon a donkey. This passage intrigued rabbinical scholars who wondered at the humble nature of the Messiah's coming. One rabbi taught that if Israel is righteous, the Messiah would come in power and glory on the clouds, while if Israel is not righteous, the Messiah would come in the lowly manner of Zechariah 9:9. Jesus specifically rode into Jerusalem to fulfill Zechariah 9:9 (Mark 11:1–11, Talmud Sanhedrin 99).[5]

Micah 5:2 states that the Messiah would be born in Bethlehem, but also indicates that the Messiah's existence antedates his birth: "But you, Bethlehem Ephrathah, though you are small among the clans of Judah, out of you will come for me one who is to be ruler over Israel." The ancient Jewish Greek translation, the Septuagint, translates, "whose goings forth were from the beginning, even from eternity." At the time of Jesus, this passage was taken to apply to the Messiah's literal birth in Bethlehem as reflected in the account of Herod and the three wise men (cf. Matthew 2:1–8; Luke 2:1–7). According to the Gospel's testimony, Jesus was so born. However, the hint that the Messiah is more than mere man and had an origin and existence before his birth is also parallel to New Testament teaching. This teaching connects Jesus with the Angel of God (Malaak Yahweh) figure in the Old Testament who is both called by the holy name of God (YHWH) and distinguished from God (Genesis 18; Exodus 3; Exodus 33:2, 14; Genesis 32:22–32; Exodus 20–24; Judges 13:1–14; Judges 2:1–3). It is not unlikely that Micah 5:2 was the source of the Rabbinical inclusion of the Messiah in the list of those things that pre-existed the creation: Torah, Wisdom, and the Messiah, etc. (Talmud Pes. 54a, Ned. 39a).

PASSAGES FROM DANIEL

The last passages we note are from the book of Daniel, which presents several visions that range over the whole of history. Daniel 2 and 7 present the succession of world empires unto the coming of the Messiah. Daniel 7 presents the Messiah as coming on the clouds of heaven and given the universal, everlasting dominion of Isaiah 9:6,7. Yeshua referred to this passage to indicate his second coming (Matthew 24:30, 26:64). Most impressive of all is Daniel's prophecy of seventy weeks (or sevens) Daniel 9:20–27. The prophecy is interpreted by Jews and Christians of varying persuasions to be speaking of weeks of years, seventy sevens equaling 490 years.[6] These seventy sevens are decreed as a time period during which transgression will be finished, an end will be put to sin, wickedness will be atoned for, and everlasting righteousness will be brought into being. Vision and prophecy are sealed up and the most holy is anointed (v. 24). Then follows greater detail concerning the process of events. First comes a period of seven sevens (49 years) and then 62 sevens (434 years). The first period will see the rebuilding of Jerusalem through troubled times. This occurred after the Babylonian captivity during the times of Ezra, Nehemiah, and Zerubbabel. Four hundred thirty-four years after this period, the anointed one (in Hebrew: Messiah) will be cut off and have nothing (or: not for Himself).

Extraordinarily, Daniel predicts that the destruction of the Second Temple, which was not yet built, would occur after this time.

Students have sought for an answer to the question of what decree was in mind. If the decree is one from a historical king (not the decree of God), the most likely one was that of Artaxerxes to the Jewish people in 445 B.C.[7]

When we add 445 years to the 483 years of the prophecy of 69 weeks, we come out to the year 38 C.E. Further calculation for lunar-solar and other calendar changes bring us to the time of the crucifixion of Jesus. Not only is there a prediction that the Messiah would die before the end of the Second Temple as an atonement, but the very time frame of his death is predicted.

This prophecy is so remarkable that anti-supernaturalists have sought various means to explain it away. Liberal humanism holds that the book of Daniel did not really come from Daniel, as Jewish tradition claimed, but was a pious fraud written to encourage Israel during the battle for freedom under the Maccabees (165 B.C.). In this view, the anointed one cut off was the high priest Onias III. Major problems exist in this interpretation.

1. Late-dating of the book of Daniel is against tradition and evidence, and mostly arises due to anti-supernatural bias.[8]

2. The temple and the city were never destroyed during this period but were destroyed after the death of Jesus, when Titus and his Roman legions set fire to the city and the temple (70 C.E.).

3. The calculation of weeks of years would be mistaken by over 190 years if the liberal interpretation is granted. This is not the case if the prophecy con-

cerns Jesus. Some of those who hold to the Onias III reference have amazingly put forth the view that the writer made a major mathematical miscalculation.

4. The prophecy has to be taken as being a sequence in which the events produce an atonement for sin and finish transgression. This does not fit Onias III, but perfectly fits Jesus. Verses 25–27 expand the meaning of verse 24. Hebrew parallelism repeats the same content in new and different ways.

Verse 27 would, under this interpretation, refer to the Messiah, who confirmed a covenant with Israel and made the Mosaic sacrificial system superfluous.[9] This is borne out by the Titus destruction of the temple. After these events Jerusalem and the temple were desolate for the decreed period. This remarkable prophecy finds fulfillment in Jesus.

A few other prophecies concerning the Second Temple period corroborate our basic interpretation of the Daniel passage.

Haggai chapter 2 gives a significant prediction that the Second Temple would be greater in glory than the first (cf. verses 2–9). This is repeated several times in the chapter. The question needs to be asked, what made the glory of the latter Temple greater than the Temple during the days of Solomon? Only one event can be identified as the fulfillment of this prophecy. This is the visit of Yeshua to the Temple and his teaching ministry there. The Second Temple period was a period of foreign domination over Israel. It was a period without the Ark, the Tablets, Urim and Thumin (lots, used to supernaturally determine the will of God), and, during the latter period, even lacking the right descendant of Aaron to serve as high priest.

Zechariah chapters 3 and 6 give more significant information. The Haggai chapter gives this word to Zerubbabel and Joshua, the Davidic ruler and the Aaronic priest respectively. However, in Zechariah, a unique prophecy is given to Joshua who is clothed with clean garments after appearing in dirty garments in a vision. He is told that he would judge the house of God (3:7) and that God would bring forth his servant the Branch (a term for the Messiah from David's house). Chapter 6 describes a vision wherein Joshua is addressed in these terms, "Behold, the Man whose name is Branch" (v. 12). Though he is a priest, not of the kingly line, we are told, "He shall sit and rule on his throne; so He shall be a priest on his throne." He is also given a kingly crown to wear (vv. 11, 14).

What is happening here? We know that Joshua never ruled as a king nor did he fulfill the full dimensions of this passage. It is clear that Zerubbabel is a foreshadowing figure of the Messiah. Yet because the Messiah is a king-priest figure, Joshua can symbolically represent him in prophecy. The Messiah will combine in his person the Aaronic functions of priest and the Davidic functions of king. Surely, it is the branch, the Messiah, that gives the Second Temple its fullest significance. Indeed, the name of this priest, Joshua, is, in Hebrew, the same as the name of Jesus in the original Hebrew (Yeshua).

Having examined prophecies concerning the Messiah of a predictive nature, and having traced the seed-promise concept from Genesis 3:15, I conclude that Jesus is the supernatural fulfillment of these prophecies. This is certainly reasonable.

We understand the fact that some prophecies were intentionally fulfilled by Jesus. They are still significant although the extent of the supernatural quality of the fulfillment for apologetic purposes is lessened. Many of the prophecies we have discussed, including His death and resurrection, are not capable of such self-fulfillment. Supernatural agency is required.

It is possible to avoid the conclusion of our argument. However, it is difficult to do so if one is seeking in an open minded way to fulfill the criteria of truth: consistency, coherence, and comprehensiveness to all the evidence. The conclusion that Jesus is the Messiah coherently ties together all of the prophetic Messianic predictive material.

📖

CHAPTER 11: STUDY QUESTIONS

1. Why is it reasonable to believe that the suffering servant of Isaiah 40-66 is primarily prophetic of Jesus?

2. How is it possible to see Psalm 22 as pointing to Jesus?

3. What is the evidence that Jesus is the Messiah from Daniel 9?

4. How do the prophecies of Zechariah connected to Joshua and Zerubbabel point to Jesus?

LATTER-DAY PROPHECIES

THE BIBLICAL PROPHETIC WORD has reference even to our day. Attempts to use latter-day prophecy in Scripture to write *detailed history* in advance are unconvincing to one that knows the many possibilities of interpretation. There are many scenarios that contradict each other. However, the broad general outline of history and of the latter days given in Scripture are amazing, to say the least.

It is important to note those misguided circles where detailed futuristic schemes take on the weight of an almost premier apologetic argument. When some supposed predictions are looked at in context, the supposed prophetic fulfillment becomes suspect. Many have stated that the Bible predicted the airplane because of its statement that the Jewish people would return to Israel on eagles' wings. However, in Exodus, Moses notes that God *brought* Israel forth from Egypt on eagles' wings. Did the ancient Israelites ride on airplanes without our knowledge? The interpreter has overlooked the fact that "eagles' wings" was a common idiom of the ancient Near East simply meaning "swiftly."

Some writers of prophecy tend to assume that passages are speaking of future events because they do not have knowledge of the historical fulfillment in the past. Sometimes this is assumed because the Hebrew prophet used highly symbolic language to bring out the intense spiritual significance of the event. This language is taken as literal and hence as unfulfilled in history. Such language as stars falling to earth, the moon turning to blood, and more would be strange in literal fulfillment. One star falling to earth would fully end earthly existence.

Yet having spoken these cautions, it is my conviction that there are broad dimensions of the prophetic word which are being fulfilled or appear to be of future fulfillment which do have apologetic value in establishing the supernatural quality of the Bible. We will only look at those passages which have a low probability of having been fulfilled in the past.

It is said that Frederick the Great asked for proof of the truth of the Bible. He was given the response, "the Jew." In other words, the Jewish people were the single greatest living proof of God's faithfulness and existence. Much of latter-day prophecy with apologetic value is connected to the Jewish people. Here are then some amazing prophecies connected to the history of Israel and the nations.

THE COURSE OF JEWISH HISTORY
IN VARIOUS LANDS

The dispersion and suffering of the Jewish nation throughout history is graphically described in Leviticus 26 and Deuteronomy 28. Yet the Scriptures promised that God would never make an end of the Jewish people, but that they would be preserved throughout history as a distinct nation despite having lost control of their national homeland: "Yet in spite of this, when they are in the land of their enemies, I will not reject them or abhor them so as to destroy them completely, breaking my covenant with them. I am the Lord their God. But for their sake, I will remember the covenant with their ancestors whom I brought out of Egypt in the sight of the nations to be their God. I am the LORD" (Leviticus 26:44).

The continued existence of the Jewish nation in dispersion is a most amazing fact of history. Yet this is no less amazing than the description of the dispersion throughout significant periods of Jewish history.

> As for those of you who are left, I will make their hearts so fearful in the lands of their enemies that the sound of a wind-blown leaf will put them to flight. They will run as though fleeing from the sword, and they will fall even though no one is pursuing them. So you will not be able to stand before your enemies. You will perish among the nations; the land of your enemies will devour you. (Leviticus 26)

In Deuteronomy 28 we read:

> The Lord will scatter you among all nations, from one end of the earth to the other . . . among those nations you will find no repose, no resting place for the sole of your foot. There the Lord will give you an anxious mind, eyes weary with longing, and a despairing heart.

THE COURSE OF WORLD EMPIRES
IN DANIEL

Daniel 2 and Daniel 7 describe the course of world empires. The image of the large statue in Daniel 2 represents the course of kingdoms from the sixth to the first centuries. The head of gold represents the Babylonian kingdom (vv. 36–38). The silver chest represents the empire of Medo-Persia; the thighs and belly of bronze, the Greek period; and the legs of iron, the Roman Empire. It is of note that Daniel sees four main kingdoms before the disintegration of the Roman Empire. Its description of the iron kingdom fits Rome.

> Finally there will be a fourth kingdom, strong as iron, for iron
> breaks and smashes everything, and, as iron breaks things to
> pieces, so it will crush and break all others.[1]

Daniel 7 gives further description to these four kingdoms as symbolized by four beasts. Some have seen the fact that this passage predicts that no long-lasting world empire will exist after the Roman empire. The ten toes of Daniel two and the ten horns of Daniel 7 probably represent a latter-day confederacy out of which will arise the anti-Messiah. He makes war on the saints (vv. 21, 25). The defeat of this figure in Daniel 7 ushers in the Messianic kingdom under the rule of God's anointed king (Daniel 7:13, 14, 26, 27). The book of Revelation and other New Testament material refer to the Anti-Christ as the personage who opposes God's people. He is finally defeated at the Messiah's coming (II Thessalonians 2:1, Revelation 19:1–21).

THE RETURN OF THE JEWISH PEOPLE
TO ISRAEL

Not only does the Bible predict the scattering of the Jewish people, but also their return to their land in the latter days. These prophecies are still in process of fulfillment. In general, Jewish people are pictured as in their land before the Messiah comes. There is also a great return after they receive the Messiah as their king.

In Isaiah 11:11 we read of a *second* regathering of the Jewish people from the nations of the world.

> In that day the Lord will reach out his hand a second time to
> reclaim the remnant that is left of his people from Assyria,
> from Lower Egypt, from Cush, from Elam, from Babylonia,
> from Hamath, and from the islands of the sea (the farthest
> corners of the earth to which they had been scattered).

The first regathering took place after the Babylonian captivity of Israel (586–
516 B.C.). This regathering was not a worldwide regathering, but primarily a
gathering from Babylonia. It only encompassed a small minority of the people.
The second latter-day regathering is much greater in scope. Jeremiah 16:14,15
notes:

> However the days are coming, declares the Lord, when men
> will no longer say, "As surely as the Lord lives who brought the
> Israelites up out of Egypt," but will say, "As surely as the Lord
> lives, who brought the Israelites up out of the land of the
> north and out of all the countries where He had banished
> them."

This prophecy is repeated in Jeremiah 23:5–8. In this latter passage, it is connected to the coming of David's righteous branch, the Messiah, and will cause
the nation to dwell in safety (v. 6).

It is of importance to note that the land of the north is especially emphasized.
In ancient times this could have referred to the area of Syria and Assyria or *to the
area north of this.* This prophecy is being fulfilled as these words are being written. Directly north of Israel, two to three million Jews have lived in captivity in
the Soviet Union. Many sensitive believers all over northern Europe expected a
great exodus of Jewry from the Soviet Union, an exodus secured by God's
supernatural intervention.[2] Thousands now are coming to Israel weekly.

Some have argued that today's regathering of the Jewish people is not prophetic fulfillment, since the Jewish people must first repent and receive Jesus as
the Messiah. Several responses can be given to this. First of all, just as all
prophecy concerning Jesus was not fulfilled all at once, nor was the turning of
the Gentiles to Jesus an all-at-once affair, should we not expect a partial
fulfillment leading up to the final fulfillment? Secondly, this is corroborated by
the amazing, yet future, prediction which pictures a Jewish people in the land of
Israel turning to the Messiah in repentance.

> And I will pour out upon the house of David and *the inhabi-*
> *tants of Jerusalem,* a spirit of grace and supplication. They will
> look upon me whom they have pierced, and they will mourn

for him as one mourns for an only child, and they shall grieve
bitterly for him as one who grieves for a firstborn son. (Zechariah 12:10)

The passage then goes on to describe massive weeping and repentance throughout the land and the opening of a fountain to cleanse them from sin and im-
purity (Zechariah 13:1).

Jesus said that not only Israel would mourn at his return, but that all of the
tribes of the earth would mourn (Matthew 24:30). How amazing are these passages. The Jewish people, not before having recognized their Messiah, mourn,
but the Gentiles who have shown their rejection by war, hate, and anti-Semitism
mourn as well. All of this assumes a large Jewish presence in the land of Israel
before the return of Jesus.

In Luke 21, Jesus predicts the destruction of Jerusalem by Roman armies and
the scattering of Israel (v. 24). He then states, "Jerusalem will be trampled on
by the Gentiles (nations) until the times of the Gentiles are fulfilled." There is
no hint here that Jewish repentance and acceptance of Jesus must take place
before there is a return to the land of Israel and Jerusalem returns to Jewish
control (1967). Instead the biblical picture is contrary to this. Luke 21 indicates
that it will be after the time of world domination by Gentile powers (times of
the Gentiles).

Although Jesus predicted the destruction of Jerusalem in Matthew 23:39, He
pictures Jerusalem again inhabited by the Jewish people before his coming, stating: "Look, your house is left to you desolate. For I tell you, you will not see
me again until you say, 'Blessed is He who comes in the name of the Lord.' "
This passage pictures a corporate call for Jesus by the nation, Jerusalem being
the representative city, *before* Jesus makes His visible appearance at the end.
Jerusalem is obviously a Jewish city before the Messiah's return.

There are other passages as well that portray Israel existing as a nation during
the last-days wars before the Messiah's return and Israel's corporate acceptance
of the Messiah. These passages amazingly describe a world situation strikingly
like today (e.g., Zechariah 14; Ezekiel 38, 39).

Thirdly, in our day an unprecedented number of Jews believe in Jesus. At
the writing of this book there are over one hundred congregations of Messianic
Jews. Almost seventy relate together in the Union of Messianic Jewish Congregations in North America. There are many such congregations in Israel. With
the return of Jewish people to Jesus, we see the parallel return to the land.
Romans 11:14,15 leads us to expect this. Paul sees a part of Israel being saved as

preceding the whole of Israel accepting the Messiah Jesus. Other prophecies concerning Israel and the land find a partial fulfillment now and will find a greater fulfillment in the Age to Come.

THE RENEWAL OF THE LAND OF ISRAEL

Ezekiel 36 prophesies the great regathering of Israel and the restoration of land which had become unproductive desert and swamp (see esp. vv. 24–32 and 34–36):

> The desolate land will be cultivated instead of lying desolate in the sight of all who pass through it. They will say, "This land that was laid waste has become like the garden of Eden, the cities that were lying in ruins, desolate and destroyed, are now fortified and inhabited."

Isaiah 35:1,2 is famous for predicting the blossoming of the desert. The fullness of these passages awaits the Age to Come. Even now we see a partial fulfillment. Anyone who visits Israel will be astonished to see the extent to which this has happened. Through modern methods of irrigation and extraordinary effort with new technologies, Israel has literally made the desert bloom. Swampland is productive today. Roses have literally become a major export business.

Ezekiel 37 describes the bones of a dead man taking on flesh and life after being seemingly dead. In this passage God says,

> Son of man, these bones are the whole house of Israel. They say, "our bones are dried up and our hope is gone; we are cut off." Therefore prophesy and say to them, "This is what the Sovereign Lord says: O my people I am going to open your graves and bring you back to Israel."

Although Israel's situation seemed hopeless at the time of Ezekiel, the limited regathering soon after that time did not lead to the fullness of Messianic blessing described in the rest of these chapters. Furthermore, this latter-day return to the land is connected to the Jewish hope of the resurrection of the dead. If we see this passage in process of fulfillment now, it is wonderfully fitting. During the holocaust of World War II, Israel said, "Our bones are dried up and our hope is gone, we are cut off." Actually the description of Ezekiel 37 describes world Jewry of the holocaust period more fittingly than any other generation. The amazing birth of the nation after the holocaust fits this chapter.

THE LINE-UP OF THE NATIONS
IN THE LAST DAYS

The Scriptures' picture of the line-up of the nations against Israel and the conditions of the world before the coming of the Messiah fits our age like no other. Ezekiel 38 speaks of the powers arrayed against Israel as Gog and Magog, the chief prince of Meshech and Tubal. The greatest of all biblical lexicographers, Gesenius, in the eighteenth century identified the latter grouping as Russia. This identification has since been questioned[3]. However, the description of the line-up of the nations mentioned in the passage (with their ancient names) closely fits the line-up of the nations against Israel today. Without basing our argument totally on Gesenius but on today's strong circumstantial evidence, we note the following. The Far North is mentioned as invading with many troops (v. 6). This could well be Russia or other nations to the north, including those which have been related to Moscow. The nations in this area of the former Soviet Union are Muslim. The period is the latter days. The Scriptural picture of the final wars before the Messiah's return shows the defeat of the northern forces on the northern mountains of Israel (Ezekiel 39:1–17).

A European confederacy is pictured in the book of Revelation. This confederacy is also defeated when the Messiah comes (Revelation 19:11–21; Daniel 2). Some Bible scholars hold to the view that the Russian confederacy is first defeated. This leads to a later defeat of the European confederacy. The picture in Ezekiel 38,39 fits this interpretation since the northern forces are defeated on the mountains of northern Israel, whereas Zechariah 14 fits the picture of the book of Revelation. The final battle picture is different than the Ezekiel picture. Zechariah depicts the defeat of these nations in the environs of Jerusalem. The passage states,

> I will gather all nations to Jerusalem to fight against it; the city will be captured, the houses ransacked, and the women raped. Half the city will go into exile, but the rest of the people will not be taken from the city. The Lord will go out and fight against these nations as he fights in a day of battle. On that day his feet will stand on the Mount of Olives, east of Jerusalem, and the Mount of Olives will be split in two from east to west forming a great valley, with half of the mountain moving north and half moving south.

This last battle precedes the ushering in of the Messianic kingdom, during which all nations send their representatives to celebrate the feast of Succoth. This is certainly the time when the prediction of Jesus comes true, that the Jewish nation through its leaders will call on the name of Jesus with the words "Blessed is he that comes in the name of the Lord" (Matthew 23:33).

Further details related to this last war are given in Zechariah 12,

> I am going to make Jerusalem a cup that sends all the surrounding peoples reeling. Judah will be besieged as well as Jerusalem. On that day when all the nations of the earth are gathered against her, I will make Jerusalem an immovable rock for all nations. All who try to move it will injure themselves (vv. 2–4) . . . On that day the Lord will shield those who live in Jerusalem, so that the feeblest among them will be like David and the house of David will be like God, and the *Angel of the Lord* going before them. On that day I will set out to destroy all the nations that attack Jerusalem.

This amazing time of victory, when world powers turn against Israel, will also be a time of mourning, when Israel shall "look upon him whom they have pierced" and receive Jesus as the Messiah.

THE ARAB NATIONS AND ISRAEL

Isaiah 19 appears to have special relevance to the Arab world today. Here the prophet looks down the corridors of history and sees conflict within Egypt as well as between Israel and Egypt. The land of Judah is said to bring terror to the Egyptians (Isaiah 19:17). This is certainly something that had not occurred until the twentieth century. Yet the passage closes on the note of reconciliation in which the land of Egypt and Assyria (present-day Iraq and Syria) turn to the God of Israel. This extraordinary passage describes Middle East hostility that fits the wars previously fought between Israel and her neighbors. Egypt's fear is fittingly seen in the wars of 1956, 1967, and 1973, in which Israel was victor. Yet the reconciliation that is predicted could occur in our day as in no other.

> In that day there will be a highway from Egypt to Assyria. The Egyptians and Assyrians will worship together. In that day Israel will be the third, along with Egypt and Assyria, a blessing on the earth. The Lord Almighty will bless them, saying, "Blessed be Egypt my people, Assyria my handiwork, and

Israel my inheritance."

All of this assumes the return of the Jewish people to the land before Israel's ultimate acceptance of the Messiah. There is great Middle East conflict and then ultimate reconciliation.

In the book of Revelation we read of other noteworthy events during these times, such as the 144,000 Jewish believers who witness to the Gospel (Revelation 7:4–8, 14:1–5), the drying up of the River Euphrates (Revelation 16:10), and the way which is thus prepared for the kings of the East. These Eastern troops are said to number 200 million (Revelation 9:14–16). This size army was totally without possibility until modern times, with the huge populations of the Far East. (We do note that the 200 million could be demonic hosts and not human soldiers.)

Whether or not there is agreement in all of the detail and order of latter-day prophecy, there is a wealth of material which has not yet been fulfilled but does fit the circumstances of our day. The cataclysmic nature of warfare, the reestablishment of Israel as a nation, and the line-up of the nations all reflect the biblical pattern of circumstances foreseen before the Messiah's return.

These future events have no clear past referent. They require the preservation of Israel and her reestablishment as a nation. In 1732, Joseph Butler, in his *The Analogy of Religion*, stated that the preservation of the Jewish people alone was an assurance that all of God's prophecies to Israel and to the world of ultimate world redemption would be fulfilled. The world situation as we know it today parallels conditions that fit the biblical picture of the last days. Time may run slowly and the present conditions of applicability may last for an age, but we also could be on the threshold of the end of this age and the inauguration of the Age to Come.

JERUSALEM'S GOLDEN (EAST) GATE

Ezekiel 40–46 describes the ideal of temple worship. Many are the interpretations of these unusual chapters. Some see them as symbolic of the worship and service of the people of God. Others see them as describing a millennial temple system whose proportions and service differs in many details from the Solomonic and Second Commonwealth temples. We tend to the latter viewpoint.

In the Ezekiel vision, the outer gate which faces east was shut:

> The Lord said to me, "this gate is to remain shut. It must not be opened, no one may enter through it. The Prince himself is the only one who may sit in the gateway to eat in the presence of the Lord. He is to enter by way of the portico of the gateway and go out the same way." (Ezekiel 44:2,3)

Although this describes rules concerning the future temple, an amazing application pointing to this prophecy has historically been maintained. The prince of the chapter is taken to be either the Messiah or the local ruling prince under him. Archaeologist Joseph P. Free, the excavator of Dothan, records the history of the Jerusalem East Gate, or the Golden Gate, which opened directly into the temple. This is the gate Jesus entered on Palm Sunday. After the destruction of Jerusalem, this gate remained blocked until an Arab caliph rebuilt the gate above the old gate (both levels can be seen today at the wall). Just before he was to make a triumphal entry through this gate, he was stricken and died. The gate was immediately sealed and remains so today. Arab peoples built a cemetery outside the gate to prevent the fulfillment of the prophecy that the Jewish Messiah would enter by it. The Messiah, being a priest, would not defile himself in a grave yard—or so it was thought. The earthquake of Zechariah 14 from the Mount of Olives (with its fault) unto the eastern wall of Jerusalem will certainly change this geography. Here is an incidence of providence preserving an entrance for the Messiah or his prince interpreted for us by an archaeologist.[4]

THE IMPACT OF THE GOSPEL

The Bible also reflects the worldwide impact of the Gospel. The book of Revelation says that the Messiah has "purchased men for God from *every tribe and language and people and nation.*" Also, His salvation is seen in the great multitude saved out of the earth "that no one could count from every nation, tribe, people, and language, standing in front of the lamb" (Revelation 7:9). The Messiah Jesus Himself predicted that the Gospel of the Kingdom would be preached throughout the whole world before the end or the Age to Come (Matthew 24:13). This indeed has come true and is yet being fulfilled in our day.

PROPHETS TODAY

Before leaving this section, a word should be stated concerning latter-day prophets. Because it is a supernatural universe, there are spiritual sources of knowledge beyond the five senses. Not all of these sources are good; some are occult and are from evil spirits. The fulfilled predictions of a Jeanne Dixon, for example, show supernatural sources, but are also connected with biblically forbidden practices of divination (e.g., crystal ball gazing). There is sufficient inaccuracy to give the lie to the prophet in these cases. It is as though the supernatural source of the information has better knowledge than mere human information. Yet since the source is not God, it can not guarantee the fulfillment of what is predicted. This is one of the key tests in the Bible for discrediting the false prophet (Deuteronomy 18)—that what is predicted does not come to past. The other is fidelity to the biblical revelation (Deuteronomy 13). Because God is in control of the universe, the one who truly speaks from God has a guarantee that his prophecy will be fulfilled. Of course, some prophecies are personal and contingent upon the hearer's response (e.g., Jonah's prophecy of Nineveh's destruction was suspended because of her repentance). Some are conditional, and some are not. We have to be careful in coming to conclusions.

The gift of prophecy in the New Covenant communities of the Messiah and the office of the prophet (I Corinthians 12; Ephesians 5:11) still are present today. All such prophecy must be tested by the written Scriptures. The examples of supernatural predictive prophecy or of supernatural knowledge granted by God are too numerous to begin to recount. Some prophets, such as Paul Cain, give detailed information about persons and circumstances for which they have no normal knowledge. Bill Hammon gives many examples in his book.[5] I have personally received several prophecies that were amazingly accurate. The tapes and books of John Wimber give many more examples. Such prophetic ministry is always secondary to the canonical Scripture. Predictive content is exceptional; most prophecies are for edification.

CONCLUSION

As we end this section, we only note that latter-day prophecy adds more credibility to the trustworthiness of the Scriptures. Along with Messianic prophecy and fulfilled prophecy concerning nations, kings, and cities, latter-day prophecy shows that the Bible is what it claims to be: the inspired Word of the God who created the heavens and the earth.

CHAPTER 12--STUDY QUESTIONS

1. How does the history of the Jewish nation point to the truth of the Bible?

2. Daniel 2 and 7 describe the course of world empires. Do these prophecies show the Bible to be accurate? How?

3. How do the pictures of last-days wars in Ezekiel 38 and Zechariah 14 more clearly fit our day than any other?

EVIDENCE FROM THE
SUPERNATURAL CHARACTER
OF JESUS

A. SHERWIN WHITE IN HIS BOOK *Roman Law and Roman Society in the New Testament* argues that the information we have concerning Jesus is of high quality and far surpasses in quality and reliability the information we have for reconstructing the life of any ancient historical figure. This evidence will be presented in Chapter Fourteen. In the present chapter, we want to look at the portrait of Jesus in the Gospels. The quality of the person presented on the pages of the Gospels is one of unsurpassing uniqueness. One can also find excellent portraits of Jesus in Everett Harrison's book *A Short Life of Christ* and in Donald Guthrie's *A Shorter Life of Christ*.

It should be noted that compassion and love well up from the pages of the Gospels. This is unparalleled in literature. Whether it is a miracle account or a parable or simply a normal human occasion in Jesus' life, the portrait is one of constant love and righteous judgment. The Gospels are not biographies in the modern sense. There is no attempt to describe the early life of Jesus. We mainly have a portrait of a man in the prime of his life and ministry, a portrait that is remarkable for its consistent quality.

The figure of Jesus towers above any other in history. The quality of his love was manifest to the downtrodden, the sinner, and the confused. Yet this did not lead to a prejudice against the "haves." Jesus could as well give a great affirmation to Zaccheus when he showed that his heart was not bound to his wealth and committed his wealth to help the needy. The love of Jesus for the sinner is well represented in the marvelous parable of the prodigal son where the father (representing God the Father) fully embraces his repentant wayward son (Luke 15).

Keen insight is given into human pride in the account of the jealous older brother as well. The parable of the one lost sheep from the flock of one hundred is a touching reflection on the heart of God (Luke 15:1–7). His love for the lost drew them to him.

Jesus was criticized because repentant prostitutes and tax collectors came to him. He ate with them, and somehow, with him, they found the power to repent and receive forgiveness. His heart was also open to children, as reflected in the words, "Suffer little children to come to me, for such is the Kingdom of God" (Matthew 19:14). We should note that tax collectors were from the wealthy class and were looked upon as betrayers for doing Rome's dirty work. Hence, both rich and poor, sinful and religious are offered the love of Jesus.

The four distinct Gospels give a unified picture of extraordinary kindness. This kindness, however, was not weakness. The same Jesus who allowed little children to be drawn to him was also the one who fashioned a whip and cleared the temple of those who would profit by financially gouging the people in the temple (Matthew 21:12ff.; Mark 11:15–19ff.). When Jesus faced hypocrites among religious leaders, He displayed righteous indignation to the fullest, saying:

> Woe to you teachers of the Law and Pharisees, you hypocrites. You are like whitewashed tombs, which look beautiful on the outside but on the inside are full of dead men's bones and everything unclean. In the same way on the outside you appear to people as righteous but on the inside you are full of hypocrisy and wickedness. (Matthew 23:27–28)

The student of comparative religions should note the unparalleled uniqueness of Jesus. He is not a figure like any other religious figure. He breaks the mold of the merely creative human mind and human legend-making ability. Let us look at several areas concerning the uniqueness of Jesus and the integrity of the Gospel material.

THE UNIQUENESS OF HIS ETHICAL TEACHING

Jesus the Messiah taught the meaning of the Law as connected to the attitudes and motives of the heart as no other man. Some seek to find parallel teachings in the recorded teaching of others—such parallels are not hard to find. However, the total coherent pattern of teaching by Jesus in the Gospels cannot be matched. Matthew 5–7 is so extraordinary that no other material is needed to establish this point.

Beginning with the moral qualities that will be blessed (enriched by God),

Jesus puts forth his teaching on the heart. The poor in spirit will be blessed because they know their need for the grace of God. The meek (those who are humble in spirit with a true view of their own real importance) will inherit the earth. Those whose hearts hunger and thirst for righteousness will be filled; the merciful will be shown mercy; and the pure in heart will see God. Peacemakers and those persecuted for righteousness' sake will be richly blessed as well.

After these beatitudes Jesus gives a unique interpretation of the key sections of the Law. "Do not murder" is expanded to show that murder arises out of a heart that hates. Forgiveness and reconciliation with a brother must precede religious ceremony (5:21–28). Adultery arises out of the lustful heart; it is the spiritual adultery of the heart which must first be healed. So important is the achievement of a spiritually pure heart that it is better to pluck out an eye or to cut off a hand than to be entrapped in lust. The high view of marital love in which divorce is not an option fits the ideal standard of God (vv. 5:31,32).

With regards to oaths, Jesus teaches that swearing should be unnecessary to the righteous. Our "yes" or "no" should be fully binding. If our hearts are right, we will practice this integrity.

Although an "eye for an eye" might guide civil authorities, even causing them to limit the ancient Near Eastern right of personal vengeance, this principle is no standard for personal righteousness in human relationships. Rather, the righteous "turns his cheek" and gives his tunic as well as his cloak. Jewish people at the time of Jesus especially despised the Roman law that gave soldiers a right of conscription whereby they could enjoin a Jew to carry a load one mile. Hatred for Roman rule enslaved the hearts of many people in a more serious way than the Roman occupation itself. Jesus taught, "If someone forces you to go one mile, go with him two miles. Give to the one who asks you and do not turn away from the one who wants to borrow from you."

The great summary of the ethic of Jesus is the "*Law of love.*" Jesus taught that to love the Lord our God with all our heart, soul, strength, and might (Deuteronomy 6:4) and to love our neighbors as ourselves was the essence of the Law (Mark 12:29–31). The Law made provision to even help an enemy whose ox had fallen under its load (Deuteronomy 23:5). Jesus taught,

> I tell you love your enemies and pray for those who persecute you, that you may be the sons of your Father in heaven. He causes his sun to shine on the evil and the good, and sends rain on the righteous and the unrighteous. If you love those who love you, what reward will you get? Are not even the tax collectors doing that? And if you greet only your brothers, what

> are you doing more than others? Do not pagans do that? Be
> perfect, therefore, as your heavenly father is perfect. (Mat-
> thew 5:44-48)

Jesus then taught on the key religious acts of Jewry, giving alms to the needy, prayer, and fasting. These actions should be done without the reward of recognition which feeds our religious pride. Religious pride and self-righteousness are constantly emphasized as grave dangers. Good deeds should be sincere, from a heart of love, and where at all possible, done privately. Then our reward will be great in heaven.

Such ethical teaching assumes the recognition of God as our loving heavenly Father. The recognition of God in these terms, and to this extent, is *uniquely* found in Jesus' teaching. Matthew 6:25-34 encourages total trust in God, who clothes the grass of the field with flowers, is aware of every fallen sparrow, and has numbered every hair on our heads. It is a central part of Jesus' ethical teaching that we are not to worry about the material needs of life but "to seek first his Kingdom and his righteousness and all these things will be given . . . as well" (Matthew 6:34). We are not to be condemning in heart toward others but forgiving in attitude (Matthew 7:1-5; 6:14–15). We are to walk the narrow way (7:13,14).

Jesus is constantly concerned with the heart. A good tree brings forth good fruit, and a bad tree, bad fruit (Matthew 7:17): "For out of the heart come evil thoughts, murder, adultery, sexual immorality, theft, false testimony, slander. These are what make a man unclean" (Matthew 15:19,20).

Jesus' exposition of the Law shows each person that there is no room for justified self-righteousness. Before God's holy standard, we are in need of grace. The parables of Jesus further demonstrate these truths. The repentant tax collector is forgiven; the self-righteous Pharisee is not (Luke 18:9-14). The repentant prodigal son is forgiven by his loving father, the self-righteous older brother misses the love of his father (Luke 15:11–31). All of heaven rejoices over the lost sheep who is found—the sinner who repents (Luke 15:1-7). The Samaritan halfbreed shows himself to be the one who loves his neighbor because he is willing to be a neighbor to the one who is placed in his path, the one in need for help in difficulty. Space does not permit the exposition of these parables, but they should be read to gain a sense of their wonderful teaching. They speak with simplicity, beauty, and depth.

We should not misunderstand Jesus to be teaching a mere sentimental love as the basis of ethics. This is no "sloppy agape." The love Jesus taught was in recognition of the fact that every man was created in the image of God. Jesus taught as well on the consequences of sin and the just judgment of God. The world to come would bring rewards for the righteous and punishment for the wicked (Matthew 25:31–46). So we read: "Every tree that does not bear good fruit is cut down and thrown into the fire . . . not everyone who says to me Lord shall enter the Kingdom of heaven, but only he who does the will of my Father who is in heaven" (Matthew 7:19-21).

The will of the Father is unqualified in requiring us to live under his Lordship in a life of sacrificial love instead of self-seeking fulfillment. Yet in taking up the cross of a life of love, in losing ourselves, we truly find ourselves (Luke 9:23–26). Fierce words of judgment are given to warn those who spurn the grace of God which would enable them to live in the way of love. Love is not mushy indulgence. Let us note Jesus' words of judgment, as sharp as any Old Testament prophet: "Upon you will come all the righteous blood that has been shed on earth, from the blood of righteous Abel to the blood of Zechariah son of Berechiah, whom you murdered between the Temple and the altar" (Matthew 23:35).

These words were spoken to corrupt religious leaders. Jesus' most fiery denunciations were for self-righteous religious leaders. The law of reaping what we sow is continually found in the teaching of Jesus. Of towns that rejected the power of God manifest in the miracles of Jesus we read: "Woe to you Chorazin. Woe to you, Bethsaida, for if the miracles that were performed in you had been performed in Tyre and Sidon, they would have repented long ago, sitting in sackcloth and ashes. But it will be more bearable for Tyre and Sidon at the judgment than for you. And you, Capernaum, will you be lifted up to the skies? No, you will go down to the depths" (Matthew 11:21-23).

Jesus was extraordinarily compassionate to the sinner, but his command was always clear, "Go thou and sin no more."

The teaching of Jesus has only been touched upon. The greatest apologetic for faith in Jesus is simply to prayerfully read the Gospels with an open mind in seeking the truth of God.

THE COMPASSIONATE LIFE OF JESUS

Search the religious literature of the world for material rivaling the quality of compassion revealed by Jesus the Messiah. You will search in vain, for there is no account like the Gospel accounts. The love displayed by Jesus gave hope to the guilty, the oppressed, and the sinner. Forgiveness was truly available. This is seen especially in his dealing with the woman at the well in John 4. She was a Samaritan woman who questioned Jesus because Jews were not willing to have unnecessary contact with Samaritans. Not only was she a Samaritan, but she was living in sin with a man who was not her husband. Previous to this she had five husbands. Did He condemn her? No, however, by a supernatural word of knowledge, He disclosed her sin and offered her the water of life. This whole scene was a surprise to the disciples (4:27). What was Jesus doing with a Samaritan woman? The woman, on the other hand, was transformed and she prepared the way for a great witness among the Samaritans. "Come see a man," she said, "who told me everything I ever did; could this be the Messiah?"

The same quality of love is revealed in the story of the woman taken in adultery (John 8:1–11). Though it is not in some of the earliest manuscripts, its quality is shown by the same unique atmosphere of love. This attests to the genuineness of the account. After turning to her accusers, Jesus says, "If anyone of you is without sin, let him be the first to throw a stone at her." When all her accusers depart, Jesus offers forgiveness in these words, " 'Woman, where are they? Has no one condemned you?' 'No one sir,' she said. 'Then neither do I condemn you,' Jesus declared, 'Go now and leave your life of sin.' "

Many are the pages that could be filled with the account of Jesus' love for the poor, the needy, and the downtrodden sinner. The parables of Jesus breathe the same amazing love. He was criticized because sinners were drawn to him (even prostitutes found their forgiveness.). Perhaps even more amazing is the love of Jesus for tax collectors. Tax collectors were often wealthy. They collaborated with Rome to tax their own people and lived off a hefty profit. The majority of the Jewish people despised these tax collectors as traitors. One of Jesus' disciples was Levi or Matthew, a former tax collector. After his call to follow Jesus, he gave a great banquet which included a large crowd of his tax collector friends (Luke 5:27–31). Jesus' love was not limited to the downtrodden sinner, but included the wealthy compromiser. He attended the banquet. The complaint among the religious leaders was, "Why do you eat and drink with tax collectors and sinners?" Jesus answered them, "It is not the healthy who need a doctor, but the sick. I have not come to call the righteous, but sinners to repentance."

In the ancient world, it would have been considered an imposition to bother a master teacher with the distractions of children. Hence, when people brought their babies to Jesus to have Him touch them, the disciples rebuked them. Jesus responded by demonstrating his love and patience for children and giving that great word wherein we are taught that the openness and teachability of a child are necessary attitudes for entering the Kingdom: "Let the little children come to me, and do not forbid them, for the Kingdom of God belongs to such as these. I tell you the truth, anyone who will not receive the Kingdom of God like a little child will never enter it" (Matthew 19:14).

Another account of Jesus' great compassion is found in John 11. Here at the grave of his friend Lazarus we read that Jesus wept (John 11:35). The word "wept" is, in Greek, a deep sorrowful weeping. Why did He so weep before performing the great miracle of raising Lazarus from the dead? Certainly it was because of his great empathy for humanity and the pain people suffer in the separation of death—the tragedy of premature loss of life and broken fellowship.

Concerning Jerusalem, we read his words of longing: "O Jerusalem, Jerusalem, how often I have longed to gather your children together as a hen gathers her chicks under her wings, but you were not willing. Look, your house is left to you desolate. For I tell you, you will not see me again until you say, 'Blessed is He who comes in the name of the Lord' " (Matthew 23:37–39).

Glimpses of his intimacy with his disciples are most precious. In John 13:3–17 Jesus demonstrates a leadership characterized by servanthood. This is his example to his disciples. During a Passover celebration, shortly before his death, we find him wrapping a towel around his waist and washing his disciples' feet. This was the task of the lowliest servants. Peter was at first so taken by this that he refused this uncustomary act. Jesus teaches on this basis, "Do you understand what I have done for you? . . . You call me 'Teacher' and 'Lord' and rightly so, for that is what I am. Now that I, your Lord and Teacher, have washed your feet, you also should wash one another's feet. I have set you an example that you should do as I have done for you."

Love is manifest through serving one another in humility. Yeshua touchingly assigned John the responsibility of being as a caring son to his mother when He was dying on the cross. "When Jesus saw his mother there, and the disciple whom He loved standing nearby, He said to his mother, 'Dear woman, here is your son,' and to the disciple, 'Here is your mother.' " (John 19:26,27). In the moment of his greatest suffering on the cross, we read the words, "Father, forgive them, for they do not know what they are doing" (Luke 23:24).

The post-resurrection accounts also breathe the same touching quality of love. We see this in John 21 when Jesus asked Peter to throw out his net on the right side of the boat after an unsuccessful night. Peter caught 153 fish. This led to an amazing dialogue in which Jesus sought to restore Peter from the state of guilt and self-rejection which ensued after his betrayal of Jesus. How appropriate that Jesus would use the miracle of fish for Peter's inner healing and recommissioning—the same type of miracle that was used to commission him (Luke 5:1-11). " 'Simon, son of John, do you truly love me?' He answered, 'Yes Lord, I love you.' Jesus said, 'Take care of my sheep.' " In this we understand that Simon was being restored and called to be a shepherd of the sheep. Similar love and concern was shown for the disciple Thomas in the midst of his doubt (John 20:24-29). Jesus gave him the direct empirical evidence he sought.

THE QUALITY OF THE MIRACLE ACCOUNTS

In speaking of the quality of miracle accounts we are not speaking of the evidence of the historicity of the Gospels, with which we will deal in our next chapter. We are here referring to the impression that these accounts make on the reader, especially on one who is aware of extra-biblical miracle stories.

A comparison of miracle accounts in the Gospels and the book of Acts with the post-canonical New Testament pseudepigrapha (unauthentic writings falsely ascribed to apostles) reveal a marked contrast. The miracle accounts of the latter are clearly fanciful. In these unauthentic writings, Jesus makes a bear come out and tear apart the children who mock him. As a youngster he blows on dead birds and makes them alive again. These miracles seem to be an attempt to fulfill the curiosity of people for information concerning the early life of Jesus. The canonical literature gives scant information from Jesus' infancy to his maturity. Although Jesus had supernatural power, it was not power used in a loose or arbitrary fashion. The miracle stories of the Gospels show a reserve that is quite apart from noncanonical stories and apart from religious miracle stories in general.

The miracle stories of the Gospels generally have these several key characteristics. They show that Jesus is empowered by the Holy Spirit in full submission to the Father. They are miracles that demonstrate redemption from sin and suffering because in Him is the manifestation of the Kingdom of God (rule of God) in person. Lastly, they are elicited by the compassionate love of Jesus for suffering humanity. They fit the same quality of what we know of authentic miracles today (a subject of a subsequent chapter) and stand apart from the miracle accounts of other religious literature and traditions.

Again and again we read, "Jesus had compassion on them," (Matthew 20:34). From the beginning of his ministry wherein He healed the demon possessed at the tombs and the paralytic lowered through the roof of a Capernaum home, unto the healing of the blind beggars near Jericho (Matthew 9:28–34; 9:1–8; 20:34ff.), the same quality is constantly in evidence. The accounts are unembellished, brief, and to the point. Let us just note a few of them.

Mark gives special insight into one of the demoniacs Jesus healed. It is a moving account (Mark 5:1–20). We read of a pathetic figure of a man living among tombs, naked and uncontrollable. We read, "Night and day among the tombs and in the hills, he would cry out and cut himself with stones" (5:5). The spirits cry out from this man in fear of Jesus. We find that it is not one spirit, but many, "My name is legion." Jesus casts them out of the man, allowing them to go into the pigs, which in fear rush down the side of the hill.

When the people of the region saw what had happened and saw the man sitting and in his right mind, they were afraid. They begged for Jesus to leave their region. It was too much for them. The conclusion is wonderful: "As Jesus was getting into the boat, the man who had been demon-possessed begged to go with him. Jesus did not let him, but said, 'Go home to your family and tell them how much the Lord has done for you, and how he has had mercy on you.' So the man went away and began to tell in the Decapolis how much Jesus had done for him, and all the people were amazed."

The receptive faith of people was an important factor for profiting from the redemptive power Jesus had to give. In Nazareth, Jesus could not do many miracles because of their unbelief (Mark 6:5). Jairus, a synagogue ruler, also sought the help of Jesus for his sick daughter. On the way there, a woman, who had been bleeding for twelve years, sought to touch the fringes of Jesus (Numbers 15:37–41), the part of the garment an observant Jew wore signifying his priestly status before God and his intention to fulfill God's commandments. She in faith said: " 'If I just touch his clothes, I will be healed.' Immediately her bleeding stopped, and she felt in her body that she was free from her suffering. At once Jesus realized that power had gone out from him. He turned and asked the crowd 'who touched me' " (Mark 5:28–30).

So many were pressing close to Jesus in the crowd that the disciples were puzzled at his question. Jesus was really asking, "Who touched me in faith so that power was released to heal?" It was his desire to combine the healing with words of encouragement. "But Jesus kept looking around to see who had done it. The woman, knowing what had happened to her came and fell at his feet and trembling with fear, told him the whole truth. He said to her, 'Daughter, your faith has healed you. Go in peace and be freed from your suffering' " (Luke

8:46–48). We are provided with a remarkably brief, vivid, and hence, believable account. The limited details fit what we know of human nature and response in such situations. After Jesus completed his journey, he gently and lovingly called Jairus' daughter back from the dead.

Other wonderful accounts are not wanting. One of the most stirring is the healing of the blind man by Jesus in John 9. For Jesus, the Sabbath was a day to celebrate redemption and to experience redemptive renewal. To receive healing on the Sabbath was perfectly appropriate. Yet his Sabbath healings provoked great antagonism among self-righteous religious legalists. This miracle was one of those Sabbath miracles. It was done through an anointing of the man's eyes with saliva and mud. The man was told to wash in the pool of Siloam. He was healed in his faith obedience. Here was one born blind, who now sees, but has not yet gotten to know Jesus. Following his healing he was interrogated harshly by religious leaders and was eventually cast out because of his answer to their accusatory questions, "Whether He is a sinner or not I don't know. One thing I do know, I was blind but now I see." At the end of the account Jesus meets him and brings him to a personal relationship with himself.

The healing of the crippled, bent-over woman in Luke 13:16 gives us Jesus' theology of healing in a nutshell. "Then should not this woman, a daughter of Abraham, whom Satan has kept bound for eighteen long years, be set free on the Sabbath day from what bound her?" (Luke 13:16). This is the character of most of Jesus' miracles. His disciples were able to minister similarly under the charge of Jesus (Luke 9:1–6, 10:1–18), showing that this was the work of the Spirit of God and was not limited to the ministry of Jesus. The same kind of miracles occurred in the book of Acts.

There are also miracles of another wonderful nature, which C. S. Lewis in his fine book *Miracles* calls miracles of creation.[1] Jesus' changing water into wine reveals God's process of creativity (John 2). This is a miracle which in the immediate shows what God always does. His feeding of the five thousand reveals God as the provider of our sustenance who always multiplies seed into food (Mark 6:30–44). His calming of the storm reveals God as supreme over nature. Lewis' insight into miracles brings joy to the reader. However, these miracles of nature reveal the authority of human beings over nature as well. This is an authority that can only be manifest through those in complete submission to the will of God. In submission to God, man recovers the dominion over the earth given to Adam at the beginning. This dominion was lost in the fall. In Jesus we see the potential of an unfallen or fully redeemed human being. As

Jesus was not subject to the peril of the storm at sea and forces of evil could not prevent him from fulfilling God's will, so natural evils (earthquakes, storms, etc.) only have power over human beings because of the fall. In Jesus we see man's dominion restored.

All in all, the miracle stories reflect the nature of truth. They have just those few details we would expect of eyewitness unembellished accounts. When we read the Gospels with an open heart we find that they have what J. B. Phillips called *the ring of truth*.[2]

THE ACCOUNT OF THE
SINLESS PERFECTION OF JESUS

The accounts amazingly portray Jesus as without sin while representing, with unrelenting honesty, the failings of the disciples. The Gospels are, however, the products of Jesus' disciples. Later generations would certainly not give us a history in which their original leadership core is represented as falling so far short of the standards of Jesus. Only Jesus is represented as ideal in his perfection; not one disciple is so represented. There is not one incident of Jesus acting in selfishness, out of jealousy, or with inappropriate anger. Aside from very few paragraphs in which a Western mind might misinterpret the actions of Jesus without understanding oriental context, there is never a violation of God's moral and ethical standards. In John 8:46 we read, "Can any of you prove me guilty of sin?" The conclusion of the epistles is derived from this Gospel material. "God made him who had no sin to be sin for us, so that we might become the righteousness of God" (II Corinthians 5:21). He is "One who has been tempted in every way, just as we are, yet was without sin" (Hebrews 4:15). We are redeemed "with the precious blood of Messiah, a lamb without blemish or defect," (I Peter 1:19). "He committed no sin, and no deceit was found in his mouth" (I John 3:5).

No Jew had ever written before (or since) that any man was sinless. What was He like to elicit this testimony? That there is such a testimony should awaken us from our slumber to see the bright evidence of the fact that in Jesus we are dealing with one who is unique. The Gospels provide us with a portrait of Jesus. Only if they provide a true portrait can we explain such a Jewish testimony to his sinlessness.

The picture in the Gospels presents one more important aspect, the claim of Jesus to be deity. In Donald Hagner's *The Jewish Reclamation of Jesus*, a forceful argument is put forth. It is that all attempts to understand Jesus as merely a human being fail. There is an element in all of the Gospels that point to an incarnational reality, the claim that Jesus is more than a mere man. This is seen in His unique use of the word *Abba* ("father") for God. It is seen in His prayer that He be glorified with the glory which was His before the world began (John 17:5). In John 8:58 He claims to be the *"I Am"* of Exodus 3:14. All three synoptic Gospels record His question to the religious authorities concerning how it was possible that King David called the Messiah, his later descendant, his Lord in Psalm 110:1 (Matthew 21:41–26). This could only be possible if David's Son was more than mere man. The ancestor was always given greater reverence, even if the accomplishments of his son were greater. Jesus' teaching and life show that He was no liar or lunatic. Therefore His claim to divinity must be taken seriously and therefore as history.

Certainly we would expect that the disciples would be represented as leading citizens of the kingdom, though not sinless. We would expect them to be portrayed as having grown beyond the petty motivations of other men. After all, they were the founding leaders of the movement. What do we find? We find that the leading disciple, Peter, denied Jesus three times in his moment of need. He showed himself to be selfish, with a desire to mainly protect his own skin when his master needed his unswerving support. His lack of courage was less than that shown by many men in danger (Luke 22:31–34).

After the holy and solemn meal of the last supper Passover, we read, "Also a dispute arose among them as to which of them was considered to be the greatest." This elicits Jesus' teaching on the nature of *servant* leadership in the Kingdom of God. Such disputes and jealousies are not lacking in other Gospel passages.

Thomas disbelieves the resurrection until he has his own personal experience with the risen Messiah (John 20:26–31). James and John's mother seeks the assurance that her sons will be highest in the Messianic kingdom under Jesus (Luke 9:46–48). Paul rebukes Peter at Antioch for not being true to the principles of the Gospel (Galatians 2:11–14). There were times when faith was lacking and his disciples could not bring deliverance to the needy (Matthew 17:14–24). Furthermore, they were blind to the revelation Jesus sought to give concerning the need for his death and resurrection (Mark 9:10; John 12:16; 16:17–18).

The striking *honesty* of the Gospels concerning the apostolic leadership in general gives great credibility to the testimony concerning the greatness of Jesus. When the disciples were changed by the reception of the Holy Spirit, they certainly became great men of God—they turned the world upside down. Yet there is no exaltation of these ordinary but supernaturally empowered men in the Bible. We can believe their testimony concerning the glorious life, death, and resurrection of Jesus. Their portrait of Jesus is unique in regard to all religious literature. It is a glorious, touching, and *believable* portrait.

This chapter is only a brief introduction for what is more important as evidence, the Gospels themselves. Read the Gospels with an open mind. Read one Gospel in one sitting to get a picture of the whole. The Gospels speak for themselves. They present testimony of one that can only be understood as Peter confessed him to be: "You are the Messiah, the Son of the Living God" (Matthew 16:16).

CHAPTER 13: STUDY QUESTIONS

1. Describe the ethical teaching of Jesus as giving credibility to the authority of Jesus.

2. How does Jesus' life reflect a unique walk of love?

3. Why do the miracles of Jesus provide us with uniquely believable supernatural events?

THE HISTORICITY OF THE GOSPELS AND THE RESURRECTION OF JESUS

WITH REGARD TO THE RELIABILITY OF THE NEW TESTAMENT DOCUMENTS, perhaps no other literature of history has been so thoroughly examined, pulled apart, and compared than the Gospel literature. Critics have looked for disharmony, and supporters have written harmonies of the Gospels. Amazingly, after 150 years of rigorous modern biblical criticism, the dean of biblical archaeologists was able to say in his mature years that the Gospels appear to be what they always were purported to be, and were believed to be, the record of Jesus' ministry with his disciples written between 40 A.D. to 90 A.D.[1] William F. Albright's conclusion was based on a study of parallel first-century literature, and especially the Dead Sea Scrolls. He saw that the Gospel literature paralleled the ideas, concepts, idioms, and situations of the first century. This is in contrast to the later Greek revisions of the meaning of Jesus. This is especially so, in his view, of the Gospel of John, which was previously dated as a late Gospel with a second-century origin. The whole atmosphere of the Gospel literature is first-century Palestinian Judaism, not the later Greek mystery religions which were supposed by earlier critics to provide the contextual parallels.

NEW TESTAMENT MANUSCRIPTS

Beyond this, we call attention to the fact that there is a plethora of early manuscripts whose discovery make a second-century date for the Gospels impossible and a mid– to later–first-century date a necessary conclusion. This is today's consensus of scholarship. Some of these manuscripts and manuscript fragments are as early as the turn of the first century. Even the Gospel of John, which used to be late dated to the mid-second century, has been represented by a manuscript fragment dated no later than 125 A.D. (the John Rylands fragment).

The student needs to be aware of two crucial implications of this plethora of manuscripts and the early manuscript evidence. The first of these is that not enough time elapsed between the purported events of the New Testament and the New Testament writings to allow for embellishment and significant myth-making. Indeed, the contemporaries of the Messiah Jesus were still living at the time the New Testament was written. This is unique among ancient religions with founding figures. For example, the earliest documentation of Buddha is hundreds of years later than the actual time in which he lived.[2] The second implication is the unchallenged trustworthiness of the New Testament Greek manuscripts used today.[3] Through the inductive scientific method applied to comparing these texts (called *lower textual criticism*), scholars have been able to produce a text which is considered by most to be 99.9% accurate to the original writings. How is this possible?

The science of text criticism is easy to understand in its most basic dimensions. If I dictate a letter to a class, most would get the correct rendering on paper, but some students would make errors. If these students then give the letter to ten others to copy, again we could believe that most would copy correctly. However, those also would make some mistakes. If these last copyists also gave these texts to others to copy, the process would repeat again. This simple process beginning with thirty students would produce three thousand copies. If the majority of these copies were lost, leaving four hundred, we could apply the inductive method to recreate the original even if the first ten copies were lost. By the method of induction we would note that the manuscripts could be grouped into families, that is, manuscripts having the same renderings. However, by noting the majority reading of a passage *from different families*, we could be quite sure of the original reading. Knowing, as well, the kind of errors a scribe might be likely to make would also be helpful (miscopying similar letters, mistaking similar words, copying a former scribal note into the text). The variety of evidence for reconstructing the original Greek text is excellent. Therefore, when one is reading the critical edition of the Greek text today, he is assured that he is virtually reading an equivalent of the original.

Ancient Old Testament texts are not nearly so vast. However, by comparing the Septuagint text (most often quoted in the New Testament), the Masoretic text, the Dead Sea Scroll text, and other useful but less important texts (Syriac, Targum, etc.) we can be reasonably confident of the basic accuracy of the Old

Testament text. In conclusion, we can be confident that the Bible we possess today is an authentic record from prophets and apostles.

THE GOSPEL MATERIAL

When we come to the Gospel material, we find several other aspects which are excellent evidences of trustworthiness. First, the Gospels and Acts reflect an amazing historical and archaeological accuracy *that is totally unique in ancient-history writing*. Wherever solid independent evidence is available from archaeology or other extant records the Bible shows itself to be accurate. This includes parallel information on places, practices, rulers, government structures, and organizations. So accurate is the New Testament that it could only have been written by those who were involved in the events at the places described in the Scriptures. Sir William Ramsey's great classic, *St. Paul, Traveler and Roman Citizen*, demonstrated this with great clarity and forcefulness.[4] His evidence has never been objectively refuted, but only denied by those with an anti-supernatural bias. In *Luke, Historian and Theologian* I. Howard Marshall brings Ramsey's work up to date and provides similar corroboration for the Gospel of Luke.[5] Ralph Martin in *Mark the Evangelist* gives similar coherent evidence for the content of our earliest Gospel.[6] Space does not permit us to review the detailed evidence of these books; the student is referred to them for reference. A good summary of all of the evidence is found in Greg Bloomburg's *The Historical Reliability of the Gospels* (see reference in bibliography).

When the Gospels are looked at historically, we find that they fit well the criteria for historical trustworthiness. These criteria are extensions of consistency, coherence, and comprehensiveness as applied to historical material. Basically, historians look for independent testimony in agreement to corroborate major events. Yet this agreement needs to reflect differences in minor detail as providing evidence that the writers are truly independent witnesses. Otherwise there may be one common source behind the testimonies, or there may be a conspiracy. Differences in detail, perspective, and even what appear to be discrepancies are important in establishing the trustworthiness of independent historical documents. With regard to these criteria, we find the highest quality of evidence when we look at the New Testament material.

1. The Gospels agree in their basic testimony concerning key events. The epistles and the writings of the early Church fathers corroborate this testimony.

2. The Gospels exhibit differences in detail, perspective, and even what at first glance appear to be discrepancies.

3. The Gospels were written near to the events which they purport to describe, as were the Epistles of the New Testament which give corroboration to this testimony.

4. The Gospels agree with external sources where there is parallel information (archaeology, other written materials, historical materials, the Church fathers, Josephus, and secular historians).

It should be noted that there is material in the Gospels that gives evidence of being from common sources. The Gospel of Mark provides a foundation of common material. Scholars have noted material common to Matthew and Luke, often called "Q." There is as well material unique to each Gospel. Common material would be expected from what we know of ancient mnemonic methods of instruction. Whole bodies of material were transmitted orally with amazing accuracy. There probably were oral materials such as the parables taught by Jesus, miracle accounts, and even the basic outline of the ministry of Jesus found in the synoptic Gospels (the first three Gospels: Matthew, Mark, and Luke). Written sources are not unlikely as well. However, we have no doubt that oral apostolic material was passed down with great accuracy. Scholars such as Reisenfeld and B. Gerhardson have given convincing evidence for this, including some of the mnemonic forms and structures found in the Gospel material. This fits the evidence of contemporary Jewish practice.[7]

However, even within this common material, differences of perspective are evident. Key testimony concerning the resurrection of Jesus shows even greater independence. The tradition of the early Church concerning the origins of the Gospels gives significant information. Papias, an early–second-century Church father, described the Gospel of Mark as the preaching and teaching of Peter which was put in written form by John Mark.[8] Matthew was described as written later by the former publican (tax collector) Matthew who was one of the twelve disciples. We are told that Matthew originally wrote his Gospel in Hebrew. This has been taken variously to be Aramaic (a cognate language to Hebrew) or to be Hebrew itself. Some believe, on the basis of the evidence of Papias, that our Gospel of Matthew is a translation from Hebrew or Aramaic. Others believe that Matthew personally composed a parallel Gospel of Matthew in Greek. It is clear, however, that the thought forms of Matthew's Gospel are Semitic more than Greek. Either of these possibilities would certainly be acceptable. Luke was written by the travel companion of Paul, who did firsthand research and interviewed eyewitnesses. John was written by the beloved disciple of Jesus in the last years of his life.

The words of Luke's introduction are especially important to the historian:

> Many have undertaken to draw up an account of the things
> that have been fulfilled among us, just as they were handed
> down to us by those who were eyewitnesses and servants of
> the Word. Therefore, since I myself have carefully investiga-
> ted everything from the beginning, it seemed good also to me
> to write an orderly account for you, most excellent Theoph-
> ilus, so that you may know the certainty of the things you have
> been taught.

Luke traveled with Paul, traveled to Israel, and visited with the eyewitnesses in
putting together his Gospel. It is now our task to look at the external sources to
give evidence for authenticity. Evidence for authenticity is found in external secular sources, Jewish sources, Church Fathers, and lastly, internally, in the New
Testament. We are not herein presenting a detailed portrait of Jesus as in our
last chapter or as is found more extensively in the works of Donald Guthrie and
Everet Harrison.[9]

There is little material outside New Testament sources that gives direct information about Jesus. There are a wealth of data confirming New Testament details about cities, events, and Jewish and Roman law practices, all of which reveal
the accuracy of the New Testament. F. F. Bruce, A. Sherwin White, I. Howard
Marshall, R. T. France, and Creig Bloomburg are only a few of the renowned
scholars who bring forth this evidence.[10] Liberal scholars writing in the last few
decades have produced new speculative theories but little in the way of any new
evidence which would count against the basic argument for the trustworthiness
of the New Testament documents.

EXTRA-BIBLICAL CONFIRMATION

There is some important material external to the New Testament. Seutonius in
the *Lives of the Caesars* speaks of one Christus whose movement was stirring up
unrest in the Empire. Tacitus notes that Christians gained their name from
Christus, who was executed by the sentence of the Procurator Pontius Pilate
when Tiberius was emperor.[11] Similar references are found in Pliny the
Younger. F. F. Bruce notes that the first Gentile writer of any import was
Thallas, who is mentioned by Josephus (*Antiquities* XVIII:6.4). Thallas' writings are referred to by Julius Africanus, a Christian writer on chronology, who
sought to refute Thallas' claim that the darkness which fell over the land when

Messiah died was an eclipse of the sun. This would be difficult to accept on astronomical grounds, since the Messiah died during the paschal full moon, a time when a solar eclipse could not take place. However, here is an early Greek writer who corroborates the testimony that darkness covered the land during the crucifixion of Jesus (Matthew 26:45; Mark 15:33–41).

The most interesting point of contact is from a Jewish writer who was not a follower of Jesus, the general and historian Josephus. His reference to Jesus is so positive and supportive of the Gospel portrait that some historians have doubted that it was in the original writing and have posited it as a later Christian addition, at least in part. Yet, there is no conflict in any of the manuscript evidence. All manuscripts preserve this testimony. The fourth-century Church historian Eusebius quotes it as it stands. It is worth repeating Josephus' statement (possible late additions are in italics):

> And there arose about this time Jesus, a wise man, *if indeed we should call him a man*, for he was a doer of marvelous deeds, a teacher of men who receive the truth with pleasure. He led away many Jews, and also many of the Greeks. *This man was the Messiah.* And when Pilate had condemned him to the cross on his impeachment by the chief men among us, those who had loved him at first did not cease; *for he appeared to them on the third day alive again, the divine prophets having spoken these and thousands of other wonderful things about him;* and even now the tribe of Christians, so named after him, has not yet died out." *(Antiquities*, Book XVIII, Chap. 3, v. 3)

Even if there were the italicized additions to the text to make the passage more affirmative of New Testament conviction, the basic material should be accepted as authentic and confirms the historicity of the New Testament. Even a traditional Jewish scholar, Joseph Klausner, who was not a disciple of Jesus, so argued in his book *Jesus of Nazareth*.[12]

The Talmud is also of value in confirming the historicity of Jesus. This literature put into written form the legal debates of various rabbinical schools concerning the application of the Law and also includes stories, parables, and legends of the Jewish people. Though compiled some centuries after the New Testament, even its negative references to Jesus show a knowledge of New Testament teaching.[13] The Talmud records earlier oral material. Its picture of Jesus is of one who was a wonder-worker who died on Passover Eve. He is called son of Pentera (Ben Pantheras)—not, as sometimes thought, as the son of a Roman soldier named Pantheras, but as a reference to *parthenos* (the Greek term for virgin). Of course, in keeping with rabbinical decisions, the Talmud ascribes his powers to magic and scorns him as a heretic.[14] This information again confirms the basic information in the Gospels.

Some very indirect information in the Talmud also notes that during the forty years before the destruction of the Second Temple (amazingly beginning after the time of the crucifixion of Jesus), the lot (for the Yom Kippur sacrifice) never was chosen by the high priest's right hand. Also, the red slip of cloth outside the Holy of Holies never turned white (a sign of God's forgiveness), and the Western candle would not light. The doors of the Sanctuary opened by themselves. Rabbi Yochanan Ben Zakkai admonished the doors saying, "Sanctuary, Sanctuary, . . . I know that you are destined to be destroyed" (Yoma 39b).

Very important evidence is found in the writings of the Church fathers. The earliest of these included men who knew the disciples. Other Church fathers knew earlier fathers who knew the disciples. The writings of these fathers can be found in *The Apostolic Fathers*, edited by Lightfoot[15], and in the *Ante-Nicean Fathers*, which is part of the classic series of early Church writings, and in the history of Eusebius, the early–fourth-century Church historian. Eusebius preserved fragments of the writings of other fathers that were lost. Rather than giving the evidence of each, since the student can read these materials for himself, we will simply name the key Church fathers and examine their basic agreement.

Clement of Rome, whose letter to the Corinthians is preserved, was a father at the end of the first century.

Polycarp was a disciple of John, the disciple of Jesus, and wrote in the early second century. He had leadership in the Church in Asia Minor.

Clement of Alexandria, a leader of the Egyptian Christian community, wrote in the mid–second century.

Justin Martyr was a leading apologist for Christianity before the mid–second century.

Eusebius was a Church historian in the early fourth century who gave important information concerning the Church fathers and their writings which are now lost. His *Ecclesiastical History* is an important source.

Ignatius of Anitoch was another important Church father whose writings stem from the early second century.

Papias, an early–second-century Church father whose writings testify to the origins of the Gospel material, is also an important figure.

These Church fathers all testify to the same basic understanding:

1. That the testimony concerning Jesus was received from the disciples of Jesus who were eyewitnesses;

2. That the Gospel material came from the original circle of disciples and apostles;

3. That Jesus was and is the Messiah, the Son of God who demonstrated the Kingdom of God in his powerful ministry of teaching, preaching, healing, and miracle-working;

4. That Jesus rose from the dead and appeared to groups of his disciples, some larger and some smaller groups, until the day of his ascension into heaven.

SUMMARY OF THE EVIDENCE

We emphasize that the evidence for Jesus and his resurrection in these sources, when taken into account altogether, is a strong confirmation of the New Testament material.   No religious figure of ancient times is as well attested as Jesus.

THE NEW TESTAMENT EVIDENCE

The New Testament itself, however, is the primary corpus of documents that give us strong evidence and testimony corroborating our faith.   It provides us with testimony from several authors and eyewitnesses:

1. The four Gospels, each of which gives independent material for the ministry of Jesus;

2. The book of Acts, which records the testimony as shared by various apostles. This history of the early Church is compiled by Luke, who wrote the Gospel of Luke and was the traveling companion of Paul;

3. The letters of Paul, an early convert to faith in Jesus, formerly a leading Pharisee, and a man who personally knew and shared with the first apostles or disciples of Jesus;

4. The writings of Peter, who in his letters gives significant testimony;

5. The letter of James, the half-brother of Jesus;

6. The letter of Jude, another half-brother of Jesus;

7. The book of Hebrews, an early letter to Jewish followers of Jesus by an unknown author variously thought to be Paul, John, or Barnabas;

8. The book of Revelation, written by the apostle John while he was exiled on the island of Patmos;

9. The Epistles or letters of John the Apostle.

I desire to save the evidence of the book of Acts for last, treating first the Gospels and then the other New Testament material.

THE GOSPELS PORTRAY JESUS IN A CONSISTENT WAY

The Gospels are in full agreement that Jesus was a great man, the anointed (Messiah) king of Israel. They portray him as living a sinless, miraculous life. In him the very rule of God broke into the dimension of our world, producing releases from demonic oppression, the healing of diseases, and a dramatic change of direction in life for many. They all agree that Jesus was baptized under the ministry of John the Baptist, who pointed to Jesus as the one to come. They all portray a man of incredible compassion to children, the needy, and the sinner, as well as showing forth great abhorrence to hypocrisy. Such power came through Jesus that He even raised people from the dead. The Gospel accounts also show unity in representing Jesus as a forceful teacher with an accomplished use of parable. He was a teacher loved by the common people. The Gospel material is uniform in its testimony that the majority of the Jewish religious establishment in Jerusalem rejected him. They all agree that He was given over to the Romans to die by this religious establishment, and that He was crucified and rose from the dead. Jesus is also seen as loyal to the Law (Torah) of God while rejecting the rabbinical applications which bypassed the heart meaning of the Law.

THE LETTERS OF PAUL AGREE WITH THE GOSPELS

In all respects, the Epistles (letters) of Paul agree with this perspective. A reading of his letters gives weighty evidence that this is what he received as the portrait of Jesus from the disciples. In all historical references to Jesus in the other New Testament books, there is total agreement with these basic facts. Some have sought to cast doubt upon this evidence by calling the ascribed authorship of the biblical books into question. However, the evidence for the traditional view of authorship is very good and is well summarized by Donald Guthrie in his excellent and revised *New Testament Introduction*. This is a standard work of scholarship.

THE BOOK OF ACTS AGREES WITH THE GOSPELS

The book of Acts itself provides a very important corroboration of the rest of the New Testament by providing an account of the early progress of the new sect of the followers of Jesus. First, it shows that all of the preaching of Peter, Phillip, Stephen, Paul, Silas, and Barnabas presented a basic outline in accord with the Gospels. Secondly, it is of the highest archaeological veracity in all points touching extra-biblical evidence.[16] Thirdly, it provides a picture of the supernatural power of God in the work of the early communities of faith which is of the same character as the supernatural power of God at work in the ministry of Jesus. The Kingdom of God was breaking into the world providing healing, deliverance, and a change in life direction. Those who have experienced the supernatural will find similarities to their own experiences with God.

One of the amazing accounts in Acts concerns the transformation of the movement for Jesus from a merely Jewish movement to a worldwide mission to all peoples. Only the account of God's supernatural interventions can explain how this took place. The Jewish conception of the time was that once Israel as a whole responded to the Gospel, the Messiah would return to deliver Israel and the Gentiles would have opportunity to be saved (Acts 3:19–21). A combination of dovetailing believable miracles changed this understanding and hence the direction of the early Jewish Church. First was a supernatural vision of the Messiah given to Saul, the persecutor of the new Messianic movement (Acts 9). His conversion was as a result of this vision of Jesus. His commission to be an apostle to the Gentiles was confirmed by Ananias. He ministered to Paul in response to a supernatural vision parallel to the vision given to Paul.

During this same time period we read of a vision given to Cornelius, a Roman centurion, who was told to send for Peter, who would give him the message of life. While men from Cornelius traveled to the place of Peter's abode, Peter was given a vision to prepare him to be willing to accompany these men to the home of Cornelius. Peter was given a vision of unclean animals and told to kill and eat. The point of the vision was not that Peter was to eat unclean food, but that he was not to consider Gentiles, who were open to the Gospel, as unclean (as was common in Jewry at the time). Peter did indeed go and preach the Gospel. While he preached, those present received the Holy Spirit with supernatural manifestations. Peter is amazed upon realizing that the Gentiles were granted repentance and faith in Jesus without becoming Jewish or without being circumcised.

This prepared the way for the Jerusalem disciples to accept the mission of Paul to the Gentiles. (Cf. Acts 11:1, Acts 15.) Paul's own conversion and mission has traditionally been seen as a great evidence for the faith. This devout Jewish Pharisee, a persecutor of the early believers, would not have accepted Jesus short of a great miracle. This is reported in the book of Acts. Furthermore, Paul was certainly familiar with the facts; his faith in Jesus shows that he knew the evidence of the resurrection of Jesus to be excellent.

Actually, the Gospel and Acts are testimonies of the many miraculous confirmations of God's Kingdom rule being present and a recording of how the miraculous gave new direction at pivotal times. These testimonies are presented as evidence for the truth of the Gospel of Jesus, since the events recorded were not merely private-subjective experiences. The fact that several witnessed the same events and that dovetailing visions and miracles were *strategically* part of the progress of the early Church gave to the early believers the clear conviction that the hand of God himself was giving supernatural manifestation and direction.

THE RESURRECTION OF JESUS

The most pronounced miracle of all recorded in the New Testament material is the resurrection of Jesus from the dead. All of the biblical writers give witness to the miraculous transformation whereby the body of Jesus did not undergo physical decomposition. Jesus was alive and manifested himself to his disciples. The resurrection accounts crucially reveal agreement in the great sweep of their testimony, while showing differences of perspective in more minor matters, which may appear contrary but are capable of harmonization.

First we call attention to the areas of agreement:

1. All testify that the tomb in which Jesus lay was empty and that a bodily resurrection (transformation) took place.

2. All testify that Jesus appeared to the women first.

3. All record the involvement of Joseph of Arimathea in the burial of Jesus (Joseph asked for the body from Pilate.

4. All record that Jesus appeared to his disciples over a period of time until his ascension. During this time the disciples were given further instruction, direction, and exhortation. During these appearances, fraught with supernatural phenomena (such as Jesus passing through a wall), Jesus also appeared to be like other unresurrected human beings.

5. All record that a disillusioned band of disciples, distressed and fearful, was turned into a fearless band of preachers and ambassadors through being with the resurrected Jesus. This transformation of the disciples was completed, according to the book of Acts, when the disciples were baptized in the Holy Spirit.

This evidence is well summarized by Paul in I Corinthians 15, an early letter of Paul's (50–52 A.D.) which is universally acknowledged as authentic. Paul, reflecting on the testimony he received directly from the disciples of Jesus says:

> For what I received I passed on to you as of first importance;
> that Christ died for our sins according to the Scriptures, that
> He was buried, and that He rose on the third day according to
> the Scriptures, and that He appeared to Peter, and then to the
> twelve. After that he appeared to more than five hundred of
> the brothers at the same time, most of whom are still alive
> though some have fallen asleep. Then he appeared to James,
> then to all the Apostles, and last of all he appeared to me also,
> as to one abnormally born. (I Corinthians 15:5–8)

All of the gathered literature of the New Testament is in agreement in testifying to this resurrection, but the I Corinthians passage we have just quoted is especially noteworthy. In this passage Paul uses the historic truth of the resurrection to prove the teaching on the future resurrection of faithful followers of Jesus. In so doing he outlines the universally accepted testimony from the disciples. The women are not included in this account, probably due to Jewish standards of acceptable legal evidence. However, Paul shows that the resurrection was objectively experienced in *group* situations. Most of the witnesses were still alive. The implication is that if Paul's readers did not believe him, they could ask the witnesses. This early testimony by Paul is of the highest value. This point cannot be overstressed. Paul was a contemporary of Jesus who personally knew the disciples. Those not greatly biased against the supernatural will recognize this evidence as excellent. This good evidence was a key to the conversion of agnostic C. S. Lewis.[17] Apologist J. W. Montgomery noted that the quality of this very evidence distinguishes Christianity from all other religions.[18] Merrill Tenney, in *The Reality of the Resurrection*, shows in much greater detail the ring of truth in these resurrection passages.[19] Tenney calls attention to the details of John's account: the accurate description of the grave clothes left behind, just as they were arranged on his body and not disturbed; the various believable responses of Mary, Peter, and John; the doubts of the disciples, and more. Tenney concludes that we have remarkably accurate and detailed testimony that fits what we know of human nature.[20]

The detailed account in the Gospel of John is artless—in other words, unforced. Indeed, although there were standards of evidence in first century Judaism, great concern with empirical details is a modern preoccupation. Yet such details are found in the Gospel accounts. Perhaps they were present because in the face of such an extraordinary miracle, witnesses, for religious not legal reasons, saw importance in these details. We now have these details, with their important function in apologetic evidence.

Tenney goes on to show how the resurrection is not simply an unusual event, but a key linchpin for understanding New Testament theology. The whole theology of the New Testament depends on the resurrection and is incomprehensible without it. The resurrection gives proof that Jesus' crucifixion had redemptive meaning, that seeming defeat was swallowed up in victory. It is the basis for a certain hope of a meaningful life after death in the restored community of the redeemed.

The historicity of the resurrection explains why the opponents could never produce the body of Jesus to stifle the new movement. It explains the birth of the New Testament Messianic movement. The account of the pouring out of the Holy Spirit in Acts 2 along with the resurrection itself can alone *adequately* account for the launching of a worldwide movement that rocked the world.

This evidence is so good that an Orthodox Jewish scholar at Bar Ilan University in Tel Aviv concludes that Jesus indeed rose from the dead. Lapide chides his liberal "Christian" colleagues for their unbelief. He uses an argument remarkably similar to classic Christian apologetics and similar to the argument used here.[21] Lapide, who claims to not have concluded that Jesus is the Messiah, would not have a bias toward believing in the resurrection of Jesus. He argues, however, that Jesus is at least an agent of God who is vindicated in the resurrection. The accounts of the resurrection have their differences. What was the order in which people went to the tomb and in which the appearances were made? Was there one angel or two? Some accounts leave out the separate visit of Peter and John to the tomb before the appearance of Jesus to Mary and later the disciples (John 20:1–15). Did Jesus send the disciples to Galilee to meet him (Mark 16:7)? Then what are we to make of the Jerusalem appearances of Jesus to his disciples? Pinchas Lapide suggests that Jesus' directive was not to go to Galilee but to the Galil, a place outside Jerusalem.[22] Yet all of these accounts can be harmonized. An excellent brief harmony of the events is given in the article "Resurrection" by Leon Morris in *The New Bible Dictionary*. A more complete summary is given by John Wenham in his *Easter Enigma: Are the Resurrection Accounts in Conflict?* The reader himself can easily see that each account is a part of the whole. Perhaps the disciples did not believe the report of the resurrection until Jesus appeared to them in Jerusalem. Then they traveled to Galilee. John and Luke record some of Jesus' appearances in Galilee. Jesus could simply have appeared in both places to strengthen the faith of the disciples and to encourage them to follow through. This provides an example of the possibilities of harmonization. These very differences in detail and perspective, however, lend credibility to the Gospels as independent witnesses.

The bias of anti-supernaturalism has caused some to try and explain away the testimony of the resurrection. Nineteenth-century writers produced the basic positions of denial.[22] With slight variations, most writers who attempt to explain away the resurrection support one of these viewpoints. A fascinating debate on the resurrection reveals this bias. In *Did Jesus Rise From the Dead?* (edited by Terry L. Maithe) a famous British skeptic and philosopher, Anthony Flew, debates three men: Christian apologist Gary Habermas, Christian philosopher Terry Maithe, and Christian religion professor W. David Bede. A significant response to the debate is given by famed theologian Wolfhart Pannenburg of the University of Munich. Pannenburg wryly notes that Flew's anti-supernatural bias shows a "reluctance to enter into a serious discussion of historical detail."[24]

THE SWOON THEORY

The "swoon theory" maintained that Jesus did not really die on the cross, but swooned. The coolness of the tomb revived him. Hence, his speaking to his disciples was taken by them to be a supernatural resurrection. Then, in their excitement, they spread the faith. This theory overlooks the testimony that there was no body of Jesus at any time to be found after the resurrection. It ignores the Gospel testimony to make up its own account. It is hard, to say the least, to believe that a bleeding, dying, but briefly revived man could have inspired the disillusioned disciples. This theory ignores the evidence of Acts 1 and 2 concerning the ascension of Jesus and the miracle of the outpouring of the Holy Spirit. The Gospel accounts report on meetings with a resurrected man, not a barely surviving man. These meetings took place over a long period of time.

THE STOLEN-BODY THEORY

A second explanation, even recorded in the Gospels, was that the disciples stole the body and proclaimed the resurrection. This explanation simply makes the disciples to be liars. Its greatest problem is why these liars would go through torture and martyrdom for a testimony they knew to be false. Furthermore, it ignores the corroborating evidence of the appearances, the ascension of Jesus, and of the miracles of the book of Acts. The conversion of Paul and his testimony concerning the five hundred who together saw him alive is conveniently ignored. Was it all made up? This is hardly believable.[25]

THE WRONG-IDENTIFICATION THEORY

Some have maintained that the women went to the wrong tomb and mistook the gardener for an angel when he said, "He is not here," and pointed to the right tomb.[26] In their emotional state they misunderstood and ran from the tomb spreading stories of the resurrection. This led to hallucinations of Jesus, it is said. We have to ask, did the other disciples also go to the wrong tomb? Did they not care to check out the women's story? Why then did not the Roman and Jewish authorities produce the body of Jesus to put an end to the movement? Furthermore, the accounts of the Gospels are not of hallucinogenic states or even visions, but of Jesus showing up in normal group situations. Together they saw him, heard him teach, and ate with him. He was *jointly* and more objectively experienced. Group hallucination has never been shown to occur. Indeed, these theories are only possible when the actual evidence of the Gospels is either ignored or selectively used.

A SPIRITUAL RESURRECTION

Others have put forth the view that Jesus did not physically rise but only rose spiritually. This ignores the clear evidence of the *empty tomb* testimony and the Jewish context of the meaning of resurrection. Jesus' resurrection is parallel to the resurrection of Lazarus in John 11. He bodily came out of the tomb. The difference in Jesus' case is that his resurrection was also a transformation to a permanent supernatural state of body. All of the New Testament evidence presupposes the transformation of a body which did not undergo decomposition.

THE PASSOVER PLOT

A most fascinating variation on these theories was created by Hugh Schoenfield in *The Passover Plot*.[27] Schoenfield proposes the theory that Jesus plotted his own death and resurrection. He planned that He would feign death, be removed from the cross, and then, after healing, would proclaim himself the risen Messiah. The soldier who pierced his side with the spear ruined the plot and Joseph of Arimathea hid the body. Schoenfield's view, however, must ignore all of the evidence of the bodily appearances of Jesus to the disciples, to the five hundred, and the evidence of the outpouring of the Spirit. It is a farfetched theory, to say the least.

THE SHROUD OF TURIN

Recently a great deal of controversy has swirled around the possible evidence of the shroud of Turin. The origin of the shroud is somewhat hazy and is based on limited traditions; therefore, if the shroud is accepted as genuine, its testimony should be understood as *secondary* corroboration, *of lesser value* than the direct testimony of the New Testament.

The shroud is purportedly the burial cloth of Jesus preserved in a church in Turin, Italy. If authentic, this shroud could provide material archaeological evidence for the crucifixion and resurrection of Jesus. A group of scientific scholars have thoroughly studied this shroud. Perhaps this is the one genuine Christian relic from ancient times. Gary Habermas, a noted apologist, has given an extensive review of the case for seeing the shroud as the burial cloth of Jesus, whose image can be explained by the energy and power present when God resurrected Jesus.[28] The shroud would thus provide an exact image of a crucified man from ancient times.

In January 1984, John Heller, a leader on the Shroud of Turin Scientific Research Project, summarized the conclusions of the team.[29] These conclusions are also summarized in Habermas' and Stevens' book noted above. Basically, the shroud provides us with several mysteries. The cloth can be traced by clear historical report to the late Middle Ages. Beyond this we have only conjecture, but there is some evidence for a first-century date for the cloth. However, here are the most salient points.

1. Computer-enhanced photos show the recording of a perfect three-dimensional image, impossible for Middle Ages painting.

2. There is no evidence that the image of the shroud was painted, since there is no clear evidence of paint pigment. Furthermore, the image is only to be found on the *surface* fibers of the cloth, unlike a painting.

3. There are no brush strokes discernable on the shroud.

4. The accuracy of the dimensions of the image of the man on the shroud is beyond the knowledge of medieval artists. This includes the proportioned depth of the three-dimensional image.

5. The shroud reflects a crucifixion through the wrists, which is historically correct for the first century but was unknown to medieval artists.

6. The shroud is the kind of image that would be made by a scorch that was very brief since the scorch is only on the surface fibers. This produces an image that is three-dimensional, since the light and dark areas of the image reflect the cloth's contact with the body. A charge of energy, such as could occur in a res-

urrection, could be the explanation of the image.

7. Other studies have detected the presence of first-century coins over the eyes in the image.

8. Blood has been detected as the origin of the stains.

9. The features of blood pooling, rigor mortis, and other aspects are anatomically accurate, far beyond the knowledge of earlier centuries.

The greatest puzzlement, in the light of the above, is recent C-14 dating, which dates the cloth of the shroud to the Middle Ages. Hence, despite all of the above points, the value of the shroud as evidence is questionable.

Recently Gary Habermas and Kenneth Stevenson authored a response to these new findings. In *The Shroud and the Controversy*, they argue that most of the basic evidence for the shroud recounted in their first book is valid in spite of the C-14 dating. They put forth several reasons to strongly question the accuracy and even the honesty of the C-14 dating experiment. In personal conversation, Habermas told me that due to the good reasons to doubt the C-14 tests, the Catholic Church was opening up the issue again.

FORM CRITICISM

A new type of approach to biblical interpretation in the twentieth century sought to analyze the biblical text in terms of the forms of the Gospel material. Some of the forms ascertained are miracle stories, parables, sayings, and narrative material.[30] Scholars, using form criticism, have sought to find the situation in life that gave rise to the particular material.[31] Some have sought to find the marks of the author who grouped the material together as we have it and to discern his particular understanding and purpose in his editing. This latter is known as *redaction criticism*.[32]

It is often the assumption of these scholars that the situation in life that gave rise to the material was not the event in the life of Jesus but a life situation in the early Church. The stories and sayings that arose spoke to these situations. They were then attributed to Jesus. The redactor tailored the material to fit his situation. The form critic often implies a radical skepticism concerning the historical Jesus. It is as if we can never get behind the Church to the real Jesus. Furthermore, there is an assumption that supernatural story material is more legendary and to be dated late. Anti-supernatural bias is often apparent.

Albert Schweitzer's *Quest for the Historical Jesus* analyzed the nineteenth-century authors who sought to recreate a true picture of Jesus by critical and selective approaches to the text. The Jesus they created was a reflection of their

own values. We cannot get behind the text to the real Jesus. The recent attempts to do this also fail. John A. T. Robinson's *New Quest for the Historical
Jesus* reveals the same problems, despite the application of form and redaction
criticism. It is interesting to note that Robinson, in recent years, has become
more and more conservative in his appreciation of the trustworthiness of the
New Testament.

Another manifestation of similar skeptical approaches has been reported in
the secular press. Members of the Jesus Seminar, a large group of liberal scholars, meet to vote on what Gospel material is authentically from Jesus and what
is not. Majority vote is then reflected in a text which highlights their vote on authenticity. These scholars begin from the skeptical basis of liberal scholarship.

An analysis of forms in the New Testament can be of value in showing the
context of parallel forms in Jewish sources. Parables can be better understood
by understanding the parable style of teaching common in first-century Rabbinic
Judaism. Redaction studies can also show valid, inspired applications of Jesus'
teaching by the apostles. Yet as a method to discount the historicity of the Gospels, it is without merit and totally the product of bias. Many of the conclusions
are subjective speculations. Some form critics only allow the authenticity of
material from Jesus if it is contrary to first-century parallel teaching in Judaism.[33] Yet Jesus both agreed with and disagreed with his contemporaries. We
can summarize our objections in the following points:

1. The theory denies that the disciples had any formative influence in the
Church or interest in the preservation of Jesus' life and teaching. This is a truly
fantastic assumption.

2. It puts forth a theory requiring us to believe that behind all the incredible
teaching and coherence of the Gospels there is not a great teacher, but only dis-
connected legends later put together.

3. It ignores the positive evidence that oral material was carefully preserved
by the disciples and hence was quoted as authoritative in the early Church. For
example, Paul in I Corinthians 7 gives his view stating that he had no direct word
from the Lord in regard to an issue, but in other places notes that he does.[34]

4. It ignores the testimony of the book of Acts as to early Church origins and
the testimony of Luke in the Gospel of Luke that he is providing a trustworthy
researched account (Luke 1:1ff.).

5. It expects us to believe that the world's greatest life-literature and teaching was produced by the legend-making imagination of several communities. Yet
we know of no social milieu that could produce such a literature.

CONCLUSION

In conclusion, we must state that the evidence for the resurrection and the historicity of the Gospels is excellent. However, we must not lose sight of the power of one's prejudice, values, and presuppositions in blunting the force of evidence. Although affirming the resurrection fulfills the criteria of consistency, coherence, and comprehensiveness, a person is still free to adopt a less coherent explanation. If his prejudice against the Gospel is great enough, he will choose one of the other more farfetched anti-supernatural explanations. It will seem to him that any other explanation is better than the resurrection. In his view, a supernatural, intervening God is unthinkable. Anti-supernatural bias and secular humanism produce mindsets that often do not see the weight of the evidence.

As we have noted earlier, it is always possible to reject conclusions by denying the premises of the argument. This is why even these powerful arguments are powerless without the work of the Holy Spirit and prayer which break through the bias and bring a person to a place where he can genuinely and fairly consider a dramatically different world view. This is why the New Testament repeatedly affirms faith as a gift of God and the essential importance of the Holy Spirit in believing. Evidence, however, has its place as an instrument of the Holy Spirit. Our faith has its corroborating evidence. Indeed, there is abundant evidence in the historicity of the Gospels and the resurrection of Jesus to strengthen the faith of any willing heart.

We have given a very brief summary of this evidence. The student is invited to pursue the books and articles mentioned in the notes and the bibliography on these subjects to gain an even fuller appreciation of this evidence.

CHAPTER 14: STUDY QUESTIONS

1. On what grounds do we hold that the Gospels are trustworthy historical documents?

2. What are the basic areas of agreement concerning the resurrection in all New Testament material?

3. Why should Gospel differences be seen as enhancing rather than discrediting our evidence for the trustworthiness of the Gospels?

4. What is form and redaction criticism?

5. Why did Albright conclude that the Gospels were early–first-century testimony?

THE EVIDENCE FROM FAITH EXPERIENCE AND CONTEMPORARY MIRACLES

THE BIBLICAL FAITH IS NOT A WORLD VIEW IN WHICH THE POWER OF GOD'S supernatural working is divorced from the moral quality of life. The miracles of the New Testament and the Old Testament were manifestations of love, power, forgiveness and deliverance from God. These manifestations have as their goal a people who reflect a moral character like unto the goodness of God. Therefore, the most wonderful manifestation of the power of the Bible is to be found in the changed lives of those who submit their lives to God through Jesus the Messiah. Whole books can and have been written about such changed lives as well as the quality of life among those in the community of faith. In our experience this has been marvelously proven out. Here are just a few areas.

First is the healing of marriages. So many have come to faith in our day whose marriages were close to disintegration. In receiving the power of God, they learn that love is the *fruit of covenant commitment*. Each receives that power to die to selfishness, the root of marital discord. In the power of the Holy Spirit they are inspired to greater acceptance and understanding for one another. Genuine selfless love grows within. In twenty two years of pastoring, we have not seen one divorce among couples in which both partners were committed to the Kingdom of God and the community of faith—the manifestation of the Kingdom of God. Indeed, these are not just cases where the people involved grit their teeth and bear the marriage because it is required. Rather, it is that both discover a power of love which replaces discord.

Similar results have been seen with regard to parents and children in the healing of families. Parents gain the power for loving consistent discipline, and children gain the power of loving obedience. I do not wish to paint an ideal picture, but the change in the truly committed is usually dramatic.

The extraordinary ability of God to change a person's life testifies as well for the truth of our faith. We have personally seen two supposedly incurable schizophrenics changed to normality by the power of prayer in a loving faith community. How many are the books on changed lives. Let us note a few.

Charles Colson, in *Born Again*, describes his great change from the ruthless lawyer and hatchet man of the Nixon administration to his subsequent change into a servant of prisoners for the sake of the Gospel. Many are the criminals who have given their lives to God and have lead productive lives as a result of their coming to faith through his ministry.

Nicky Cruz was a gang member, burned out on drugs. He was transformed and became a leading evangelist. This he attributes to the power of God. The account of his story and many more is in David Wilkerson's *The Cross and the Switchblade*.

Tom Skinner, a Harlem gang leader, was also transformed by the power of God and is now the leading black evangelist in America.

How many have been saved from alcohol, drugs, compulsive behavior, criminal lifestyles, and destructive patterns of life. No faith compares to the biblical faith in offering testimonies of life-saving power.

However, it is not only the changes God can bring, but the sustaining power to bring a person through all difficulties. Where will one go to find a similar testimony to Richard Wurmbrand's *Tortured for Christ*. This pastor from Romania describes his amazing ability to be at peace through terrible tortures, his power in Messiah to rejoice in faith, and his ability to love and forgive his tormentors. To read this man's books, or better yet to hear him speak, is to be transported into the presence of the Spirit.

It is also worth mentioning Corrie Ten Boom. This simple spinster was taken prisoner by the Nazis for helping Jews to escape the horrors of the Nazis. Her many books reflect the vibrant faith of her father and her family, which enabled them to persevere in faith, hope, and forgiveness.[1]

Two noted psychiatrists who carefully observed the inmates in the Nazi camps noticed that some easily succumbed to the shame and cruelty. They became camp zombies. Others, however, had an unbreakable spirit and psychologically held together through all difficulties. What was the difference? Both authors discovered it to be a vital faith in the God of the Bible.[2] Both Bruno Bettelheim and Victor Frankel are now famous in their fields, the former for his work with children. He describes his experience in his marvelous book, *The Informed Heart*. Frankel was famous for his development of *logo-therapy*, a theory based on the concept that meaning in life is essential to human fulfillment. His experience in the camps was a key to developing his theory.

Faith in the God of the Bible is a foundation for stable families and societies. It gives an abiding sense that life has meaning and purpose in an ultimate sense. It motivates moral behavior. It lets us know that the beautiful sunset is not some delusion of the imagination but is the product of the Artist behind the universe. The experience of beauty thus rises to praise and adoration; all of life is enhanced. Faith in the Scriptures elevates man—he is created in the image of God. His sexuality is a gift to be reserved for that one special person in the expression of covenant commitment, love, and intimacy. Life is seen as a sacred gift, the earth as a stewardship from God. The values that sustain a rich life cannot long be maintained without the biblical world and life view that gives rise to these values.

One of the aspects of religious experience which is worthy for examination is the miraculous. To adequately reflect on the evidence of the miraculous, it is necessary to give an explicit apologetic definition of "miracle." The common use of the word miracle is broader than this definition.

Many people commonly use the term *miracle* to connote anything wonderful that conveys the sense of the divine to them. Many have been awed in witnessing the birth of their children and speak of it as miraculous. Surely this is the kind of event which shouts against a view of the world as only the product of time, plus chance, plus matter. For many, the birth of a child, the glory of a wedding, the flowers in bloom, a mountain landscape, the starry sky at night, and the depth of friendship can be a catalyst to faith in God. The word *miracle* is used for them all. Especially, this is the case with the miracle of our own existence, the extraordinary powers of our brains, our ability to feel, to love, to hate, to create and to destroy. Man is a creature of great wonder.

However, for apologetic purposes, I wish to reserve the word *miracle* for events which are beyond normal explanation. Normal explanation can be divided into two aspects. The first is that the event is explainable by the laws of material cause and effect. This would include mathematics and the laws of matter in motion. As we have argued earlier, however, we do not believe that normal, everyday experience can be tied together by the terms of material causation. Our thoughts, our volitional acts, etc., all require concepts of explanation that are not merely extensions of the laws of physics, chemistry, or even biology. Hence, the second aspect includes the usual explanations that are part of ordinary human life and speech. We could say, for example, that she slapped him because he needled her to the point of anger.

The non-usual or non-normal events and explanations point us beyond the simplistic notion that the world of our five senses is the whole of reality—a very strange and suspect assumption indeed. There are such events, according to biblical and some nonbiblical orientations. Two books of note that first pushed me beyond a naturalistic viewpoint were on the occult and psychic phenomena. The first was G. N. Tyrell's *Science and Psychical Phenomena*. Tyrell gives documented evidence of several phenomena not amenable to our present concepts of physical law. These include telepathy (knowledge gained without the benefit of the five senses); clairvoyance (knowledge of future and distant events before their occurrence); poltergeist phenomena (the noisy-ghost manifestations in some houses); telekinesis (moving an object without physical contact); and mediumistic powers of knowledge and communication. Tyrell recounts only the most documented cases. My evaluation of Tyrell is that he was a careful researcher whose evidence the openminded will not discount.[3]

Such cases as Tyrell's leave only two conclusions. Either there is a nonmaterial realm of existence (or at least another dimensional realm of spirits, consciousness centers, forces) that impinges upon our space-time world and is subject to different laws, or there are natural-physical explanations for these phenomena that are merely extensions of known physical laws. The latter conclusion seems to be very forced; it is the position of a naturalistic precommitment. These psychical phenomena are so extraordinary that to begin to apply known physical principles to explain them seems foolish. For example, telepathic knowledge is transmitted and received without any apparent space-time travel aspects, such as we know in radio waves. There is an immediacy of knowledge from one point of the world even to the other side of the earth.

Dr. S. Mbiti, a brilliant and well-educated philosopher, in *African Religions and Philosophy* chides Westerners for their materialist and skeptical bent. Noting that there are powers in primitive religions that are beyond Western scientific categories of understanding, Mbiti gives a powerful example. He cites a construction project blocked by a small sacred tree. The local witch doctor placed incantations on this tree to prevent its removal. As astonishing as it might seem, no bulldozer could budge this modest-sized plant; the machinery just bounced off the tree.[4]

The second major book to influence me in this regard was Kurt Koch's monumental *Christian Counseling and Occultism.*[5] He puts forth the thesis that there are unseen powers and spirit beings that can be tapped into in occult experience. After studying thousands of cases, Koch concluded that most mediumistic and clairvoyant claims were fraudulent. Yet Koch documented many that he believed to be unquestionably genuine. Koch found most such occult experiences to be destructive of the persons involved and even destructive to their descendants. Often, such experimentation brought accompanying depression, oppressive fears, spook-phenomena manifestations, and even suicide. Renunciation and prayer in the name of Jesus were effective in delivering many who were oppressed after occult involvements (ouija boards, table-lifting, palm reading, divining with a rod or pendulum, crystal-ball gazing).

This brings me to conclude that supernatural experience in a biblical faith context is qualitatively different. Biblically based supernatural experiences often deliver from oppression—they give hope and motivate to a better life. There are many miraculous manifestations occurring today in biblical faith contexts. Such miracles do not contradict the laws of nature, but show that God can intervene in the world which He created—a most normal implication of the doctrine of creation.   Miracle accounts are often misleading.   Sometimes they are exaggerated; sometimes they are imaginary. I will emphasize the authentic.

For apologetic purposes I categorize miracles into three types. The first is a type "A" miracle. This is one that is so immediate and extraordinary that all but the most closed-minded are forced to see supernatural intervention since there is no conceivable other explanation. A type "B" miracle is one where the most appropriate explanation is supernatural intervention. A farfetched natural explanation is conceivable, but the circumstances, timing, and the event clearly point beyond the merely natural. A type "C" miracle is one wherein a person of faith would rightly see intervention but nothing significant would be seen by many unbelievers. In the following discussion we limit ourselves to type "A" and "B" miracles that are significantly documented.

Richard Casdorf has written a book called *The Miracles*[6] which documents five significant miracles occurring during the healing ministry of Kathryn Kuhlman. Casdorf has superb credentials for this research as an M.D. and a Ph.D. medical researcher. In Casdorf's book we are presented with X-rays and medical records. Advanced cancer was shown to be immediately reversed in one case. However, most astonishing was the re-creation and response of a damaged heart, including a deformed valve. The deformed valve was replaced by a healthy one. Casdorf concludes that although there are known cancer remissions without apparent explanations in contexts where there is no known prayer or religious intervention, there are no cases of *immediate reversals* as seen when people are prayed for in the name of Jesus. Nor are there any reversals in the kind of physiological heart conditions like the ones he illustrates in his book. The reader is told that he is choosing the best examples from among hundreds that have significant evidential value.

Christianity Today magazine recently did a series on healing, including articles representing different viewpoints. As part of this series, *Christianity Today* printed the account of the healing of a multiple sclerosis patient named Barbara Cummiskey. This was no mere slight case; she had MS of a more rare and severe form that attacks the body's organs. Totally confined to bed, Cummiskey was in severe physical distress. She was subject to chronic lung disease, pneumonia, and asthma, and had an ileostomy for the bowel and a catheter for the bladder. She was on a respirator to breathe with a tracheotomy in the neck. Great chest pain was unceasing, legs were spindly and dangling, arms and hands were turned in, and her eyesight had reached the point of technical blindness. Beyond all of this, tumors grew on her hands and feet. At 31 she was taken to a hospice to die. On June 7, 1981, a local radio station mentioned her situation and asked for prayer. The article continues,

> On this summer day, a Sunday, Barbara sat in bed as two women from her church read cards to her. Barbara (but not the other two women) heard a voice over her shoulder. It was not a booming voice, but a calm one, and it said, "My child, get up and walk." Barbara assumed it was God, at last answering in kind after all those hours of her audible address. She told the two women she was going to walk, and that they should alert her family. Since Barbara had not walked in two years, the women were confused, but they left the room.
>
> Barbara could not wait for her parents. She says she "jumped" out of bed. Elated, she started down the hall, where her mother met her. Barbara's legs, atrophied from lack of exercise, now had muscle tone and firmness. Her mother's first words were a shout: "Calves! You have calves!"
>
> Her father, when Barbara met him downstairs, could summon no words. He grabbed his daughter and danced around the living room with her. After waltzing with her father, Barbara did ballet steps, standing on her toes leaping and laughing.
> . . .

MS is an incurable disease. Barbara Cummiskey, her doctors admit, never should have gotten well, but not only did the
MS leave (conclusive spinal taps show no trace), Barbara's
caved-in lung, dormant for years, should have been no good. It
was completely healthy and functioning. The chronic lung disease, also "incurable," was gone. So were the hand and feet
tumors. Even if the woman somehow recovered from MS,
there should have been permanent brain damage. There was
not. Fortunately, the surgeon performing Barbara's ileostomy
had not removed the entire bowel. Now the bowel was functioning, so the ileostomy was reversed. Likewise the tracheotomy. Health was entirely restored, instantaneously.

Today Barbara is training to be a surgeon's assistant. A man
she trains under was one of her doctors. He delights in intro-
ducing her to classes. "Here is a woman who used to lay under
my knife. I said she would not live. I said she would never
walk. Now she hands me the knife. You can see how good my
predictions are."[7]

The nature of a miracle like this has the potential to shatter naturalistic bias.
It catapults us beyond secondary and physical explanations to ask those ultimate
questions of the nature of our world. It is worthwhile to note that *Christianity
Today* is not the news magazine of an evangelistic healing ministry, but the conservative, reserved, and scholarly organ of Evangelical Christianity in North
America. This is very unusual content for this magazine, but the evidence war-
ranted its inclusion.

When we come face to face with the Divine in such a way, it can produce
awe and conversion. Peter fell face down in awe before Jesus after a miracle of
a great instantaneous catch of fish. He was awed by the sense of the in-breaking
of the Divine.

Attempts to explain away a miracle such as Barbara Cummiskey's are lame
indeed. Shall we posit little-known mechanisms in the body of instant creativity
and healing that somehow were tapped into? Did some genetic mechanism get
released so that flesh was restored to her arms and legs, and healing was brought
to nerves, bowels, and lungs instantaneously? How foolish. The physical is
merely one type of conscious experience, and the physical is subject to spiritual
laws or the laws of the Spirit.

Another extraordinary account of healing is found in the story of T. H. Welsh
by Jerry Parrick.[8] This account was originally shared on Pat Robertson's "700
Club." Robertson makes a practice of thoroughly checking out miracle testi-

monies before airing to be certain of documented authenticity.

Welsh was injured in a logging accident after falling from a trestle over the logging river and severely banging his head in the fall. He was not pulled from under the water until after forty-five minutes had passed. To all appearances he was dead. This was the clear consensus of all involved. However, one couple continued to fervently pray for Welsh. This is the account.

> She placed one hand in the blood on my head and the other on my heart. A young man took her hand off my head and protested to Mabel, "Can't you see that's were he's hurt?"
>
> With blood oozing out between her fingers, Mabel persisted and prayed her short, simple supplication to spare my life and save my soul because, by her firebrand calipers, I wasn't a Christian.

Welsh goes on to describe his supernatural vision of hell and of Jesus during the time he was apparently dead. After this experience, his body came to life, and, to everyone's amazement, he was breathing again. T. H. Welsh was taken to the hospital with several internal injuries, a concussion and broken ribs. His head was sewn and his chest taped for a six-to-eight-week healing. He was placed in intensive care. He hovered between life and death. At this point in the story Welsh recounts being given a word from God asking him to share the vision he had previously received. After his affirmative answer was given to God, Welsh, who was not even yet given much hope to live, was supernaturally healed. All his broken bones were immediately knit and healed, and his injuries to the head healed. Welsh was immediately able to leave the hospital. There were no effects from the skull fracture or the lung puncture. From this experience, Welsh went on to become a powerful preacher of the Gospel.

This account is important because it includes the affidavits of eyewitnesses. Another account worthy of mention is the testimony of Petty Wagner, heiress of the Peet family of the Palmolive company. Wagner is a Ph.D. and a leading businesswoman. Her book recounts a horrifying story of swindling, kidnapping, and torture as part of the plot of her assailants to acquire her wealth. This remarkable book[9] also retells an after-death–type experience; she had a vision of Jesus after which she was given a spiritual sense of God's aid and instruction for escaping. Also, she was asked to pray for each of her captors before each died in very unusual freak accidents and circumstances.

Testimony is given in this book of many remarkable instantaneous healings, reversing the damage inflicted through numerous beatings and tortures suffered at the hands of her captors. Wagner, a scientist and savvy businesswoman, gives no mere rumor or hearsay, but documents her account. This book is well worth reading.

Other information of significance is reported by Peter Wagner of Fuller Theological Seminary.[10] He gives several accounts from eyewitnesses in the mission field that are astonishing. Wagner is a noted scholar who is not rash in his reporting.

Up to this point we have mostly noted supernatural healings, yet there are many other types of events which show the hand of God's intervention. One is the exact answers to prayer received by saintly people of God. Another is knowledge about situations without normal means of knowledge.

The testimony of George Mueller found in numerous biographies gives an amazing account of an abundance of exact answers to prayer—far too many to be explained as coincidence. Mueller established several children's orphanages in Britain. When funds seemed depleted and food reserves were at an end, Mueller and his staff would pray in detail. Often, exact amounts would be given by unexpected sources in answer to prayer. Mueller made a practice of this method of prayer and eschewed publicity and fund-raising as a means of provision.[11]

Francis Schaeffer records numerous answers to prayer of this exact kind. Financial gifts given met required needs *to the penny* when Schaeffer was beginning the L'Abri ministry. This all came in answer to prayer, as recorded in the book by Edith Schaeffer.[11]

Amazing answers to prayer are also recorded in the book *Rees Howells, Intercessor*.[13] The Welsh Bible college run by Howells was a school of prayer. When Howells would call his students to pray, astounding things happened. Great men of prayer often testified of a sense of victory being attained when the burden of prayer was lifted. This is an intuitive sense of having completed the work. A story is told of one prayer meeting which was called by Howells when the British troops were trapped at Dunkirk. When the students were fervently praying with Howells during this time, they had a sense of the victory. Howells then dismissed the meeting and announced that the battle had been won. The next day they read of the "mysterious" cloud cover which provided for the evacuation of troops from the mainland. Historians believe that this escape was a major factor in Hitler's eventual defeat.

We should convey that these kinds of prayer answers do not take place for just anyone who voices something to God. They rather are consistently a part of the lives of those who have learned to walk with God and have wholly dedicated their lives to His service.

Another wonderful account of answered prayer is given in the book *Sit, Walk, Stand*[14] by Watchman Nee. Nee records the triumph of the Gospel over an island off the coast of China. This conquering came by prayer and a word of knowledge. The leaders of the pagan cult had celebrated the feast of their gods for scores of years on perfectly clear days, due to weather forecasting by the island's fishermen. Nee's assistant assured the islanders that it would rain on the feast day when he had an intuitive sense that God was telling him to do so. They stood in faith and saw torrential rain come after a clear early morning. A re-scheduled feast day gave occasion to repeat the prophecy. Once again the rain came. It increased in great torrents when the missionaries were led to pray for heavier rain. Unknown to them, the people of the island had just brought out their idol-god to halt the rain. The intense storm caused the islanders to drop the idol. It was broken. In masses the islanders turned to faith in Jesus and the Bible.

Other documented accounts can be briefly mentioned. There are the accounts in the writings and tapes of Derek Prince, a former Cambridge professor of philosophy and logic. Prince is an accurate reporter of many extraordinary miracles. His wife's instant healing of a deteriorated spine is especially significant.[15]

The tapes and books of John Wimber are especially good sources for documented miracles. Wimber was formerly the director of the Fuller Evangelistic Association. His church of over seven thousand has mushroomed in part due to the presence of the Spirit of God doing many signs and wonders. Wimber is a careful, scholarly teacher who provides a theological and philosophical context for understanding the miraculous.[16]

The writings of Francis McNutt, a well-educated former Catholic (now Episcopal) priest who has been called to the healing ministry, also provide many significant examples.[17]

Another is the former president of the Reformed Church of America, Robert Wise. He was raised off his deathbed, healed of an incurable kidney disease, and has since had a significant healing ministry.

I would be remiss if I did not personally mention the miracles which I have personally witnessed and received. I will give these experiences in chronological order.

My wife has been given several prophetic dreams. The first occurred several years ago, when we were pastoring a congregation in Chicago. One of the couples there had been unable to bear children for over fifteen years of married life. They had adopted two dear children who were then eight and ten. My wife dreamed that our friend would be pregnant. When she told her she laughed. Medical tests had shown that neither she nor her husband were able to produce children. Nevertheless, shortly thereafter she became pregnant. The amazed gynecologist-obstetrician, a secular Jewish man, asked how this could be possible. She told him that it was God. His response was, "I'll believe it was God if you have a boy and he is born circumcised." Later it was found that our friend was pregnant with twins—she gave birth to a girl and a boy and the boy was born circumcised, to the astonishment of the physician.

Shortly after moving to Washington, D.C., my problems with anxiety diarrhea increased. This was a long-term, chronic problem which I developed in the intense skepticism and depression of college years. Despite the fact that I was living a fulfilling life, the pressures of ministry continued to exacerbate this problem. As a matter of fact, for over fifteen years I rarely had a solid bowel movement. Medication was continually necessary. I still wonder if my purchases kept the Pepto-Bismol company in business. Shortly before a tour to Israel, one of my congregants came to me with a prophecy saying that the problem that I had suffered from for so long would be cured in Israel. Those who travel to Israel are aware of the fact that diarrhea is a common problem for travelers. All are encouraged to bring medicine to counter it. Many on the tour did suffer accordingly. However, I experienced the first full relief ever—I was normal for the first time and have continued to be normal since that time.

Upon visiting a pastor in the Boston area, we began to share on some of the wonderful miracles God was doing today. He proceeded to share concerning a former parishioner who was the recipient of an amazing continuing miracle. This parishioner was missing an eye and wore a glass eye in its place. Upon being prayed for some years previously, she was given the ability to see perfectly through the glass eye as though she had a normal eye. I was very skeptical, but he assured me that this was real and that she had taken eye tests to prove it. He then astonished me with the words, "Why, you may know the minister who prayed for her, Sammy Oppenheim." Sammy is a good friend of mine in El Paso, Texas. He had never spoken of this miracle, however. The Boston pastor gave me the phone number of the woman who was healed. I proceeded to verify the account, both by talking to Sammy and by calling the home of the woman. Both calls provided verification. Although the woman was not home, her husband assured me that the miracle was real and continues to this day. The woman can read her Bible with her normal eye shut. Sammy well stated that this was one of the most astonishing miracles that he had ever witnessed.

Periodically my wife continues to receive astonishing dreams. One occurred shortly before our Rosh Hashana (new year) service. I was minister in a Messianic Jewish context. During the week Patty was given several segments of information in a dream. She saw a young man wearing a particular shirt. She saw the same man on a stage and was given a name. She also saw him wearing female clothing. Then in another segment she saw him enter our services, but then leave. She walked to the parking lot and saw him sitting in his car on the passenger side of the front seat. In the dream she went up to the car and asked him if he would like to be made whole? Would he come for prayer? He said he would and did.

The details of this dream were confirmed in every detail as this young man, a homosexual transvestite, came to the service. Indeed, the name given was a nickname used with actor friends. My wife first saw him after she had a distinct impression that he was there and looked in the parking lot to find him. There he was, sitting on the passenger side in the front seat of the car. He had entered the service, but left. He felt called to drive all night from a far distance to be at our services. He came for prayer as in the dream. All of the details were true, though my wife had never met the man.

In a dream shortly after this Patty saw a young man who had suffered a bitter youth. She saw him writing in volumes of hard-bound blue journals about his sad experiences growing up. She saw that these journals were holding him in bondage and were keeping him from moving forward in his walk with God. Patty announced this at a service and invited the young man to come forward for prayer for healing. He did so and was dramatically touched by God. Patty had interpreted these books as symbolic of his continued preoccupation with his past. However, a few weeks later the young man gave a testimony of his healing and brought in several copies of hard-bound journals in which he had been writing just as revealed in the dream.

The most dramatic healing in our family occurred when my son Samuel was just a year old. He was taken seriously ill with a condition known as myocarditis, a severe viral inflammation of the heart. Samuel's heart was described as blown up like a balloon. The doctors gave little hope for his survival and were certain that if Samuel did survive, he would live a very limited life and would need a heart transplant. When the heart stretches to such a great extent it does not recover, but becomes full of scar tissue. After much prayer, Samuel had a recovery that astonished the medical staff at Georgetown University Hospital. Although echocardiograms showed a terribly enlarged and damaged heart, Samuel exhibited normal energy and activity during the period between his discharge from the hospital and his six-month check up. He was expected to relapse and to be readmitted many times. He never had another problem. Within a year his heart function and size returned to normal. The full story of this recovery is told in a little booklet available from Beth Messiah Congregation. Medical records and testimony from doctors and nurses are included.

These kinds of experiences, healings, supernatural dreams, prophetic knowledge, etc., are not uncommon among people of faith. Furthermore, there are enough type "A" and "B" miracles to make naturalistic explanations impossible. Yes, lame explanations can be given about the possibility of the existence of unknown genetic powers to create new organs and produce healings; or perhaps there are even yet-unknown mental transmitting abilities for transmitting and receiving knowledge by physical laws that transcend what we presently know about space, time, and the nature of how knowledge is gained. I have heard these explanations.

The essential problem is well brought out in the tapes and books of John Wimber.[18] Wimber argues rightly that Westerners are post-Enlightenment people who look at the world with an extraordinary predilection for material-cause explanations. It is difficult for them to even entertain miracle reports. The kind of experiences that we have noted seem too farfetched. Peter Berger in his *Sociology of Knowledge*[19] talks about precognitive presuppositions. These are foundational concepts or categories which are often unexamined. Their value is that they enable us to dismiss huge amounts of false information without wasting time and energy to look into many dead-end directions. However, these same categories limit our potential in receiving experiences and creative conceptions that do not fit within their scope. Enlightenment scientific materialism is one such concept. Even religious people reserve the miraculous for ages gone by and go about their daily existence on the basis of these limits.

Hence, the response of many to such testimonies is utter disbelief. The testimonies seem farfetched to them because *they simply do not fit into their framework of understanding.* They are dismissed as fabrications; it is thought that it would be a waste of time to look into them. Yet such judgments only follow from the framework of a naturalistic world view.

Others may admit the legitimacy of such testimony, but will still hold out for some as-yet-unknown explanation within a naturalistic context. Yet to do so is a great error, for we have *no analogous concepts* whatsoever from the natural realm to explain these events. We are speaking on a level that by its very nature transcends the concepts of scientific materialism. This is what philosophers have called a *category mistake*, seeking to explain one type of reality in terms of another type of reality. It is a total cop-out to simply assert "scientific" naturalism in the face of such evidence. Such a response is more a faith assertion than a reasonable response.

The question is not whether or not the person of naturalistic bent can continue to foolishly assert his naturalistic commitment. Of course he can. The question is whether or not such a person can be brought to risk questioning after this fashion: "Within the present state of our knowledge and experience, which world view is best able to make sense of the testimony of the miraculous in human experience?" The *value pervasity* principle in discovering truth implies that we cannot force a naturalist from his commitments. The work of the Holy Spirit is crucial in his coming to an open attitude.

We should note that the miraculous events reported in the latter part of this chapter are within the context of prayer and the laying on of hands in the *name of Jesus*. The evidence is very significant. In my studies, I have seen that the supernatural is present in many religious traditions. However, to date I have found that only within a biblical context are the following aspects regularly present. Generally, miracles within the context of biblical faith produce long-term moral, spiritual, and psychological health without negative repercussions. Secondly, I have found no documented miracles of a type "A" character in these other traditions (although a few type "B" and several type "C" ones seem to be present). Creative miracles, such as restoring a bodily part or reversing a severe condition instantly, as in the case of Barbara Commiskey, are unknown to me outside of a New Testament faith context. This gives further credence to the biblical world view. Several have asked why, if such incredible events are occurring, they are not reported in the press or on the evening news. I have reflected upon this question for some twenty years. First of all, the mechanism spoken of before, relative to dismissing what seems fantastic, is pervasive in the press. Surveys have shown that the men and women of the press are religiously far more skeptical and unbelieving than the population as a whole.

Secondly, people tend to move in circles of like-minded people with similar frames of reference. Newspeople do not usually run into such reports. If they did, they might quickly dismiss them as psychosis. Their own limited experience is the foundation for judgment. Furthermore, there is enough fancy and fraud to muddy the waters and obscure the real miracles. Personally, I examined many exaggerated claims before I found one of real substance. It is a principle of human life that believers and unbelievers each tend to be part of separated communications flows and networks that usually do not intersect. News anchors choose as news what seems important from their frame of reference.

An example of the above would be the progress of charismatic Christianity in the nation of South Korea. In Seoul we find the congregation of Paul Cho with over 600,000 members, built in part on the testimonies of marvelous miracles. This is only one part of the story. Several churches approach 50,000 to 100,000 members. At the present rate of church growth, South Korea will be a charismatic Christian people by the turn of the century. A Buddhist nation is being turned upside down. In confrontation with a supernatural Christianity, Buddhism is losing. Yet there is no report on the major networks—no account of the miracles. We read of the student unrest, political problems, and the trade balance, but nothing more. To our media, Christianity in Korea (and Africa, South America, etc., where amazing changes are taking place) is not news. South Korea is no backward nation, but a modernized industrial miracle in East Asia. It is clear that the spirit of unbelief, not open examination, pervades our world and prejudices the examination. Even seventy years ago this was less so. The Seattle *Press*, for example, reported on the astonishing miracles of John Lake as real and credible.

In conclusion, it is well to restate that the evidence of miracles and faith experience lends credibility to the biblical world view. Societies where biblical faith is pervasive are healthier, stronger, and more prosperous. This is the result of biblical values. Contemporary miracles provide further evidence of the biblical world and life view. Indeed, they provide one more confirmation of the truth of the concepts of creation, fall, and redemption as the ultimate categories for understanding human existence.[20]

CHAPTER 15: STUDY QUESTIONS

1. What does the evidence from supernatural phenomena in general say to us concerning the nature of reality?

2. What is the nature of the evidence from biblically grounded supernatural phenomena today (prophecy, healings, signs and wonders, etc.)? What does this evidence lead us to conclude?

3. Why is the evidence from miracles today rarely reported in major media outlets?

THE INSPIRATION
OF THE BIBLE

A S WE HAVE LOOKED AT THE SCRIPTURES, we have found them to be unparalleled in quality. The Bible bears a supernatural mark in fulfilled
prophecy and in the extraordinary presentation of the nation of Israel and its
God. The incomparable ethical teaching, throughout the pages of Scripture, and
the moving portrait of Jesus as the perfect man confound the reader. Jesus is
portrayed as the revealer of God, and the One who brought the power of the
Kingdom to earth. Our examination of the Bible has brought us to the point
where it is reasonable to at least revere it as a reliable witness and interpreter of
God's intervention in the world. The Bible is the product of those human witnesses who saw the works of God and heard the voice of God. As such, on historical grounds, the Bible shows itself to be basically reliable and to be the most
trustworthy guide to faith (religion) and practice (ethics).

But is the Bible *more* than just a good human witness to the revelation of
God? Are there areas of error in the Bible which reason, through the guidance
of Holy Spirit, must transcend? Some, as in the neo-orthodox and liberal-
evangelical schools of thought would say "yes" in answer to these questions. Or
is the Bible, as classic Christian (and Jewish, for the Hebrew Scriptures) teaching has affirmed, *the Word of God* and not just basically and generally trustworthy with human limits of reporting, prejudice, and misinterpretation? These
are questions commonly covered under the topic of "Inspiration."

In the view that the Bible is the Word of God, it is taught that all that the
Bible teaches is true or without error. Hence, doctrinal and ethical issues are
settled by appeal to the Bible's teaching. In the other viewpoint, such issues
would be settled by looking at the Bible, examining the limitations of the biblical
writer, by looking at history to see if the doctrinal or ethical outworking of the

issue shows the biblical teaching to be fruitful, and by examining one's sense of the Spirit to see if one confirms Scripture's teaching. The searching person may come out with the same viewpoint from either position. However, the neo-orthodox view leaves great room for human reason and subjective opinion in matters of doctrine and ethics.

Thus the doctrine of inspiration is a most practical issue. For example, should we teach that premarital sex is wrong? All conservatives who believe that the Bible is the Word of God would say "yes" because Scripture says so. However, a person with a weaker concept of inspiration could say that the Bible reflects the views and limits of the Pharisees. Therefore, although marriage is a high level of sharing love, other forms of mutual sharing should not be rejected as sin if they are expressions of a caring relationship. Of course, the person may, on the other hand, hold that on the basis of the biblical tradition—its outworking in human experience—and on the basis of comparison with other cultures, we can agree with the Bible that premarital sex is wrong.

The preacher or counselor who holds to the limited inspiration view cannot just say, "the Bible says" and thereby settle the issue. He must also appeal to reason as to why he agrees with the Bible. A congregant may consider the preacher to be merely bound to tradition. He may have a different "sense in the spirit." It is much more difficult to maintain unity in doctrine and morals without a clear and final revelatory authority. Through human reason will come many different conclusions. A "sense in the spirit" will produce as many variations. Some will be conservative in their conclusions, and some will not (e.g., Karl Barth is conservative by this method, and Paul Tillich is not).

Hence, the debates rage in denominations that do not hold to a traditional view of inspiration. Is homosexual marriage a valid form of loving commitment? Was Paul overly influenced by his society's prejudice against homosexuality? Is the husband really to be the head of the home, or was Paul influenced by an overly patriarchal society? As one coed said to me during seminary days, "Paul was a male chauvinist pig." Should we really accept the view of a future bodily resurrection for human beings, or is not this merely a reflection of the limits of Jewish understanding that could not conceive of life after death without a body?

The weak view of inspiration leads to what Kenneth Kantzer called a subjective sieve.[1] Each interpreter approaches the Bible with his own mental strainer. If it has small holes, his reason and intuitive sense accept just about all the Bible teaches in doctrine and ethics as true. This is the case with Karl Barth.[2] If his sieve has larger holes, some doctrines will be maintained but much will fall

through, as in the theology of Emil Brunner.[3]   However, if the individual is
greatly influenced by modern trends, almost nothing of the biblical faith will be
left in the strainer. This is the case with Rudolph Bultmann.   Bultmann maintains very little of traditional Christian doctrine.   Even the resurrection of Jesus
is rejected as impossible to believe in a day when men turn electric lights on and
off.[4]

Yes, through the grace of God, a person may be led to maintain biblical doctrine and ethics despite a weak view of inspiration.   However, the assurance of
an objective test for doctrine and ethics in God's revealed Word will be lost;
those great doctrines and ethical teachings traditionally believed and practiced
will be more difficult to preserve at best. Man's reason and subjective sense will
produce an abundance of varying opinions.   Furthermore, when the chips are
down, how will this affect our ability to stand in faith on the promises found in
the Bible?

One other view has recently come to the fore that holds to the Bible as fully
true in all doctrinal and ethical matters, but not in scientific and historical matters. This view overlooks that much doctrine is built on historical connections.
The resurrection doctrine is based, in part at least, on the historical event of the
resurrection of Jesus. The exodus, the judgments, and the fulfilled prophecies
show us the intertwining of history and doctrine. Perhaps one would hold that
the Bible is historically true whenever history would affect doctrine. However,
those who hold to this modified conservative view of inspiration must wrestle
with what that Bible says about its own inspiration. To this we must now turn.
Suffice it to say that a Bible that was untrustworthy in historical matters would
not be as credible for other matters.

We cannot justly believe the traditional doctrine of inspiration merely because there are negative consequences. Yet seeing these consequences could
cause us to hope that a loving God would provide a more sure foundation for
our instruction. With this in mind, it is our task to briefly outline the case for
the belief that the Bible is the Word of God. The doctrine of inspiration is a
course in itself; however, the doctrine is also an issue of apologetics.[5]

Two great questions must be answered in a discussion of inspiration. The
first is, What do we mean when we claim that the Bible is the inspired Word of
God? The second is, How do we know that the books within our Bible are the
inspired books? The Bible is a compilation of several pieces of literature spanning a 1,500-year period. The last question concerns *canonicity*, that is, what
books are included in the canon (having authority, as in canon law). Finally, sec-

ondary issues need to be addressed which seem to undercut the traditional view
of inspiration, such as the supposed contradictions and errors in the Bible.
Other supposed problems arising from comparing the Bible with information
from archaeological and historical sources and from scientific information are
also discussed as part of these issues.

As stated previously, I have already shown the Bible to be an awesome book
with its prophecies, fulfillments, accounts of God's interventions in the history
of Israel and in the early Church, its miracle accounts, and its portraits of Jesus.
This does not, however, prove its full inspiration or even define the meaning of
inspiration. Indeed, it is the teaching of Jesus and his apostles which most def-
initely establish the meaning of inspiration and its doctrinal validity. It is true
that we appeal to the New Testament for this teaching. However, we do not
thereby argue in a circle. Rather, our appeal is to the New Testament as com-
pendium of the primary source documents which by *historical evidence* are good
sources to ascertain the view of Jesus and his disciples.

The late Benjamin B. Warfield in his article "It Says, Scripture Says, God
Says" thoroughly examined every chapter of the Gospel material and concluded
that for Jesus, if the Old Testament Scriptures taught something, it was truth
and could be quoted to settle the issue. Thus, in the Gospels statements are attributed to God, when in the Old Testament the statements are attributed to
Moses or the prophets. In other words, "It says," "Scripture says," "It is written," and "God says" are equivalents in the teaching of Jesus. Any student may
read Warfield's article or study the evidence directly.[6] Furthermore, with the
following words Jesus explicitly taught that the Bible was from God and wholly
true:

> Do not think that I have come to destroy the law or the proph-
> ets; I have not come to abolish them, but to fulfill them. I tell
> you the truth, until heaven and earth disappear, not the small-
> est letter, not the least stroke of a pen, will by any means dis-
> appear from the law until everything is accomplished. Anyone
> who breaks one of the least of these commands and teaches
> others to do the same will be called least in the Kingdom of
> Heaven, but whoever practices and teaches these commands
> will be called great in the Kingdom of Heaven. (Matthew 5:17–
> 19)

The NIV translation well carries the meaning of the Hebrew "jot" or "tittle"
as showing that God's oversight of Scripture's inspiration extends to the least
letter and pen stroke. This is reflected as well in John 10:35, where Jesus

quotes an obscure phrase from Psalm 82:6 to settle a controversy and then says of it, "The Scripture cannot be broken." The evidence is overwhelming; Jesus held to and believed in the full trustworthiness of the whole Old Testament. This was also the predominant Jewish view of the day, as reflected in the teaching of the Pharisees. Even the famous atheistic New Testament scholar at Harvard, the late H. J. Cadbury (no friend of the doctrine of the divine inspiration of the Bible), held on to the basis of the evidence that Jesus both believed and taught the same.

Warfield thus puts the issue well. If Jesus is our ultimate authority as teacher and mentor, how can we accept his doctrinal and ethical teaching in some areas and reject his teaching on the trustworthiness of Scripture? Indeed, we have more evidence for this doctrine in the teaching of Jesus, from a historical point of view, than we have for other doctrines.

Other biblical passages bring out what Jesus and the apostles understood by the doctrine of inspiration. Remembering that Paul was a trained Pharisee, it is not unreasonable to hold that he would be a good source for understanding the first-century Jewish view, as would other Jewish sources, such as Josephus' writings (Josephus was the noted first-century Jewish general and historian) and the Talmud. Paul was part of the first-century apostolic circle (Acts 9, 15, Galatians 2). He would also reflect their view. All of the New Testament books, including Paul's, reflect the same high regard for the Old Testament. Quoting it settled the issue at hand. Paul writes,

> All Scripture is God-breathed (inspired by God) and is useful for teaching, rebuking, correcting, and training in righteousness, so that the man of God may be thoroughly equipped for every good work. (II Timothy 3:16)

Once again the NIV brings out the sense of the Greek, which means "breathed out" by God. This doctrine is also reflected in II Peter 2:19–21:

> And we have the word of the prophets made more certain, and you do well to pay attention to it, as a light shining in a dark place, until the day dawns and the morning star arises in your hearts. Above all you must understand that no prophecy of Scripture came about by the prophets' own interpretation. For prophecy never had its origin in the will of man, but men spoke from God as they were carried along by the Holy Spirit.

This has traditionally been understood as the power of God so superintending the writers of Scripture, that what they wrote was what God desired to write.

Hence, the writing itself was inspired (verbal inspiration) and this inspiration extends equally to all of Scripture (plenary inspiration). Opponents of this teaching have attributed to its supporters a dictation theory—that God dictated the words of Scripture and the writers acted as secretaries. This is simply not what its supporters hold. To be sure, there are examples of dictation. Jeremiah is told to "Write these words in a scroll." There are trances and visionary experiences later recorded as the book of Revelation. However, the Scriptures in many passages reflect the personalities and backgrounds of the writers. Matthew and John reflect Essene backgrounds. Paul's writings reflect a more rabbinic or Pharisaic background. When, however, a man is in the power of the Spirit, his desires are parallel to God's desires, he wills what God wills. Hence, his unique personality is made use of by the Holy Spirit to convey what God wanted conveyed.

Jesus taught, "Abide in the vine and you may ask what you will," (John 15:7ff.). Proverbs taught, "Delight yourself in the Lord and He will give you the desires of your heart" (Proverbs 37:4). Scripture teaches that when we abide in Him and delight in Him our desires are His desires. Thus the biblical writer is writing his desire and will, but in the Spirit it is also God's desire and will. What he writes is God-breathed. This doctrine is called *confluence*, meaning that the writer and God flow together in the production of Scripture. This is well reflected in the II Peter 2:21 passage. Therefore I hold that God so superintended the writing of Scripture that what the biblical writer wrote was also what God wanted written and that it is the word of God without error in all its intended teaching. This is indeed close to the view of first-century Judaism.

It is important to ascertain just what a passage is teaching. This is the task of hermeneutics (biblical interpretation). The original language and culture is the necessary background for accurate interpretation. In this regard, I hold that the Bible is *true in all that the biblical writer was claiming to teach as true*. This immediately eliminates many foolish charges of supposed errors in the Scriptures. For example, the Scriptures speak in ordinary phenomenological language. When we say the sun rose at 6:32 A.M., we are not claiming to teach something that contradicts the idea of the earth's revolution around the sun. Furthermore, when we quote what President Reagan said, or what the Congressional Record said, we are claiming accuracy for our quote, but not necessarily endorsing every detail of what the president said as truth or what the congressman said within the Congressional Record as fully accurate.

The Scriptures quote other sources without necessarily claiming the full accuracy of those sources. The Scripture quotes the Chronicles of the Kings of Israel and Judah as Israel's official national record. The Scripture quotes Stephen's speech in Acts 7 in which he says that seventy-five descendants of Abraham went down to Egypt, while Genesis 46:47 says seventy. Stephen may have been mistaken, but Luke, as inspired, was accurate in quoting Stephen. (The Septuagint version of the Old Testament with which Stephen was familiar with does say seventy-five; furthermore, there are different ways to calculate who was to be counted; cf. G. Archer, *Bible Difficulties*). What Luke was claiming to teach was without error; he wasn"t claiming that every speaker he quoted was exactly accurate in his speeches. He was claiming a basic accuracy in his recounting of events. The Scriptures even quote the words of a fool who says in his heart, "There is no God."

Scripture also gives estimates and is full of poetry and symbol. In other words, we must not impose upon Scripture a criterion of claiming to speak scientifically or with such exactitude unless it claims to do so within its own context. We must not assume that Scripture is claiming to teach something as true unless the context and intent of the author give evidence of such. We must ask of every passage, What is Scripture claiming to teach in this verse or passage? When this is ascertained, if the interpretation is correct, it is truth without error. It is important to keep this in mind in studying the Gospel portraits. Each Gospel writer took the memorized body of material in his possession, possible written sources, and his own memories of Jesus, and each created, under the inspiration of the Spirit, a portrait of Jesus. The same teaching is quoted in different contexts because much teaching was repeated in different contexts by Jesus. Some material is paraphrased, but all is under the inspiration of the Spirit and in accord with the author's specific purposes in writing his Gospel.

The traditional doctrine of inspiration only claimed total trustworthiness for the original autographs (original copies). From multiple copies of ancient manuscripts, it becomes clear that copyists made errors. By comparing them, we can reconstruct a text that is very close to the original. Some have said that the doctrine of inspiration and inerrancy are of no use, since we do not possess the original copies anyway. This objection is clearly wrongheaded. It implies that our quest for a more accurate textual rendering gets us no closer to a trustworthy document than what we have. Those who believe in the classical doctrine of inspiration take textual work seriously because they believe that the more adequate a text we produce the closer we come to the original and hence to a fully trustworthy Bible. Our text reconstruction for the Old Testament can be considered very accurate and trustworthy because of the discovery of the Dead Sea Scrolls, the existence of the Septuagint translation, and the Masoretic Text, as well as other more minor recensions. For the New Testament, with hundreds of early texts, our reconstruction can be considered to be 99.98 percent accurate.[8] Therefore when the student reads the Nestle text of the Greek New Testament or the Baumgarten Hebrew Old Testament (prepared through careful manuscript comparisons by the science of lower textual criticism), he can be assured that he is almost essentially reading the original and can have a similar respect for it. Furthermore, the differences between text traditions are so limited that not one biblical doctrine would be in question from one version to another.

We have left out some gaps in our case. First of all, when Jesus and the apostles taught the inspiration of the Scriptures, what books did they refer to? This raises the question of the Old Testament canon. Furthermore, when Jesus and his apostles used the Scriptures as their authority for teaching, how does this imply the inspiration of the New Testament books? Why are the twenty-seven books of the New Testament accepted as inspired and not others?

As briefly mentioned before, Josephus gives credence to the view that just those books in the Hebrew Bible (the same as the Protestant Bible) were accepted as having authority (canonical). Extra-biblical sources show that when Jewish people referred to Scripture, they referred to our thirty-nine Old Testament books and no other. Josephus, for example, states that the Jewish nation held to just twenty-two God-inspired books. Since the twelve minor prophets were one scroll, Ezra and Nehemiah were one scroll, Kings and Chronicles were one, and Joshua and Judges were one, scholars are universally agreed that Josephus referred to the thirty-nine books of the Protestant Bible.[9] Other books written after the time of these books were not accepted as God-inspired, though they might have been valued. Jewish tradition held that the Spirit of prophecy was absent after the Old Testament period. Of course, this Spirit is essential in producing Scripture. This is reflected in the letter of Ben Sirac. Even the books of Maccabees, accepted as Scripture in Catholic circles, do not claim inspiration, but record that the Maccabees were puzzled concerning what to do with a defiled altar. There was no prophet to give direction. Therefore, they buried it, looking toward the day that the gift of prophecy would be restored.[10] Thus, the Jewish Bible includes just those books included in the Protestant Bible. When Jesus and his disciples referred to the law and the prophets or the Scriptures, they are approving just those thirty-nine books in our Old Testament.

Exactly how these books were preserved is uncertain. The New Testament claims that the Jewish people were given the privilege of receiving the oracles of God and preserving them (Romans 2). Most certainly the Temple was a locale in which the books considered to be from true prophets were preserved during Israel's faithful periods. Henry Thiele, in his remarkable *The Mysterious Numbers of the Hebrew Kings*, also presents evidence that prophetic schools existed on the border between the northern and southern divisions of Israel and Judah.[11] They preserved the prophetic tradition, including very possibly the works of the writing prophets. The stories of Elijah and Elisha in I and II Kings make several references to the school of the prophets. We are safe in trusting the wisdom of Jewish tradition, especially in the light of its acceptance by Jesus and his disciples, with regard to the issue of inspiration and canonicity.

What of our New Testament books? First of all, if God would make provision to accurately interpret the great events of salvation history in the Old Testament period through inspired prophets, would it not be likely that the same inspiration would be present to interpret the life, death, and resurrection of Jesus and the progress of the early communities of faith? This is indeed confirmed when we realize that Jesus chose twelve apostles to be the witnesses and the authoritative prophetic teachers in the early Church. This circle also had the authority to expand and include others in its circle of authority. Clearly this was so of James, the brother of Jesus, as seen in Acts 15 and 21, of Paul in Acts 9, 15 and Galatians 2, and perhaps of Barnabas as well in Acts 9:27 and 11:22–26.

R. Laird Harris, in his excellent summary on the inspiration and the canonicity of the Bible, argued that the main test of inspiration is a connection to this apostolic circle.[12] Indeed, the early Church fathers attributed most of our New Testament books to this circle. The writings of Papias in the first century (preserved in the quotations in Eusebius), Irenaeus, Clement of Rome, Clement of Alexandria, Ignatius of Antioch, and Polycarp are the earliest sources. The only definite extra-biblical evidence from these fathers and other traditions of the early Church provide these accounts:

1. Matthew was originally issued in Hebrew and later translated into Greek. Its author was the disciple Matthew (Papias in Eusebius and Jerome).

2. Mark was the John Mark of the New Testament and wrote under the authority of Peter. Mark contains the material orally presented by Peter.

3. Luke was the travel companion of Paul. He wrote Luke and Acts under Paul's authority and with close contact with the other apostles through his visits

to Jerusalem.

4. John was written by the beloved disciple John himself, as were I, II, and III John and Revelation.

5. Romans – II Timothy was authored by Paul.

6. James was authored by James, the apostle and brother of Jesus.

7. Jude was authored by another brother of Jesus, also accepted into the apostolic circle.

8. I, II Peter was authored by none other than Peter the disciple.

9. Hebrews is a book of disputed attribution. Paul, Barnabas, and John have all been suggested as authors, but there is no certainty, though Paul was traditionally accepted to be the author by a majority. The style has more Essene touch points, as do Matthew and John's writings. Paul's writings reflect a more Pharisaic background. Yet all agree that Hebrews is inspired with an extraordinary quality and coherence with the rest of the New Testament.

Within the New Testament itself, we do find a realization of inspired authority within the writings. Paul notes in I Corinthians 14:37 that a prophetic person should confirm that his writing is a command of God. Peter puts Paul's writings in the category of Scripture when he speaks of other Scriptures alongside of Paul's writing in II Peter 3:16. Throughout the Pauline corpus, there is a clear claim of a teaching authority to be received and obeyed. At the same time, Paul shares that his knowledge of the Gospel was also received from the other apostles (I Corinthians 15:3–7).

The student of the Scriptures will also be amazed in a comparison of the New Testament with post–New Testament noncanonical writings. The quality difference is vast. It is as if the noncanonical writers wrote within their limitations —including foolish ideas as well as good thoughts.[13] Yet the Scriptural writers seem to be on a different plane altogether. These writings have a timeless superiority unhindered by human fallibility. Hence, we note two primary tests of canonicity in the early Church. As the Scriptures were collected into the New Testament, long before Church councils proclaimed our twenty-seven books as the inspired writings of the New Testament, these tests already had caused our twenty-seven books to be generally accepted. These tests were:

1. Early testimony to the apostolic origins of the writings—that these books came from the original apostolic circle.

2. The witness of the Spirit to the hearts of the believing community—that the writing was of the quality of Scripture.

In this second criterion, of course, such features as the quality of the writing and the coherence of its teaching within and with the other Scriptures were certainly weighed. A fuller account of the evidence from the Church fathers than we have given can be found in Harris. Actually, few other books were serious contenders for acceptance (e.g., perhaps the *Didache*, the first-century ethical training book for new believers).

The doctrine of the inspiration and the canonicity of the Bible as presented here has been accepted throughout history as the classical position of the Church and within Judaism with regard to the Old Testament. This doctrine has been attacked by those claiming to find fault with Scripture. Moral faults have been supposedly exposed, along with internal contradictions and historical errors. Often these errors are put forth as new discoveries in our "scientific age." Most such problems and supposed errors were well known to the classical formulators of the doctrine of inspiration and canonicity. A summary of classical solutions to these questions can be found in Haley's *An Examination of the Alleged Discrepancies in the Bible*.[15] An updated response can be found in the recent work by Old Testament scholar Gleason Archer.[16] Most of the so-called problems are answerable when we simply understand what the biblical writer is claiming to teach as true. A better appreciation of first-century Jewish culture is greatly aiding our understanding. There are reasonable solutions to most of the problems raised. The works mentioned are worthy of pursuit by the student of apologetics. They catalogue most of the problem texts usually put forth.

Therefore, in conclusion we maintain that the classical doctrine of inspiration and canonicity is the best viewpoint in the light of the totality of the evidence. Other theories of the origins of the biblical material ignore the positive testimony of history and early Church tradition. These theories are speculative hypotheses. The Bible, therefore is a sure foundation for faith and doctrine. As Jesus fully endorsed the Old Testament, He provided an apostolic authority to give rise to the New Testament.

CHAPTER 16: STUDY QUESTIONS

1. What is the classical view on the inspiration of the Bible?

2. What are the practical implications of this classical doctrine? What are the possible conclusions for those who believe the Gospel message but do not hold to the classical doctrine of inspiration?

3. What are the essential reasons for believing in the full inspiration and authority of the Bible?

4. What is the meaning of *canonicity*?

5. Why are the books in the Bible accepted as canon instead of others?

CONCLUSION

WE HAVE NOW PUT FORTH THE VIEW THAT THE BIBLICAL WORLD VIEW is the most consistent, coherent, and comprehensive way to understand human existence. We now put forth the additional point that the Bible, which is the source of this world view, is a trustworthy revelation from God to man. It is a secure foundation for faith. We can stand upon the biblical promises.

We have given a summary of the basic concerns of apologetics. Hopefully it is an adequate summary—a summary to stimulate further reading. We must, however, reaffirm our view that the knowledge of God is no mere intellectual quest. Since the human heart is deceptive, no apologetic is adequate to convince the skeptic. Only the work of the Holy Spirit can open the eyes of the blind so that the light of the Gospel can shine forth. There is great evidence, but the principle of value pervasity shows that this evidence is available only to the humble, repentant, open, and genuinely searching heart. The knowledge of God is more akin to the blinders being ripped off when we repent than a computer solution to a problem. It is more like coming to trust another human being.

Blaise Pascal argued that there was sufficient evidence for faith for the willing but insufficient for the stubbornly unwilling. Therefore, in my pastoral work of witness, I share this thought with any reader who might not yet be a follower of Jesus. Do you want to know the truth? If you find it, are you willing to live your life by it? Why not open yourself up to God by this prayer:

> Dear God, if you are there, please show me if the Gospel is true. I commit myself to search out this question. Lead me as I search. I commit myself to live by the truth you reveal.

Then begin to search the Bible; or perhaps review the evidences in this text. I have never known one to sincerely pray this prayer and follow through who did not become convinced. The Bible says, "You will seek me and find me when you shall search for me with all your heart," (Jeremiah 29:13). "If any man's will is to do God's will, he shall know of the doctrine thereof" (John 7:17).

Perhaps you are already convinced, at least to a probable degree. Then you may receive eternal life by simply placing your trust in Jesus. Why not do so through this prayer if you have never done so before.

> Dear Father, I now confess myself to have broken your law and to have sinned before you. However, I now receive Jesus as my Messiah, my Lord and Savior from sin and the source of new life. By faith in Him I am now born again and invite your Holy Spirit to take up residence in my life.

Jesus said, "Him that comes to me I will in no way cast out."

CHAPTER NOTES

CHAPTER 1

1 Sören Kierkegaard, *Concluding Unscientific Postscript*.

2 Karl Barth, *Nine (No.)*. This booklet is his response to Emil Brunner's position on the existence of limited common ground from which to dialogue with unbelievers.

CHAPTER 2

1. H. P. Rickman, *Meaning in History: William Dilthey's Thoughts on History and Society* (London, 1961).

2. Gordon Clark, *Religion, Reason, and Revelation*, Chapters 1 and 2.

3. For a survey of this movement see H. Spiegelburg, *The Phenomenological Movement* (The Hague: Martinus Nijhoff, 1969).

4. See Zeno in Joseph Katz and Rudolph Weingartner, *Philosophy in the West (Readings)* (New York: Harcourt, Brace, and World, 1963), pp. 17, 18.

5. On this question, see Jerome Shaffer, *Philosophy of Mind* (Englewood Cliffs, New Jersey: Prentice Hall, 1968). For Descartes, pp. 61, 62; for Melebranche, pp. 62-68.

6. As applied in Frederick Ferre, *Basic Modern Philosophy of Religion*, pp. 336-370.

7. Ferre, p. 386.

8. Karl Popper, *The Logic of Scientific Discovery* (London: Hutcheson, 1959).

9. David Wolfe, *Epistemology, The Justification of Belief*.

10. Arthur F. Holmes, *Christian Philosophy in the Twentieth Century*.

CHAPTER 3

1. The following books are most helpful resources in these areas: Stuart Barton Babbage, *The Mark of Cain*; C. S. Lewis, *The Abolition of Man*; Os Guiness, *The Dust of Death*; Hans Rookmaaker, *Modern Art and the Death of Culture*.

2. Francis Schaeffer, *The God Who Is There*.

3. Oscar Cullman, *Christ and Time* (Philadelphia: Westminster Press, 1964). This book gives a significant summary of key differences in Greek and Hebrew thought.

4. See Heraclitus in Joseph Katz and Rudolph Weingartner, *Philosophy in the West (Readings)* (New York: Harcourt, Brace, and World, 1963), pp. 9-13.

5. For a summary of Pythagoras, see Frederick C. Copleston, *A History of Philosophy*: Vol. 1, Part 1 (Garden City, New York, 1962), pp. 45-53.

6. *Ibid.*, pp. 166-232 for a discussion of Plato. Also see Plato's *Timeaus. Collected*

Dialogues, ed. Edith Hamilton and Huntington Carins (New York: Pantheon, 1961), pp. 1051-1212. Also in the same volume see Plato's *Laws*, pp. 1225-1317. Plato argues that the goal of existence is the soul's contemplation of the forms.

7. *Ibid.*

8. Copleston, Vol. 2, Part 1, pp. 232-238, for Copleston's treatment on the Middle Age rediscovery of Aristotle.

9. *Ibid.*

10. For dealing with the religious language problem, see Langdon Gilkey, *Naming the Whirlwind*. Also see Frederick Ferre, *Language, Logic, and God*.

11. Cullman, *Christ and Time*, pp. 63-68.

12. See the excellent presentation of Michael Polanyi in his Gifford Lectures, *Personal Knowledge*.

13. On Descartes, see Copleston, Vol. 4, pp. 74-160. Also Descartes, *Dialogues*.

14. Mircea Eliade, *The Sacred and Profane*, for a summary of the primitive understanding of reality.

15. Floyd Matson, *The Broken Image*. Matson shows how the mathematical model of meaning leads to meaninglessness.

16. Martin Gardner, *Relativity for the Millions*.

17. Martin Heidegger, *Being and Time*, pp. 73, 74, 101, 140. As an existentialist, Heidegger was no friend of biblical theism. However, his analysis of reductionism is potent.

18. C. E. M. Joad, *The Recovery of Belief*. See especially his discussion of the tasteless, colorless, odorless world of scientific language, pp. 107-152.

19. Herbert Spiegelburg, *The Phenomenological Movement* (The Hague: Martinus Nijhoff, 1969).

20. John Locke, *A Common Place Book to the Holy Bible* (New York: American Tract Society, 1858).

21 Immanuel Kant, *Critique of Pure Reason*.

22 Immanuel Kant, *Critique of Practical Knowledge*; see also Copleston sections on Kant, Vol. VI, Part 2.

CHAPTER 4

1. George F. W. Hegel. *Phenomenology of Mind* (London: G. Allen and Unwin, 1931). On Hegel's historiography, see Copleston, Vol. VII, Part I, pp. 210-241.

2. Karl Marx, *Manifesto of the Communist Party* in *Basic Writings on Politics and Philsosophy* (Garden City, New York: Doubleday Anchor, 1959). Also *Das Kapital* (Chicago: Charles H. Kerr and Co., 1919). For a critique of Marxism, see Thomas Sowell, *Marxism* (New York: William Morrow and Co., 1986).

3. For a presentation of this, see Herbert Butterfield, *Chrisitanity and History* (London: Collins, Fontana Books, 1957).

4. For a summary of these theories and a case for traditional views, see R. K. Harrison, *Introduction to the Old Testament*, pp. 19-82.

5. *Ibid.* see presentations on the authorship and date of each book.

6. On prophecy after the event, see William Foxwell Albright, *From the Stone Age to Christianity*, pp. 3-75 of the introduction.

7. Alfred Jules Ayer, *Language, Truth, and Logic*.

8. C. E. M. Joad, *A Critique of Logical Positivism* (Chicago: University of Chicago Press, 1951).

9. Heidegger, *Being and Time*, pp. 73,74.

10. Herman Dooyweerd, *A New Critique of Theoretical Thought*, pp. 333-362.

11. Michael Polanyi, *Personal Knowledge*.

12. A second-century Church father.

13. For a full analysis see Lit Sen Chang, *Zen Existentialism*.

14. Ayer, pp. 41, 87-101.

15. C. L. Stevenson, *Ethics and Language* (New Haven, Connecticut: Yale University Press, 1944), pp. 22-24.

16. For an excellent critique of relativism, see C. S. Lewis, *The Abolition of Man*.

17. For representative liberal views see: L. Harold deWolf, *The Case for Theology in Liberal Perspective* (Philadelphia: Westminster Press, 1959); Harry Emerson Fosdick, *The Living of These Days* (New York: Harper and Brothers, 1956); Henry P. Van Dusen, *The Vindication of Liberal Theology* (New York: Scribner, 1963).

18. Karl Barth, *Church Dogmatics* (Edinburg: T. T. Clark, 1956), Vol. 1, pp. 457-660, and *Evangelical Theology: An Introduction* (London: Collins, Fontana, 1965). I am indebted to Kenneth S. Kantzer of Trinity Evangelical Divinity School, Deerfield, Illinois, for his brilliant exposition of Barth's epistemology and its effect in the erosion of neo-orthodoxy in Brunner, Bultmann, and Tillich.

19. Rudolph Bultmann, *Jesus Christ and Mythology*.

20. Paul Tillich, *Dynamics of Faith* (New York: Harper Torchbooks, 1958).

21. Mordecai Kaplan, *Judaism without Supernaturalism* (New York: Reconstructionist Press, 1958).

22. For the death-of-God theologies see J. J. Altizer and William Hamilton, *Radical Theology and the Death of God* (London: Penguin, 1968); Paul Van Buren, *The Secular Meaning of the Gospel* (London: Penguin, 1963); and Richard Rubinstein, *After Auschwitz: Radical Theology and Contemporary Judaism* (Indianapolis, Indiana: Bobbs-Merrill, 1966).

23. Harvey Cox, *The Secular City* (New York: Macmillan, 1965).

24. *Ibid.*, p. 96.

CHAPTER 5

1. see *Doors of Perception* and *Heaven and Hell*.

2. Rookmaaker, pp. 96.

3. *Ibid.*, p. 108.

4. *Ibid.*, p. 109.

5. *Ibid.*, p. 110.

6. *Ibid.*, p. 174.

7. For an excellent presentation of the challenge and meaning of modern art see A.

Neihmeyer, *The Quest for Meaning in Modern Art.*

8. Bertrand Russell, *Mysticism and Logic* (London: Longmans, Green, 1925), pp. 47, 48, 56, 57.

9. See the excellent summary in Schlossburg, *Idols for Destruction.*

CHAPTER 6

1. Antony Flew, *New Essays in Philosophical Theology* (New York: The Macmillan Company, 1955).

2. Richard Rubinstein, *After Auschwitz: Radical Theology and Contemporary Judaism* (Indianapolis, Indiana: Bobbs-Merrill, 1966).

3. Gordon Clark, *Religion, Reason, and Revelation*, pp. 194-241.

4. For a summary of Leibnitz on this see F. C. Copleston, Vol. IV, pp. 330-335.

5. F. R. Tennant, *Philosophical Theology*, (Cambridge: Cambridge University Press, 1928), Vol. II, pp. 180-208.

6. Frederick Sontag, *The God of Evil* (New York: Harper and Row, 1970).

7. For finite-god solutions, see Edgar Sheffield Brightman, *A Philosophy of Religion*, (Englewood Cliffs, New Jersey: Prentice Hall, 1940). For a recent solution along similar lines, see Rabbi Harold Kushner, *When Bad Things Happen to Good People* (New York: Schocken Books, 1981).

8. John Hick, *Evil and the God of Love*, pp. 43-95.

9. This is argued by an amazing variety of thinkers, including George F. Moore in *Principia Ethica* (Cambridge: Cambridge University Press, 1966), pp. 1-36; Edmund Husserl, *The Ideas* (New York: Collier, 1962), pp. 133-154; Jean-Paul Sartre, *Being and Nothingness* (New York: Philosophical Library, 1956), pp. 25-45; and C. S. Lewis, *Mere Christianity*, pp. 17-30.

10. Michael Polanyi, *Personal Knowledge.*

11. Gabriel Marcel, *The Mystery of Being* (Chicago: Henry Regnery, 1969), pp. 121-139. See also Paul Ricoeur, *Fallible Man* (Chicago: Henry Regnery, 1965).

12. Alvin Plantinga, *God and Other Minds* (Ithaca, N.Y.: Cornell University Press, 1967).

13. John Hick, pp. 217-220.

14. C. S. Lewis, *The Problem of Pain*, pp. 69-81.

15. Augustine, *Confessions* (Philadelphia: Westminster Press, 1955).

16. Jean-Paul Sartre, *Being and Nothingness* (New York: Philosophical Library, 1956), pp. 25-45.

17. C. S. Lewis, *The Problem of Pain*, pp. 129-143.

18. *Ibid.*, pp. 138-140.

19. C. E. M. Joad, *The Recovery of Belief*, pp. 46-82.

20. Oscar Cullman, *Christ and Time*, pp. 51-67.

21. I am indebted to Dr. Kenneth S. Kantzer and Dr. David L Wolfe as the sources of these ideas.

22. Dorothy Sayers. *The Mind of the Maker* (London: Methuen, 1941).

23. In *Christianity Today*, April 8, 1983.

24. *Ibid.*
25. William Temple, *Nature, Man, and God*, pp. 198-221, p. 149.

CHAPTER 7

1. David Hume, *Enquiry Concerning Human Understanding* (1776; rpt. New York: Bobbs-Merrill, Library of Liberal Arts, 1955) and *Treatise on Human Nature* (New York: E. P. Dutton, 1934).
2. Sigmund Freud, *The Future of an Illusion* (New York, 1953).
3. David Baken, *Sigmund Freud and the Jewish Mystical Tradition* (Princeton, N.J.: Princeton University Press, 1958).
4. William Lloyd Warner, *The Family of God* (New Haven, Connecticut: Yale University Press, 1961) and Mary Douglas, *Natural Symbols* (New York: Pantheon, 1982).
5. Max Weber, *The Protestant Ethic and the Spirit of Capitalism* (New York: Scribner, 1958) and *The Sociology of Religion* (Boston: Beacon Press, 1963). See also Ernst Troeltsch, *Christian Thought, Its History and Application* (London: University of London Press, 1923).
6. For an example of sociological analysis supporting classical theistic views, see Peter Berger, *A Rumor of Angels*; George Gilder, *Wealth and Poverty* (New York: Basic Books, 1981).

CHAPTER 8

1. F. C. Copleston, *A History of Philosophy*, Vol. 4, pp. 108-120; also René Descartes, *Meditations* (New York: Bobbs-Merrill, 1951), pp. 33-49.
2. Norman Malcolm, "The Ontological Argument Revisited."
3. Norman Geisler, *Christian Apologetics*, pp. 237-250; also Stuart C. Hackett, *The Resurrection of Theism*.
4. A. E. Taylor, *Does God Exist?*
5. C. S. Lewis, *Mere Christianity*, pp. 17-36; also Edward John Carnell, *Christian Commitment*.
6. Floyd W. Matson, *The Broken Image*, pp. 64, 65, 244-247.
7. Martin Heidegger, *Being and Time*.
8. Henry Bergson, *Creative Evolution*.
9. A. E. Wilder-Smith, *Man's Origin, Man's Destiny*.
10. *Ibid.*, pp. 55-58.
11. Michael Denton, *Evolution, A Theory in Crisis*, pp. 228, 230,233-248, 324.
12. A. E. Taylor, *Does God Exist?*, Denton, p. 62.
13. See Kierkut.
14. C. S. Lewis, *Mere Christianity*.
15. See the brilliant analysis of Darwin's and Huxley's motivation in John P. Koster, *The Atheist Syndrome*.
16. In a lecture at Wheaton College, Wheaton, Illinois, fall 1967.
17. Frederick Ferre, *Basic Modern Philosophy of Religion*; William Temple, *Nature, Man, and God*.

18. See summary of Hartman in Herbert Spiegelburg, *The Phenomenological Movement* (The Hague: Martinus Nijhoff, 1969), pp. 358-389.

19. C. S. Lewis, *Mere Christianity*, pp. 31,32.

20. E. M. Blaiklock, *Is it or Isn't It* (Grand Rapids, Michigan: Zondervan, 1968), pp. 16-31.

21. Lewis, *Mere Christianity*, Part I, "The Case for Christianity."

22. C. S. Lewis, *The Abolition of Man.*

23. E. J. Carnell, *Christian Commitment*, pp. 80-116.

24. Emielle Caillet, *The Recovery of Purpose*, pp. 144-179.

25. Immanuel Kant, *Critique of Practical Knowledge.*

26. In philosophy, this is called the problem of the relationship of the one and the many; see Edward J. Carnell, *An Introduction to Christian Apologetics.*

27. On God's triunity, see Francis Schaeffer, *Escape from Reason*, pp. 86-89.

28. Some have noted similarities to the existential cosmological argument of Catholic philosopher Etienne Gilson.

CHAPTER 9

1. Edward J. Young, *My Servants the Prophets* (Grand Rapids, Michigan: Eerdmans, 1952); R. K. Harrison, *An Introduction to the Old Testament*, pp. 741-763; William Foxwell Albright, *From the Stone Age to Christianity*, see introduction; Gerhard Von Rad, *An Old Testament Theology*, Vol. II, pp. 6-98.

2. Harrison, *Introduction to the Old Testament*, pp. 901-918.

3. Peter Stoner, *Science Speaks* (Chicago: Moody Press, 1963). This is the source for the probability agrument used in many apologetics works.

4. On dating biblical books, see the following: R. K. Harrison, *An Old Testament Introduction*; Gleason Archer, *A Survey of Old Testament Introduction*; Donald Guthrie, *New Terstament Introduction.*

5. On the issue of prophecy after the event, see W. F. Albright, *From the Stone Age to Christianity*, introduction.

6. *Ibid.*, and as referenced in note four.

7. See Rudolph Bultmann, *Jesus Christ and Mythology* (New York: Scribners, 1958). For a refutation see John W. Montgomery, *The Shape of the Past.*

8. For helpful sources, see Josh McDowell, *Evidence that Demands a Verdict;* also J. Barton Payne, *An Encyclopedia of Biblical Prophecy* (New York: Harper and Row, 1973).

9. The stele says literally, "I have up Hezekiah as a bird."

10. As recorded in Herodotus, also see Floyd Hamilton, *The Basis of the Christian Faith* (New York: Harper and Row, 1964), p. 279; Joseph P. Free, *Archaeology and Bible History*, pp. 262.263; and J. Barton Payne, *An Encyclopedia of Biblical Prophecy*, pp. 362-364.

11. H. L. Ellison, *Ezekiel, The Man and His Message*, Grand Rapids, Michigan: Eerdmans, 1951).

12. Payne, p. 431.

CHAPTER 10

1. Peter Stoner, *Science Speaks*, on the probability quotients used as evidence for fulfilled prophecy.

2. Robert Culver, "Were the Old Testament Prophecies Really Prophetic?" in *Can I Trust My Bible* (Chicago: Moody Press, 1963).

3. Merrill Tenney, *New Testament Times* (Grand Rapids, Michigan: Eerdmans, 1965), pp. 88-106.

4. Wayne Meeks, *The Prophet King* (New York: Abington, 1967).

5. K. Stendahl, *The School of St. Matthew and its Use of the Old Testament* (Philadelphia: Fortress, 1968). See also Richard Longenecker, *Biblical Exegesis in the Apostolic Period* (Grand Rapids, Michigan: Eerdmans, 1975).

6. Walter Kaiser, *The Uses of the Old Testament in the New* (Chicago: Moody Press, 1985).

7. *Ibid.*, pp. 61-76.

8. Meridith Kline, *The Structure of Biblical Authority*.

9. Raymond Brown, *The Gospel of John* (Garden City, New York: Doubleday and Co., 1966), pp. 205-415.

10. *Babylonian Talmud, Sukkot* 52.

11. Walter Kaiser, pp. 103-144.

12. F. Kenton Beeshore, *The Messiah of the Targums, Talmuds, and Rabbinical Writers* (Los Angeles: World Bible Society, 1971); also Raphael Pattai, *The Messiah Texts* (Detroit: Wayne State University Press, 1979).

13. Beeshore on David Kimchi on Gen. 3:15, p. 1.

14. H. Wheeler Robinson, *Corporate Personality in the Old Testament* (Philadelphia: Fortress Press, 1964).

15. Beeshore, p. 5.

16. Pinchas Lapide, *The Resurrection of Jesus, A Jewish Perspective*, p. 114.

17. Wayne Meeks, *The Prophet King*.

18. Sigmund Mowinkle, *He That Commeth* (New York: Abington, 1954), pp. 114-120.

19. *Sanhedrin* 98 in *Babylonian Talmud*.

CHAPTER 11

1. See references in Arthur Kac, *The Messianic Hope* (Grand Rapids, Michigan: Baker Book House, 1975), pp. 58-105. See also Raphael Pattai, *The Messiah Texts*, pp. 104-121.

2. For a full description of the suffering-Messiah concept in Judaism and the two-Messiah concept, see R. Pattai, pp. 104-121, 165-170.

3. For Qumranic backgrounds, see R. N. Longenecker, *Biblical Exegesis in the Apostolic Period* (Grand Rapids, Michigan: Eerdmans,1975) on the book of Hebrews.

4. Wayne Meeks, *The Prophet King*.

5. For various references see Beeshore, also W. D. Davies, *Paul and Rabbinic Judaism* (Philadelphia: Fortress Press, 3d edition, 1980), pp. 147-176.

6. For a full exposition of the passage, see Edward J. Young, *The Prophecy of Daniel* (Grand Rapids: Eerdmans, 1948).

7. Robert Culver, *Daniel and the Latter Days* (Chicago: Moody Press, 1954), pp. 135-160.

8. For a full account, see R. K. Harrison, *Introduction to the Old Testament*, pp. 1110-27.

9. See Edward J. Young, commentary on relevant sections.

CHAPTER 12

1. See Young on relevant sections.

2. See Steve Lightle, *Exodus II* (Kingwood, Texas: Hunter Books, 1983).

3. Edward M. Yamauchi, "Ezekiel 38, 39 and the Latter Days" in *The Journal of the Evangelical Theological Society*, Spring, 1971.

4. Joseph P. Free, *Archaeology and Bible History* (Wheaton, Ill.: Scripture Press, 1950), p. 225, and in Moody Bible Institute fall presentation on the Bible and archaeology with Dr. Free.

5. See Bill Hammon, *Prophets and Personal Prophecy* (Shippensburg, Pa.: Destiny Image, 1987).

CHAPTER 13

1. C. S. Lewis, *Miracles*.

2. J. B. Phillips, *Ring of Truth*.

CHAPTER 14

1. William Foxwell Albright, *From the Stone Age to Christianity*, pp. 19-23.

2. F. F. Bruce, *The New Testament Documents, Are They Reliable?* See also A. Sherwin White, *Roman Law and Roman Society in the New Testament*.

3. Sir Frederick Kenyon, *Our Bible and the Ancient Manuscripts* (London: A. V. Adams, 1895, rev. 1958).

4. Sir William Ramsey, *St. Paul, Traveler and Roman Citizen*.

5. I. Howard Marshall, *Luke, Historian and Theologian*.

6. Ralph Martin, *Mark the Evangelist*. See R. T. France, and Greg Bloomburg, *The Historical Reliability of the Gospels*, p. 344.

7. Donald Guthrie, *A Shorter Life of Christ* (London, 1979), and Everett Harrison, *A Short Life of Christ* (Grand Rapids, Michigan: Eerdmans, 1968).

10. See bibliography for titles. Also Bloomburg and France.

11. F. F. Bruce, *The New Testament Documents*.

12. Joseph Klausner, *Jesus of Nazareth* (New York: Macmillan, 1925).

13. R. Trevor Herford, *Christianity in Talmud and Midrashim* (1903; rpt. Clifton, New Jersey: Reference Book Publishers, 1966).

14. Klausner, pp. 18ff.

15. J. B. Lightfoot, ed., *The Apostolic Fathers* (1891 edn., New York: MacMillan; rpt.

Grand Rapids, Michigan: Baker Book House, 1956).

16. See Marshall and Ramsey.

17. C. S. Lewis, *Surprised by Joy* (New York: Harcourt, Brace, and World, 1953).

18. J. W. Montgomery, *Where Is History Going?*

19. Merrill C. Tenney, *The Reality of the Resurrection.*

20. *Ibid.*

21. Pinchus Lapide, *The Resurrection of Jesus, A Jewish Perspective.*

22. *Ibid.*, pp. 113, 114.

23. Summarized in J. N. D. Anderson, *The Resurrection of Jesus, the Witness of History.*

24. Terry Maithe ,ed., *Did Jesus Rise from the Dead?*

25. *Ibid.*, also, see Frank Morrison, *Who Moved the Stone?*

26. Kirsopp Lake, *The Historical Evidence for the Resurrection of Jesus Christ* (New York: G. P. Putnam's Sons, 1907), pp. 250-253.

27. Hugh Schoenfield, *The Passover Plot* (London: Hutchenson, 1965).

28. Gary Habermas, *Verdict on the Shroud* (Ann Arbor, Michigan: Servant, 1981).

29. See also Heller, *Report on the Shroud of Turin* (Boston: Houghton Mifflin, 1983).

30. George Ladd, *The New Testament and Criticism* (Grand Rapids, Michigan: Eerdmans, 1967).

31. As found in the writings of Gunkel and Bultmann.

32. For a good summary, see Ladd, *The New Testament and Criticism.*

33. Reginald Fuller, *Foundations of New Testament Christology* (New York: Scribners, 1965).

34. Everett Harrison, "*Gemeindetheologie:* The Bane of Gospel Criticism," in Carl F. H. Henry ed., *Jesus of Nazareth, Savior and Lord* (Grand Rapids, Michigan: Eerdmans, 1966).

CHAPTER 15

1. Corrie Ten Boom, *Father Ten Boom* (Old Tappan, New Jersey: Flemming Revell, 1978), and *The Hiding Place* (Minneapolis: World Wide Pictures and Chosen Books, 1971).

2. Bruno Bettelheim, *The Informed Heart* (Glenco, Illinois: Free Press, 1960) and Victor Frankel, *Man's Search for Meaning* (New York: Washington Square Press, 1963).

3. G. N. Tyrell, *Science and Pyschical Phenomena* (London: O. P.) and Gardner Murphy, *The Challenge of Psychical Research* (New York: Harper and Brothers, 1961).

4. S. Mbiti, *African Religions and Philosophy* (Garden City, New York: Doubleday Anchor, 1963).

5. Kurt Koch, *Christian Counseling and Occultism.*

6. Richard Casdorf, M.D. , Ph.D., *The Miracles.*

7. From "One Who Left Her Bed," in *Christianity Today*, Vol. 27, No. 19, Dec. 16, 1983.

8. Jerry Parrick, *Twentieth-Century Miracle* (Plainfield, New Jersey: Logos, 1981).

9. Petty Wagner, *Murdered Heiress, Living Witness* (Shreveport, La.: Huntington House), 1984.

10. Dr. Peter Wagner on tape in series, *Wimber Interpretes Wagner* (Anaheim, Ca.: Vineyard Ministries Int., n.d.).

11. Roger Steer, *George Mueller, Delighted in God* (Wheaton, Ill.: Harold Shaw, 1981).

12. Edith Schaeffer, *The L'Abri Story* (Wheaton, Ill.: Tyndale, 1969).

13. Norman Grubb, *Rees Howells, Intercessor* (Ft. Washington, Pa.: Christian Literature Crusade, 1973).

14. Watchman Nee, *Sit, Walk, Stand* (Ft. Washington, Pa.: Christian Literature Crusade, 1962).

15. Derek Prince, *How I Learned to Do Miracles*, a tape series (Ft. Lauderdale, Fla.: Derek Prince Ministries).

16. John White, M.D., *When the Spirit Falls with Power* (Downers Grove, Ill.: Intervarsity Press, 1989). A psychiatrist gives testimony to supernatural power and miracles.

17. Francis McNutt, *The Power to Heal* (Notre Dame, Ind.: Ave Maria Press, 1977).

18. John Wimber, *Power Evangelism* (New York: Harper and Row, 1986).

19. Peter Berger, *The Social Construction of Reality.*

20 Recently William de Artega in *Quenching the Spirit* (Creation House: Altemonte Springs, Florida 1993) gave an excellent defense of contemporary Christian miracles as evidence for the truth of our faith. His book is a remarkable study of why some Christians do not see the value of miraculous experiences (analogous to the Bible) in sharing the truth of the biblical world view. His analysis of philosophical influences and his comments on epistemology and metaphysics are amazingly parallel to our presentation. I highly recommend his book.

CHAPTER 16

1. Kenneth Kantzer, unpublished notes from class, "Revelation and Inspiration," at Trinity Evangelical Divinity School (Deerfield, Ill.) in 1970.

2. See Karl Barth, *Evangelical Theology, An Introduction* (London: Collins, 1963).

3. Emil Brunner, "Nature and Grace." in *Natural Theology* (London: G. Bles, The Centenary Press, 1946).

4. Rudolph Bultmann, *Jesus Christ and Mythology* (New York: Scribners, 1958).

5. Key works on inspiration are: Benjamin Warfield, *The Inspiration and Authority of the Bible* (Philadelphia: Presbyterian and Reformed Publishing, 1970); R. Laird Harris, *The Inspiration and Canonicity of the Bible* (Grand Rapids, Michigan: Baker Book House, 1970); Edward J. Young, *Thy Word Is Truth* (Grand Rapids, Michigan: Eerdmans, 1957).

6. Warfield, pp. 299-347.

7. H. J. Cadbury as quoted in K. Kantzer.

8. Sir Frederick Kenyon, *Our Bible and the Ancient Manuscripts*, 4th edn. (New York: Harper, 1958),and Norman Geisler and William Nix, *A General Introduction to*

the Bible (Chicago: Moody Press, 1969).

    9. Josephus, *Antiquities*, in *Complete Works of Josephus* (Grand Rapids, Michigan: Kregal, 1960). R. Laird Harris, pp. 141ff.

    10. I Macabees 2:44-48.

    11. Henry Theile, *The Mysterious Numbers of the Hebrew Kings.*

    12. R. Laird Harris, pp. 219-235.

    13. The student could do well to read New Testament pseudepigrapha available in various collections. For example, M. R. James, *The Apocryphal New Testament* (Oxford: Clarendon Press, 1924).

    14. See R. Laird Harris, "The Patristic Test of Canonicity," pp. 236ff.

    15. A. A. Haley, *An Examination of the Alleged Discrepancies in the Bible.*

    16. Gleason Archer. *Encyclopedia of Bible Difficulties.*

BIBLIOGRAPHY

Albright, William Foxwell. *From the Stone Age to Christianity*. New York: Doubleday, 1957.

Anderson, J. N. D. *Christianity, the Witness of History*. London: Tyndale, 1969.

Archer, Gleason. *A Survey of Old Testament Introduction*. Chicago: Moody Press, 1964.

Augustine. *Confessions*. New York: Random House, 1949.

Ayer, A. J. *Language, Truth, and Logic*. New York: Dover, 1936.

Babbage, Stuart Barton. *The Mark of Cain*. Grand Rapids, Mich.: Eerdmans, 1966.

Berger, Peter. *A Rumor of Angels*. New York: Doubleday, 1969.

————. *The Social Construction of Reality*. Garden City, N.Y.: Doubleday Anchor, 1966.

Bruce, F. F. *The Defense of the Gsopel in the New Testament*. Grand Rapids, Mich.: Eerdmans, 1959.

————. *The New Testament Documents, Are They Reliable?.* Grand Rapids, Mich.: Eerdmans, 1960.

Bultmann, Rudolph. *Jesus Christ and Mythology*. New York: Scribners, 1958 .

Butler, Joseph. *The Analogy of Religion*. New York: Frederick Unger Publishing, 1961; from 1736 edition.

Calliet, Emile. *The Recovery of Purpose*. New York: Harper and Brothers, 1959.

Carnell, Edward John. *The Case for Orthodox Theology*. Philadelphia: Westminster Press, 1959.

————. *Christian Commitment*. New York: Macmillan, 1957.

————. *An Introduction to Christian Apologetics*. Grand Rapids, Mich.: Eerdmans, 1948.

————. *The Kingdom of Love and the Pride of Life*. Grand Rapids, Mich.: Eerdmans, 1960.

————. *A Philosophy of the Christian Religion*. Grand Rapids, Mich.: Eerdmans, 1952.

Casdorf, Richard. *The Miracles*. Plainfield, New Jersey: Logos, 1976.

Clark, Gordon. *A Christian View of Men and Things*. Grand Rapids, Mich.: Eerdmans, 1951.

————. *Religion, Reason, and Revelation*. Philadelphia: Presbyterian and Reformed Publishing, 1961.

Chang, Lit Sen. *Zen Existentialism*. Philadelphia: Presbyterian and Reformed Publishing, 1969.

Coleman, James A. *Relativity for the Layman*. New York: American Library, Signet Books, 1958 .

Creig, William. *Apologetics: An Introduction*. Chicago: Moody Press, 1985.

Dooyweerd, Herman. *A New Critique of Theoretical Thought*. Philadelphia: Presbyterian and Reformed Publishing, 1969.

Eliade, Mircea. *The Sacred and the Profane*. New York: Harcourt, Brace, and World, 1959.

————. *Patterns of Comparative Religion*. New York: Sheed and Ward, 1958.

Evans, C. Steven. *Philosophy of Religion: Thinking About Faith*. Downers Grove, Ill.: Intervarsity Press, 1982.

Ferre, Frederick. *Basic Modern Philosophy of Religion*. New York: Scribners, 1967.

————. *Language, Logic, and God*. New York: Harper and Row, 1961.

Flew, Antony and Alisdair MacIntyre. *New Essays in Philosophical Theology*. New York: Macmillan, 1955.

Fuller, Daniel. *Easter Faith and History*. Grand Rapids, Mich.: Eerdmans, 1965.

Gardner, Martin. *Relativity for the Millions*. New York: Macmillan, 1962.

Geisler, Norman. *Christian Apologetics*. Grand Rapids, Mich.: Baker Book House, 1976.

Gilkey, Langdon. *Naming the Whirlwind*. New York: Bobbs Merrill, 1969.

Guernsey, Otis L. *The Best Plays of 1985*. New York: Dodd, Mead, 1987.

Guthrie, Donald. *An Introduction to the New Testament*. London: Tyndale Press, 1962.

Habermas, Gary and Ken Stevenson. *Verdict on the Shroud*. Ann Arbor, Mich.: Servant, 1981.

————. *The Shroud and the Controversy*. Nashville: Thomas Nelson, 1990.

Hackett, Stuart C. *A Westerner's Guide to Eastern Thought*. Madison, Wisc.: Univ. of Wisconsin Press, 1979.

————. *The Reconstruction of the Christian Revelation Claim*. Grand Rapids, Mich.: Baker Book House, 1984 .

————. *The Resurrection of Theism*. Chicago: Moody Press, 1957.

Haley, John W. *An Examination of the Alleged Discrepancies in the Bible*. Nashville: Gospel Advocate, 1951, from 1874 edition.

Hannigan, M. *Homosexuality*. New York: Paulist Press, 1988.

Harrison, R. K. *Introduction to the Old Testament*. Grand Rapids, Mich.: Eerdmans, 1969 .

Hartshorn, Charles. *The Logic of Perfection and Other Essays in Neoclassical Metaphysics*. LaSalle, Ill.: Open Court Publishing, 1962.

————. *A Natural Theology for Our Time*. LaSalle, Ill.: Open Court Publishing, 1967.

Heidegger, Martin. *Being and Time*. New York: Harper and Row, 1962 .

Hick, John. *Evil and the God of Love*. London: Macmillan, 1966.

Holmes, Arthur F. *Christian Philosophy in the Twentieth Century*. Nutley, N.J.: Creig Press, 1969 .

————. *Faith Seeks Understanding*. Grand Rapids, Mich.: Eerdmans, 1971.

Joad, C. E. M. *The Recovery of Belief*. London: Farber and Farber, 1951 .

Kant, Immanuel. *A Critique of Practical Knowledge*. New York: Bobbs-Merrill, 1956, from 1788 German edition.

————. *A Critique of Pure Reason*. New York: St. Martin's Press, 1965, from 1781 German edition .

————. *Religion within the Limits of Reason Alone*. New York: Harper and Row, 1960, from 1794 German edition.

Kline, Meredith. *The Structure of Biblical Authority*. Grand Rapids, Mich.: Eerdmans, 1972.

Koch, Kurt. *Christian Counseling and Occultism*. Grand Rapids, Mich.: Kregal Publications, 1965.

Kramer, Hilton. *The Revenge of the Philistines*. New York: Free Press, 1985.

Kung, Hans. *Does God Exist?*. Garden City, N.Y.: Doubleday, 1980.

———. *Eternal Life*. Garden City, N.Y.: Doubleday, 1984.

Lapide, Pinchas. *The Resurrection of Jesus: A Jewish Perspective*. Minneapolis, Minnesota: Augsburg Pub., 1987.

Lewis, C. S. *The Abolition of Man*. New York: Macmillan, 1947.

———. *Mere Christianity*. New York: Macmillan, 1952.

———. *Miracles*. New York: Macmillan, 1947.

———. *The Pilgrim's Regress*. Grand Rapids, Mich.: Eerdmans, 1958.

———. *The Problem of Pain*. N.Y., Macmillan, 1962.

Locke, John. *The Works of John Locke*. London: Harry G. Bohn Co., 1854.

Maithe, Terry, ed. *Did Jesus Rise from the Dead?* New York: Harper and Row, 1987.

Malcolm, Norman. "The Ontological Argument Revisited." *Philosophical Review*. Vol. 69, No. 4, 1960.

Marshall, I. Howard. *Luke, Historian and Theologian*. Grand Rapids, Mich.: Zondervan, 1971.

Martin, Ralph. *Mark the Evangelist*. Grand Rapids, Mich.: Zondervan, 1971.

Matson, Floyd W. *The Broken Image: Man, Science, and Society*. Garden City, N.Y.: Doubleday Anchor, 1966.

Mavrodes, George. *Belief in God*. New York: Random House, 1970.

McDowell, Joshua. *Evidence That Demands a Verdict*. San Bernardino, California: Campus Crusade, 1972.

Montgomery, John W. *History and Christianity*. Downers Grove, Ill.: Intervarsity Press, 1965.

———. *The Shape of the Past*. Ann Arbor, Mich.: Edwards Brothers, 1962.

———. *Where is History Going?* Grand Rapids, Mich.: Zondervan, 1969.

Moreland, J. P. *Scaling the Secular City*. Grand Rapids, Mich.: Zondervan, 1987.

Niemeyer, Alfred. *The Quest for Meaning in Modern Art*. New York: Metropolitan Museum of Art, 1967.

Novak, Michael. *Will it Liberate?*. New York: Paulist Press, 1986.

Orr, James. *A Christian View of God and the World*. Edinburgh: Andrew Elliot, 1902.

Payne, J. Barton. *An Encyclopedia of Biblical Prophecy*. New York: Harper and Row, 1973.

Phillips, J. B. *Ring of Truth*. New York: Macmillan, 1967.

Polanyi, Michael. *Personal Knowledge*. Chicago: University of Chicago Press, 1962.

Ramm, Bernard. *Protestant Christian Evidences*. Chicago: Moody Press, 1953.

———. *A Christian View of Science and Scripture*. Grand Rapids, Mich., 1954.

Ramsey, Sir William. *St. Paul, Traveler and Roman Citizen*. Grand Rapids, Mich., 1954.

Rookmaaker, Hans. *Modern Art and the Death of Culture*. Downers Grove, Ill.: Intervarsity Press, 1970.

Schaeffer, Francis. *Death in the City*. Downers Grove, Ill.: Intervarsity Press, 1970.
———. *Escape from Reason*. Downers Grove, Ill.: Intervarsity Press, 1968.
———. *The God Who is There*. London: Hodder and Stoughton, 1968.
———. *How Shall We Then Live?* Old Tappan, N.J.: Fleming Revell, 1976.
Schlossburg, Herbert. *Idols for Destruction*. New York: Thomas Nelson, 1983.
Sire, James. *The Universe Next Door*. Downers Grove, Ill.: Intervarsity Press, 1976.
Smith, Wilbur. *Therefore Stand*. Boston: W. A. Wilde, 1945.
Stoner, Peter. *Science Speaks*. Chicago, Moody Press, 1963.
Taylor, A. E. *Does God Exist?*. New York: Macmillan, 1947.
Temple, William. *Nature, Man, and God*. New York: St. Martin's Press, 1934.
Tenney, Merrill. *The Reality of the Resurrection*. New York: Harper and Row, 1963.
Thiele, Henry. *The Mysterious Numbers of the Hebrew Kings*. Chicago: University of
    Chicago Press, 1951.
Tyrell, G. N. *Science and Psychical Phenomena*. London: Society for Psychical Research,
    1915, O.P.
Van Til, Cornelius. *The Defense of the Faith*. Philadelphia: Presbyterian and Reformed
    Publishing, 1967.
Wenhem, John. *Easter Enigma: Are the Resurrection Accounts in Conflict?* Grand
    Rapids, Mich.: Zondervan, 1986.
White, A. Sherwin. *Roman Law and Roman Society in the New Testament*. London:
    Oxford University Press, 1961.
Wildersmith, A. E. *The Creation of Life: A Cybernetic Approach to Evolution*. Wheaton,
    Ill.: Harold Shaw, 1970.
———. *Man's Origin, Man's Destiny*. Wheaton, Ill.: Harold Shaw, 1980.
Wolfe, David L. *Epistemology, the Justification of Belief*. Downers Grove, Ill.: Intervar-
    sity Press, 1960.

INDEX

ENDORSEMENTS FOR
THE BIBLICAL WORLD VIEW, AN APOLOGETIC

By Daniel C. Juster Th.D.

Dr. David L Wolfe. Prominent Christian Philosopher. Wheaton College and later Gordon College. Author Epistemology. The Justification of Belief. The key work on epistemology from a Christian point of view.

"The Biblical World View is a comprehensive treatment of Christian apologetics addressed to an intellectually aware general audience. Dr. Juster draws on decades of careful and serious reflection, dialogue and teaching on these matters. Unlike many such attempts, it is philosophically responsible and critical. It would be an excellent choice as a textbook for a course in general apologetics".

Dr. Craig Keener. Adjunct Professor of New Testament. Eastern Baptist Theological Seminary. Author. The IVP Bible Background Commentary and other significant publications.

"The Biblical World View integrates information from different academic disciplines relevant to apologetics. It does so with accuracy. It is unusual to find a text which deals with philosophical, historical and Biblical studies in such a way that scholars in various disciplines will find that their own area of study is treated with solid understanding. I found that my own discipline of Biblical Theology and exegesis was handled deftly whereby I had little to correct. The book is coherent and forceful. I strongly recommend it."

Dr. Dennis Lindsay. President Christ For The Nations Institute.

"It was at L'Abri Fellowship in Switzerland, under the teaching of the late Dr. Francis Schaeffer, that I was suddenly made aware of the monumental significance of biblical apologetics. My life was dramatically and positively changed. As a result I have been teaching Apologetics for the last 25 years. Dan Juster's recent book has once again reminded me of the far reaching implications and the need for every believer to obtain a strong apologetic support in order to add substance to one's faith. Dan's book is superb and has skillfully provided one, not only with a reason to believe that God exists, but that He has revealed Himself to man in a meaningful and trustworthy revelation. The book is on a par with any book that I have read on the subject."

Rev. Isaac Rottenburg, former General Secretary, the Reformed Church in America
"We all face some fundamental issues which pastors who want to address questions that are on their members minds cannot avoid. Christians are often accused of answering all sorts of questions nobody is asking. That is not true of this book. Juster deals with the many theories and philosophies that compete with the message of the Gospel in our society today. But he is not a crusader who uses hype in defense of the faith. I found his discussions to be balanced and thought provoking. There are points where one might want to argue about details. But in the main, this book represents a broadly evangelical perspective in line with the historic faith of One Holy Catholic and Apostolic Church."

Dr. Stan deKovan. President of Vision University
"An excellent and comprehensive treatment of Apologetics which we have selected as the text book in apologetics of our university."

Dr. Jay Grimstead, Director of Coalition on Revival, Coordinator of National Think Tank

"This book, The Biblical World View, is a balanced, comprehensive yet concise Apologetic of the basic historic orthodox theology and philosophy held by most of the great heroes of the faith down through the ages from the early church to the late Francis Schaeffer. I can recommend this book for all students who want an understanding of the biblical world view as it is contrasted with the major philosophies which have challenged that world view. The next generation of Christian leaders needs this book on their shelves."